RICHARD M. ABRAMS was born and educated in New York City (Columbia College, A.B., 1953; and Columbia University, A.M., 1955, and Ph.D., 1962). His academic achievements are further exemplified by an enviable list of honors which includes Phi Beta Kappa, 1953; Columbia University Fellowships, 1953-1955; Social Science Research Council Pre-Doctoral Fellowship, 1960-1961; Newcomen Society of North America Prize, 1962; Social Science Research Council Post-Doctoral Fellowship, 1964 1965; and a Fulbright Lectureship in History, University of London, Institute of United States Studies, 1968-1969.

Now an associate professor of history at the University of California at Berkeley, Dr. Abram's published works include the following books: *The Issue of Federal Regulation in the Progressive Era, Conservatism in a Progressive Era: Massachusetts Politics, 1900-1912*, and (with Lawrence W. Levine) *The Shaping of Twentieth-Century America*.

The Issues of the Populist
and Progressive Eras,
1892-1912

The Issues of the Populist and Progressive Eras, 1892-1912

Edited by

RICHARD M. ABRAMS

THE UNIVERSITY OF SOUTH CAROLINA PRESS
Columbia, South Carolina

THE ISSUES OF THE POPULIST AND
PROGRESSIVE ERAS, 1892–1912

Introduction, editorial notes, and compilation copyright ©
1969 by Richard M. Abrams.

Printed in the United States of America.

First edition: HARPER PAPERBACKS, 1969,
Harper & Row, Publishers, Incorporated,
49 East 33rd St., New York, N.Y. 10016.

This edition published in 1970 by the University of
South Carolina Press, Columbia, S.C.,
by arrangement with Harper Paperbacks, from
whom a paperback edition is available (HR/1428).

Standard Book Number: 87249-164-1

Library of Congress Catalog Card Number: 76–625503.

Contents

Foreword

WHEN the editors asked me to participate in this series, my first reaction was: Why another collection of so-called documents? There are literally scores of such collections, and especially for the Populist and Progressive eras. Surely all the really important documents have been reproduced and are already in handy volumes. In an effort to prove my point, I asked an assistant to catalogue the contents of about twenty of the more popular editions. The results truly surprised me. There was, of course, some of the expected repetition of standard material, such as Bryan's "Cross of Gold" speech, but what was astonishing was the mass of esoterica reproduced—little-known speeches, letters, or editorials designed to illustrate some point of especial interest to the editor. Some of these collections are well done, but most of them present such severely truncated excerpts that the purpose of some selections remains an enigma even when "clarified" by individual prefaces. Most remarkable of all, however, is how few of the standard historical documents have been reproduced, at least in any substantial part.

Satisfied that I might yet make a contribution, I have proceeded first of all to select public documents that, as a teacher of the period, I should expect every student to know. Some of these appear in none of the general collections, while even the more specialized collections fail to contain more than a couple of pages of, for example, the Dillingham Immigration Commission's Report of 1911, or the New York Tenement House Report of 1903. The Pittsburgh Survey was one of the most powerful contemporary accounts of industrial conditions to appear in the Progressive Era, but I found no collection that presented any part of the multivolume report. One reason such documents are not included, I suppose, is that the excerpts must be rather lengthy to be meaningful. Yet if the purpose of directing students to documents is, as I have taken it to be, to acquaint them with contemporary tone and style—to let them immerse themselves in contemporary discourse—then it is necessary that they be exposed at length to documents that contributed substantially to such discourse.

This collection, in sum, is designed to make available extensive passages from what I think most historians will agree are many of the basic documents of the Populist-Progressive period. It includes many familiar pieces, of course: what collection can do without at least one chapter from Steffens's *The Shame of the Cities?* or some commentary by "Mr. Dooley"? or the Populists' "Omaha Platform"? I should like to think, however, that no documentary history can properly do without such other contemporary landmarks as Turner's "The Significance of the Frontier," F. W. Taylor's *Scientific Management,* the *Plessy v. Ferguson* ("separate but equal") decision (and *not* merely Harlan's dissent), Booker T. Washington's Atlanta Exposition address, or Robert Hunter's pioneering study, *Poverty.* There are, finally, a few documents that express my own peculiar perceptions—for example, Herbert Croly on Mark Hanna, Congressman Samuel McCall's demurrer against federal railroad legislation, and Adna Weber's scholarly defense of the city. I hope these do not appear as esoterica. They are intended to illustrate vital themes that I consider on a par with the themes expressed in the better-known documents, but which so far have failed to become a significant part of the historiographical consensus.

Instead of presenting an introductory essay on the Populist-Progressive period that would be necessarily too short to say anything a student is not likely to find in the Harper *New American Nation* series (which this selection ostensibly parallels), I have saved the space in order to allow for detailed headnotes to each separate document.

J. William T. Youngs, Jr., is the assistant who ably persuaded me that there was ample room for a good documents collection; and my colleague, Professor Gunther Barth, has my thanks for his suggestions on the problem of the city in the Populist-Progressive period.

The Issues of the Populist and Progressive Eras, 1892-1912

I

America Transformed

1. Frederick Jackson Turner,
"The Significance of the Frontier"

PERHAPS the most persistent theme underlying the turmoil of the
Populist-Progressive period was that some essential, invigorating force
had gone out of American life forever. The presumed loss of that force
helped contemporaries account for the severe depression of the 1890's,
the violence that accompanied it, and especially the shockingly wide-
spread appeal—so "un-American" in character—for the federal government to commit itself on behalf of particular interest groups which
events ostensibly beyond their influence had placed in critical difficulties.
Constriction of economic opportunity seemed to be the principal complaint voiced. Contemporaries differed, however, over the causes of that
constriction. The Populists generally argued that the consolidation of
business enterprise and monopolistic control over the country's money
supply had effectively subverted rugged individualism in farming and in
business, thereby undermining the foundations of the American democratic social structure. This argument had the virtue of presenting visible
villains to accompany the visible victims. The remedies would thus seem
simple and clear: hit the trusts, put an end to monopoly and privilege,
restore the conditions of equal opportunity that had made America
great. Less "radical" observers generally preferred more subtle arguments.
One which gained increasing currency during the 1892–1912 period was
that America's continental resources had begun to be noticeably depleted—most conspicuously though not exclusively the resource of "free
land." The implications of this fact were the theme of the paper delivered at the American Historical Association convention in Chicago
in summer 1893 by Frederick Jackson Turner, then an assistant professor
of history at the University of Wisconsin. Probably for most contemporary historians attention centered on Turner's challenge to orthodox
historiography's argument that American democratic institutions were
founded in the traditions of Anglo-Saxon and Teutonic Europe. Turner
argued that the remarkable personal liberty and economic vigor that
existed in America rested more certainly on the country's own distinctive
geographical attributes. One feature of Turner's thesis thus appeared to

exalt the pristine West over the more tradition-bound, Europe-oriented East. But the broader implication of "the closing of the frontier," to which Turner calls attention at the outset, was that it had brought to an end the most potent force behind the development of America's exceptional progressive qualities. This theme was given considerable emphasis by many contemporary Progressives, notably Herbert Croly, a sample of whose work follows in Document 4.

Since the so-called Turner Thesis remains probably the most debated problem in American historiography, the literature on it is extraordinarily large. The most complete recent bibliography may be found in Ray Allen Billington (ed.), The Frontier Thesis: Valid Interpretation of American History? (New York, 1966).

SOURCE: Frederick Jackson Turner, "The Significance of the Frontier in American History," *Annual Report of the American Historical Association for the Year 1893* (Washington, D.C., 1894), pp. 199–227.

In a recent bulletin of the Superintendent of the Census for 1890 appear these significant words: "Up to and including 1880 the country had a frontier of settlement, but at present the unsettled area has been so broken into by isolated bodies of settlement that there can hardly be said to be a frontier line. In the discussion of its extent, its westward movement, etc., it can not, therefore, any longer have a place in the census reports." This brief official statement marks the closing of a great historic movement. Up to our own day American history has been in a large degree the history of the colonization of the Great West. The existence of an area of free land, its continuous recession, and the advance of American settlement westward, explain American development.

Behind institutions, behind constitutional forms and modifications, lie the vital forces that call these organs into life and shape them to meet changing conditions. The peculiarity of American institutions is, the fact that they have been compelled to adapt themselves to the changes of an expanding people—to the changes involved in crossing a continent, in winning a wilderness, and in developing at each area of this progress out of the primitive economic and political conditions of the frontier into the complexity of city life. Said Calhoun in 1817, "We are great, and rapidly—I was about to say fearfully—growing!" So saying, he touched the distinguishing feature of American life. All peoples show development; the germ theory of politics has been sufficiently emphasized.

In the case of most nations, however, the development has occurred in a limited area; and if the nation has expanded, it has met other growing peoples whom it has conquered. But in the case of the United States we have a different phenomenon. Limiting our attention to the Atlantic coast, we have the familiar phenomenon of the evolution of institutions in a limited area, such as the rise of representative government; the differentiation of simple colonial governments into complex organs; the progress from primitive industrial society, without division of labor, up to manufacturing civilization. But we have in addition to this a recurrence of the process of evolution in each western area reached in the process of expansion. Thus American development has exhibited not merely advance along a single line, but a return to primitive conditions on a continually advancing frontier line, and a new development for that area. American social development has been continually beginning over again on the frontier. This perennial rebirth, this fluidity of American life, this expansion westward with its new opportunities, its continuous touch with the simplicity of primitive society, furnish the forces dominating American character. The true point of view in the history of this nation is not the Atlantic coast, it is the great West. Even the slavery struggle, which is made so exclusive an object of attention by writers like Professor von Holst, occupies its important place in American history because of its relation to westward expansion.

In this advance, the frontier is the outer edge of the wave—the meeting point between savagery and civilization. Much has been written about the frontier from the point of view of border warfare and the chase, but as a field for the serious study of the economist and the historian it has been neglected.

The American frontier is sharply distinguished from the European frontier—a fortified boundary line running through dense populations. The most significant thing about the American frontier is that it lies at the hither edge of free land. In the census reports it is treated as the margin of that settlement which has a density of two or more to the square mile. The term is an elastic one, and for our purposes does not need sharp definition. We shall consider the whole frontier belt, including the Indian country and the outer margin of the "settled area" of the census reports. This paper will make no attempt to treat the subject exhaustively; its aim is simply to call attention to the frontier as a fertile field for investigation, and to suggest some of the problems which arise in connection with it.

In the settlement of America we have to observe how European life entered the continent, and how America modified and developed that life and reacted on Europe. Our early history is the study of European germs developing in an American environment. Too exclusive attention has been paid by institutional students to the Germanic origins, too little to the American factors. The frontier is the line of most rapid and effective Americanization. The wilderness masters the colonist. It finds him a European in dress, industries, tools, modes of travel, and thought. It takes him from the railroad car and puts him in the birch canoe. It strips off the garments of civilization and arrays him in the hunting shirt and the moccasin. It puts him in the log cabin of the Cherokee and Iroquois and runs an Indian palisade around him. Before long he has gone to planting Indian corn and plowing with a sharp stick; he shouts the war cry and takes the scalp in orthodox Indian fashion. In short, at the frontier the environment is at first too strong for the man. He must accept the conditions which it furnishes, or perish, and so he fits himself into the Indian clearings and follows the Indian trails. Little by little he transforms the wilderness, but the outcome is not the old Europe, not simply the development of Germanic germs, any more than the first phenomenon was a case of reversion to the Germanic mark. The fact is, that here is a new product that is American. At first, the frontier was the Atlantic coast. It was the frontier of Europe in a very real sense. Moving westward, the frontier became more and more American. As successive terminal moraines result from successive glaciations, so each frontier leaves its traces behind it, and when it becomes a settled area the region still partakes of the frontier characteristics. Thus the advance of the frontier has meant a steady movement away from the influence of Europe, a steady growth of independence on American lines. And to study this advance, the men who grew up under these conditions, and the political, economic, and social results of it, is to study the really American part of our history.

Stages of Frontier Advance

In the course of the seventeenth century the frontier was advanced up the Atlantic river courses, just beyond the "fall line," and the tidewater region became the settled area. In the first half of the eighteenth century another advance occurred. . . .

From decade to decade distinct advances of the frontier occurred. By the census of 1820 the settled area included Ohio, southern Indiana and Illinois, southeastern Missouri, and about one-half of Louisiana. . . .

The rising steam navigation on western waters, the opening of the Erie Canal, and the westward extension of cotton culture added five frontier states to the Union in this period. . . .

In the middle of this century the line indicated by the present eastern boundary of Indian Territory, Nebraska, and Kansas marked the frontier of the Indian country. Minnesota and Wisconsin still exhibited frontier conditions, but the distinctive frontier of the period is found in California, where the gold discoveries had sent a sudden tide of adventurous miners, and in Oregon, and the settlements in Utah. As the frontier has leaped over the Alleghanies, so now it skipped the Great Plains and the Rocky Mountains; and in the same way that the advance of the frontiersmen beyond the Alleghanies had caused the rise of important questions of transportation and internal improvement, so now the settlers beyond the Rocky Mountains needed means of communication with the East, and in the furnishing of these arose the settlement of the Great Plains and the development of still another kind of frontier life. Railroads, fostered by land grants, sent an increasing tide of immigrants into the far West. The United States Army fought a series of Indian wars in Minnesota, Dakota, and the Indian Territory.

By 1880 the settled area had been pushed into northern Michigan, Wisconsin, and Minnesota, along Dakota rivers, and in the Black Hills region, and was ascending the rivers of Kansas and Nebraska. The development of mines in Colorado had drawn isolated frontier settlements into that region, and Montana and Idaho were receiving settlers. The frontier was found in these mining camps and the ranches of the Great Plains. . . .

Having now roughly outlined the various kinds of frontiers, and their modes of advance, chiefly from the point of view of the frontier itself, we may next inquire what were the influences on the East and on the Old World. A rapid enumeration of some of the more noteworthy effects is all that I have time for.

Composite Nationality

First, we note that the frontier promoted the formation of a composite nationality for the American people. The coast was preponderantly English, but the later tides of continental immigration flowed across to the free lands. . . . Such examples teach us to beware of misinterpreting the fact that there is a common English speech in America into a belief that the stock is also English.

Industrial Independence

In another way the advance of the frontier decreased our dependence on England. The coast, particularly of the South, lacked diversified industries, and was dependent on England for the bulk of its supplies. In the South there was even a dependence on the Northern colonies for articles of food. . . . Before long the frontier created a demand for merchants. As it retreated from the coast it became less and less possible for England to bring her supplies directly to the consumer's wharfs, and carry away staple crops, and staple crops began to give way to diversified agriculture for a time. The effect of this phase of the frontier action upon the northern section is perceived when we realize how the advance of the frontier aroused seaboard cities like Boston, New York, and Baltimore, to engage in rivalry for what Washington called "the extensive and valuable trade of a rising empire."

Effects on National Legislation

The legislation which most developed the powers of the National Government, and played the largest part in its activity, was conditioned on the frontier. Writers have discussed the subjects of tariff, land, and internal improvement, as subsidiary to the slavery question. But when American history comes to be rightly viewed it will be seen that the slavery question is an incident. In the period from the end of the first half of the present century to the close of the civil war slavery rose to primary, but far from exclusive, importance. . . . The growth of nationalism and the evolution of American political institutions were dependent on the advance of the frontier. . . . The pioneer needed the goods of the coast, and so the grand series of internal improvement and railroad legislation began, with potent nationalizing effects. Over internal improvements occurred great debates, in which grave constitutional questions were discussed. Sectional groupings appear in the votes, profoundly significant for the historian. Loose construction increased as the nation marched westward. But the West was not content with bringing the farm to the factory. Under the lead of Clay—"Harry of the West"—protective tariffs were passed, with the cry of bringing the factory to the farm. The disposition of the public lands was a third important subject of national legislation influenced by the frontier.

The Public Domain

The public domain has been a force of profound importance in the nationalization and development of the Government. The effects of the struggle of the landed and the landless States, and of the ordinance of 1787, need no discussion. Administratively the frontier called out some of the highest and most vitalizing activities of the General Government. The purchase of Louisiana was perhaps the constitutional turning point in the history of the Republic, inasmuch as it afforded both a new area for national legislation and the occasion of the downfall of the policy of strict construction. But the purchase of Louisiana was called out by frontier needs and demands. As frontier States accrued to the Union the national power grew. . . .

When we consider the public domain from the point of view of the sale and disposal of the public lands we are again brought face to face with the frontier. The policy of the United States in dealing with its lands is in sharp contrast with the European system of scientific administration. Efforts to make this domain a source of revenue, and to withhold it from emigrants in order that settlement might be compact, were in vain. The jealousy and the fears of the East were powerless in the face of the demands of the frontiersmen. . . .

National Tendencies of the Frontier

It is safe to say that the legislation with regard to land, tariff, and internal improvements—the American system of the nationalizing Whig party—was conditioned on frontier ideas and needs. But it was not merely in legislative action that the frontier worked against the sectionalism of the coast. The economic and social characteristics of the frontier worked against sectionalism. . . .

> One of the main causes of discontent which led to this convention, that which had the strongest influence in overcoming our veneration for the work of our fathers, which taught us to contemn the sentiments of Henry and Mason and Pendleton, which weaned

us from our reverence for the constituted authorities of the State, was an overweening passion for internal improvement. I say this with perfect knowledge, for it has been avowed to me by gentlemen from the West over and over again. And let me tell the gentleman from Albemarle (Mr. Gordon) that it has been another principal object of those who set this ball of revolution in motion, to overturn the doctrine of State rights, of which Virginia has been the very pillar, and to remove the barrier she has interposed to the interference of the Federal Government in that same work of internal improvement, by so reorganizing the legislature that Virginia, too, may be hitched to the Federal car.

It was this nationalizing tendency of the West that transformed the democracy of Jefferson into the national republicanism of Monroe and the democracy of Andrew Jackson. The West of the war of 1812, the West of Clay, and Benton, and Harrison, and Andrew Jackson, shut off by the Middle States and the mountains from the coast sections, had a solidarity of its own with national tendencies. On the tide of the Father of Waters, North and South met and mingled into a nation. Interstate migration went steadily on—a process of cross-fertilization of ideas and institutions. The fierce struggle of the sections over slavery on the western frontier does not diminish the truth of this statement; it proves the truth of it. Slavery was a sectional trait that would not down, but in the West it could not remain sectional. . . . Nothing works for nationalism like intercourse within the nation. Mobility of population is death to localism, and the western frontier worked irresistibly in unsettling population. The effects reached back from the frontier and affected profoundly the Atlantic coast and even the Old World.

Growth of Democracy

But the most important effect of the frontier has been in the promotion of democracy here and in Europe. As has been indicated, the frontier is productive of individualism. Complex society is precipitated by the wilderness into a kind of primitive organization based on the family. The tendency is anti-social. It produces antipathy to control, and particularly to any direct control. The tax-gatherer is viewed as a representative of oppression. . . . The frontier individualism has from the beginning promoted democracy. . . .

So long as free land exists, the opportunity for a competency exists, and economic power secures political power. But the democracy born of free land, strong in selfishness and individualism, intolerant of administrative experience and education, and pressing individual liberty beyond its proper bounds, has its dangers as well as its benefits. Individualism in America has allowed a laxity in regard to governmental affairs which has rendered possible the spoils system and all the manifest evils that follow from the lack of a highly developed civic spirit. In this connection may be noted also the influence of frontier conditions in permitting lax business honor, inflated paper currency and wild-cat banking. The colonial and revolutionary frontier was the region whence emanated many of the worst forms of an evil currency. The West in the war of 1812 repeated the phenomenon on the frontier of that day, while the speculation and wild-cat banking of the period of the crisis of 1837 occurred on the new frontier belt of the next tier of States. Thus each one of the periods of lax financial integrity coincides with periods when a new set of frontier communities had arisen, and coincides in area with these successive frontiers, for the most part. The recent Populist agitation is a case in point. Many a State that now declines any connection with the tenets of the Populists, itself adhered to such ideas in an earlier stage of the development of the State. A primitive society can hardly be expected to show the intelligent appreciation of the complexity of business interests in a developed society. The continual recurrence of these areas of paper-money agitation is another evidence that the frontier can be isolated and studied as a factor in American history of the highest importance.[1]

Attempts to Check and Regulate the Frontier

The East has always feared the result of an unregulated advance of the frontier, and has tried to check and guide it. . . . But the

1. I have refrained from dwelling on the lawless characteristics of the frontier, because they are sufficiently well known. The gambler and desperado, the regulators of the Carolinas and the vigilantes of California, are types of that line of scum that the waves of advancing civilization bore before them, and of the growth of spontaneous organs of authority where legal authority was absent. Compare Barrows, United States of Yesterday and To-morrow; Shinn, Mining Camps; and Bancroft, Popular Tribunals. The humor, bravery, and rude strength, as well as the vices of the frontier in its worst aspect, have left traces on American character, language, and literature, not soon to be effaced.

attempts to limit the boundaries, to restrict land sales and settlement, and to deprive the West of its share of political power were
all in vain. Steadily the frontier of settlement advanced and carried
with it individualism, democracy, and nationalism, and powerfully
affected the East and the Old World.

Missionary Activity

The most effective efforts of the East to regulate the frontier
came through its educational and religious activity, exerted by
interstate migration and by organized societies. . . . The New
England preacher and school-teacher left their mark on the West.
The dread of Western emancipation from New England's political
and economic control was paralleled by her fears lest the West cut
loose from her religion. . . . As seaboard cities like Philadelphia,
New York, and Baltimore strove for the mastery of Western trade,
so the various denominations strove for the possession of the West.
Thus an intellectual stream from New England sources fertilized
the West. Other sections sent their missionaries; but the real
struggle was between sects. The contest for power and the expansive tendency furnished to the various sects by the existence of a
moving frontier must have had important results on the character
of religious organization in the United States. The multiplication
of rival churches in the little frontier towns had deep and lasting
social effects. The religious aspects of the frontier make a chapter
in our history which needs study.

Intellectual Traits

From the conditions of frontier life came intellectual traits of
profound importance. The works of travelers along each frontier
from colonial days onward describe certain common traits, and
these traits have, while softening down, still persisted as survivals
in the place of their origin, even when a higher social organization
succeeded. The result is that to the frontier the American intellect
owes its striking characteristics. That coarseness and strength combined with acuteness and inquisitiveness; that practical, inventive
turn of mind, quick to find expedients; that masterful grasp of
material things, lacking in the artistic but powerful to effect great
ends; that restless, nervous energy; that dominant individualism,
working for good and for evil, and withal that buoyancy and

exuberance which comes with freedom—these are traits of the frontier, or traits called out elsewhere because of the existence of the frontier. Since the days when the fleet of Columbus sailed into the waters of the New World, "America has been another name for opportunity," and the people of the United States have taken their tone from the incessant expansion which has not only been open but has even been forced upon them. He would be a rash prophet who should assert that the expansive character of American life has now entirely ceased. Movement has been its dominant fact, and, unless this training has no effect upon a people, the American energy will continually demand a wider field for its exercise. But never again will such gifts of free land offer themselves. For a moment, at the frontier, the bonds of custom are broken and unrestraint is triumphant. There is not *tabula rasa*. The stubborn American environment is there with its imperious summons to accept its conditions; the inherited ways of doing things are also there; and yet, in spite of environment, and in spite of custom, each frontier did indeed furnish a new field of opportunity, a gate of escape from the bondage of the past; and freshness, and confidence, and scorn of older society, impatience of its restraints and its ideas, and indifference to its lessons, have accompanied the frontier. What the Mediterranean Sea was to the Greeks, breaking the bond of custom, offering new experiences, calling out new institutions and activities, that, and more, the ever retreating frontier has been to the United States directly, and to the nations of Europe more remotely. And now, four centuries from the discovery of America, at the end of a hundred years of life under the Constitution, the frontier has gone, and with its going has closed the first period of American history.

2.   Bishop William Lawrence,
"The Relation of Wealth to Morals"

FEW DOCUMENTS *seem to bespeak so well the lag of intelligence behind the march of industrial development as Episcopal Bishop William Lawrence's paean to wealth. Progressive-minded historians have usually delighted in serving up passages from the article to illustrate the fatuousness of the "gospel of wealth." "It is only to the man of morality that wealth* comes," averred Lawrence in one choice passage; and again: "If ever Christ's words have been obeyed to the letter, they are obeyed today by those who are living out His precepts of the stewardship of wealth." In an important way, however, to excerpt Lawrence's article is to run an unusual risk of wrenching it from its historical context. Lawrence was indeed pressing to the point of exaggeration a traditional American religious belief that God's will could be read in worldly events and that therefore there had to be, as a general rule, a harmony of morality and material success; moreover, there is no doubt—at least in retrospect—that his premise blinded him, as it did so many of his day, to the evidence all around him of how imperfect that supposed harmony really was. Yet it must not be overlooked that Lawrence was writing at the end of the third year of a hearty prosperity and at the end of a century in which the United States had emerged as the most productive industrial nation in the world. It was natural for the country to feel optimism and exultation, not least about how America's great wealth had helped make it the exemplar of the success of democratic institutions and the great hope of the demoralized everywhere. If Lawrence made too easy a link between excellence and affluence, his contention specifically included the point that "grinding poverty does grind down" and that it grinds down the spirit (character) as well as the body. This was an argument entirely consistent with the environmentalism of the most advanced Progressives, who tended to assume that moral uplift was implicit in the material redemption of the poor. Lawrence's point, it should be remembered, contrasts distinctly with the common quietisms of the day, such as, "Blessed are the poor in spirit: for theirs is the kingdom of heaven"; and, "Better is the poor that walketh in his uprightness, than he that is perverse in his ways, though he be rich."

SOURCE: Bishop William Lawrence, "The Relation of Wealth to Morals," *The World's Work*, I (January 1901), pp. 286–292.

There is a certain distrust on the part of our people as to the effect of material prosperity on their morality. We shrink with some foreboding at the great increase of riches, and question whether in the long run material prosperity does not tend toward the disintegration of character.

History seems to support us in our distrust. Visions arise of their fall from splendor of Tyre and Sidon, Babylon, Rome, and Venice, and of great nations too. The question is started whether England is not to-day, in the pride of her wealth and power, sowing the wind from which in time she will reap the whirlwind.

Experience seems to add its support. Is it not from the ranks of the poor that the leaders of the people have always risen? Recall Abraham Lincoln and patriots of every generation.

The Bible has sustained the same note. Were ever stronger words of warning uttered against the deceitfulness of riches than those spoken by the peasant Jesus, who Himself had no place to lay His head? And the Church has through the centuries upheld poverty as one of the surest paths to Heaven: it has been a mark of the saint.

To be sure, in spite of history, experience, and the Bible, men have gone on their way making money and hailing with joy each age of material prosperity. The answer is: "This only proves the case; men are of the world, riches are deceitful, and the Bible is true; the world is given over to Mammon. In the increase of material wealth and the accumulation of riches the man who seeks the higher life has no part."

In the face of this comes the statement of the chief statistician of our census—from one, therefore, who speaks with authority: "The present census, when completed, will unquestionably show that the visible material wealth in this country now has a value of ninety billion dollars. This is an addition since 1890 of twenty-five billion dollars. This is a saving greater than all the people of the Western Continent had been able to make from the discovery of Columbus to the breaking out of the Civil War."

If our reasoning from history, experience, and the Bible is correct, we, a Christian people, have rubbed a sponge over the pages of the Bible and are in for orgies and a downfall to which the fall of Rome is a very tame incident.

May it not be well, however, to revise our inferences from history, experience, and the Bible? History tells us that, while riches have been an item and an indirect cause of national decay, innumerable other conditions entered in. Therefore, while wealth has been a source of danger, it has not necessarily led to demoralization.

That leaders have sprung from the ranks of the poor is true and always will be true, so long as force of character exists in every class. But there are other conditions than a lack of wealth at the source of their uprising.

And as to the Bible:—while every word that can be quoted against the rich is as true as any other word, other words and deeds are as true; and the parables of our Lord on the stewardship of wealth, His association with the wealthy, strike another and complementary note. Both notes are essential to the harmony of His life and teachings. His thought was not of the conditions, rich or poor, but of a higher life, the character rising out of the conditions—fortunately, for we are released from that subtle hypocrisy which has beset the Christian through the ages, bemoaning the deceitfulness of riches and, at the same time, working with all his might to earn a competence, and a fortune if he can.

Man "Born to be Rich"

Now we are in a position to affirm that neither history, experience, nor the Bible necessarily sustains the common distrust of the effect of material wealth on morality. Our path of study is made more clear. Two positive principles lead us out on our path.

The first is that man, when he is strong, will conquer Nature, open up her resources, and harness them to his service. This is his play, his exercise, his divine mission.

"Man," says Emerson, "is born to be rich. He is thoroughly related, and is tempted out by his appetites and fancies to the conquest of this and that piece of Nature, until he finds his well-being in the use of the planet, and of more planets than his own. Wealth requires, besides the crust of bread and the roof, the freedom of the city, the freedom of the earth." "The strong race is strong on these terms."

Man draws to himself material wealth as surely, as naturally, and as necessarily as the oak draws the elements into itself from the earth.

The other principle is that, in the long run, it is only to the man of morality that wealth comes. We believe in the harmony of God's Universe. We know that it is only by working along His laws natural and spiritual that we can work with efficiency. Only by working along the lines of right thinking and right living can the secrets and wealth of Nature be revealed. We, like the Psalmist, occasionally see the wicked prosper, but only occasionally.

Put two men in adjoining fields, one man strong and normal, the other weak and listless. One picks up his spade, turns over the earth, and works till sunset. The other turns over a few clods, gets a drink from the spring, takes a nap, and loafs back to his work. In a few years one will be rich for his needs, and the other a pauper dependent on the first, and growling at his prosperity.

Put ten thousand immoral men to live and work in one fertile valley and ten thousand moral men to live and work in the next valley, and the question is soon answered as to who wins the material wealth. Godliness is in league with riches.

Now we return with an easier mind and clearer conscience to the problem of our twenty-five billion dollars in a decade.

My question is: Is the material prosperity of this Nation favorable or unfavorable to the morality of the people?

The first thought is, Who has prospered? Who has got the money?

I take it that the loudest answer would be, "The millionaires, the capitalists, and the incompetent but luxurious rich;" and, as we think of that twenty-five billion, our thoughts run over the yachts, the palaces, and the luxuries that flaunt themselves before the public.

Who the Rich Are

As I was beginning to write this paper an Irishman with his horse and wagon drew up at my back door. Note that I say his horse and wagon. Twenty years ago that Irishman, then hardly twenty years old, landed in Boston, illiterate, uncouth, scarcely able to make himself understood in English. There was no symptom of brains, alertness, or ambition. He got a job to tend a few cows. Soon the American atmosphere began to take hold. He discovered that here every man has his chance. With his first earnings he bought a suit of clothes; he gained self-respect. Then he sent money home; then he got a job to drive a horse; he opened an account at the savings bank; then evening school; more money in the bank. He changed to a better job, married a thrifty wife, and to-day he owns his house, stable, horse, wagon, and bicycle; has a good sum at the bank, supports five children, and has half a dozen men working under him. He is a capitalist, and his yearly earnings represent the income on $30,000. He had no "pull"; he has made his own way by grit, physical strength, and increasing intelligence. He has had material prosperity. His older brother, who paid his passage over, has had material prosperity, and his younger brother, whose passage my friend paid, has had material prosperity.

Now we are beginning to get an idea as to where the savings are. They are in the hands of hundreds of thousands of just such men, and of scores of thousands of men whose incomes ten years ago were two and five thousand, and are now five and ten thousand; and of thousands of others whose incomes have risen from ten to thirty thousand. So that, when you get to the multi-millionaires, you have only a fraction to distribute among them. And of them the fact is that only a small fraction of their income can be spent upon their own pleasure and luxury; the bulk of what they get has to be reinvested, and becomes the means whereby thousands earn their wages. They are simply trustees of a fraction of the national property.

When, then, the question is asked, "Is the material prosperity of this nation favorable or unfavorable to the morality of the people?" I say with all emphasis, "In the long run, and by all means, favorable!"

In other words, to seek for and earn wealth is a sign of a natural, vigorous, and strong character. Wherever strong men are, there they will turn into the activities of life. In the ages of chivalry you will find them on the crusades or seeking the Golden Fleece; in college life you will find them high in rank, in the boat, or on the athletic field; in an industrial age you will find them eager, straining every nerve in the development of the great industries. The race is to the strong. The search for material wealth is therefore as natural and necessary to the man as is the pushing out of its roots for more moisture and food to the oak. This is man's play, his exercise, the expression of his powers, his personality. You can no more suppress it than you can suppress the tide of the ocean. For one man who seeks money for its own sake there are ten who seek it for the satisfaction of the seeking, the power there is in it, and the use they can make of it. There is the exhilaration of feeling one's self grow in one's surroundings; the man reaches out, lays hold of this, that, and the other interest, scheme, and problem. He is building up a fortune? Yes, but his joy is also that he is building up a stronger, abler, and more powerful man. There are two men that have none of this ambition: the gilded, listless youth and the ragged, listless pauper to whom he tosses a dime; they are in the same class.

We are now ready to take up the subject in a little more detail. How is it favorable? The parable of my Irish friend gives the answer.

In the first place, and as I have already suggested, the effort to make his living and add to his comforts and power gives free play to a man's activities and leads to a development of his faculties. In an age and country where the greater openings are in commercial lines, there the stronger men and the mass of them will move. It is not a question of worldliness or of love of money, but of the natural use and legitimate play of men's faculties. An effort to suppress this action is not a religious duty, but a disastrous error, sure to fail.

Self-Respect and Self-Mastery

Besides this natural play of the faculties comes the development of self-respect and ambition. In the uprise from a lower to a higher civilization, these are the basal elements. Watch the cart-loads of Polish or Italian immigrants as they are hauled away from the dock. Study their lifeless expression, their hang-dog look, and their almost cowering posture. Follow them and study them five years later: note the gradual straightening of the body, the kindling of the eye, and the alertness of the whole person as the men, women, and children begin to realize their opportunities, bring in their wages, and move to better quarters. Petty temptations and deep degradations that might have overwhelmed them on their arrival cannot now touch them.

With this comes also the power of self-mastery. The savage eats what he kills and spends what he has. In the movement towards civilization through material wealth, questions come up for decision every hour. Shall I spend? Shall I save? How shall I spend? How can I earn more? Shall I go into partnership with a capital of ten dollars, or shall I wait until I have fifty dollars?

Wage earners are not to-day, as they were in earlier days, hungering for the bare physical necessities of life. They are hungering now, and it marks an upward movement in civilization, for higher things, education, social life, relaxation, and the development of the higher faculties.

To be sure, a certain fraction wilt under the strain, take to drink, to lust, to laziness. There is always the thin line of stragglers behind every army, but the great body of the American people are marching upwards in prosperity through the mastery of their lower tastes and passions to the development of the higher. From rags to clothes, from filth to cleanliness, from disease to health; from bare walls to pictures; from ignorance to education; from narrow and petty talk to books and music and art; from superstition to a more rational religion; from crudity to refinement; from self-centralization to the conception of a social unity.

Here in this last phrase we strike the next step in development. In this increase of wealth, this rapid communication which goes with it, this shrinking of the earth's surface and unifying of peoples through commerce, men and women are realizing their relations to society.

That there are those who in the deepest poverty sustain the spirit of unselfishness and exhibit a self-sacrifice for others which puts their richer neighbors to the blush we know by experience. At the same time, the fact is that for the mass and in the long run grinding poverty does grind down the character: in the struggle for bare existence and for the very life of one's children there is developed an intense self-centralization and a hardness which is destructive of the social instinct and of the finer graces. When, however, through the increase of wealth man has extended his interests, his vision, and his opportunities, "he is thoroughly related." His lines run out in every direction; he lays his finger upon all the broader interests of life, the school, the church, and the college. He reaches through commerce to the ends of the earth. He discovers one bond which is essential to the social unity in this commercial age—the bond of faith in other men; for in credit, on belief in others, our whole social and commercial fabric is built. And when a man has reached this point, he has indeed reached one of the high plateaus of character: from this rise the higher mountain peaks of Christian graces, but here he is on the standing-ground of the higher civilization.

As I write I can almost feel the silent protest of some critics. Are not these qualities, self-respect, self-mastery, a sense of social unity, and mutual confidence, the commonplaces of life? Is this the only response of material wealth in its relation to morality?

These are to us now the commonplaces of life: they are at the same time the fundamentals of character and of morality. If material prosperity has been one of the great instruments (and I believe it has) in bringing the great body of our people even to approach this plateau of character, it has more than justified itself.

One might, however, mention other and finer qualities that follow in these days the train of prosperity. I instance only one. We will strike up one mountain peak: it is that of joyful and grateful service.

The Privilege of Grateful Service

In other days we have heard much of "the sweet uses of adversity": the note still lingers in sermons and will linger as long as Christianity stands. There is, however, the other note that sounds strong in these days,—the privilege of grateful service.

I have in mind now a man of wealth (you can conjure up many like him) who lives handsomely and entertains; he has everything that purveys to his health and comfort. All these things are tributary to what? To the man's efficiency in his complete devotion to the social, educational, and charitable interests to which he gives his life. He is Christ's as much as was St. Paul, he is consecrated as was St. Francis of Assisi; and in recognition of the bounty with which God has blessed him he does not sell all that he has, but he uses all that he has, and, as he believes, in the wisest way, for the relief of the poor, the upbuilding of social standards, and the upholding of righteousness among the people. The Christian centuries, with all their asceticism and monasticism, with their great and noble saints, have, I believe, never witnessed a sweeter, more gracious, and more complete consecration than that which exists in the lives of hundreds of men and women in the cities and towns of this country, who, out of a sense of grateful service to God for His bounty, are giving themselves with all joy to the welfare of the people. And if ever Christ's words have been obeyed to the letter, they are obeyed to-day by those who are living out His precepts of the stewardship of wealth.

As we think of the voluntary and glad service given to society, to the State, the Church, to education, art, and charity, of the army of able men and women who, without thought of pay, are serving upon directories of savings banks and national banks, life insurance companies, railroads, mills, trusts and corporations, public commissions, and offices of all sorts, schools and colleges, churches and charities; as we run our thoughts over the free services of the doctors, of the lawyers, for their poorer clients, we are amazed at the magnitude of unpaid service, which is now taken for granted, and at the cheerful and glad spirit in which it is carried through. Material prosperity is helping to make the national character sweeter, more joyous, more unselfish, more Christlike. That is my answer to the question as to the relation of material prosperity to morality.

Again I feel a silent protest. Is not the writer going rather far? We did not believe that our twenty-five billions would lead to orgies; but is he not getting rather close to the millennium? Are there no shadows and dark spaces in the radiance which he seems to think that wealth is shedding around us?

Yes, my friendly critic, there are, and to a mention of a few of them I give the pages that are left.

The Spirit of Commercialism

First and most pervasive, I name the spirit of commercialism. It crops up in many forms and places, hydra-headed.

Is it any wonder? When one realizes that in the last ten years seventy millions of people have earned their living, paid their bills, and have at the same time increased the property of the Nation by twenty-five billions of dollars, we reach a slight conception of the intensity, the industry, the enterprise, and the ability with which those people have thought, worked, and reaped. One wonders that religion, charity, or culture have survived the strain at all. When the eye and ambition of a strong man are set upon a purpose, he sometimes neglects other considerations; he is not over nice about the rights of others; he occasionally overrides the weak, crushes out the helpless, and forgets to stop and pick up those that have fallen by the way.

We know how that was in England: we remember the report of the Commission by Lord Shaftesbury as to the horrible condition of the miners, men, women, and children. That was simply one phase in the development of the great movement of modern industrialism. It was a neglect and forgetfulness under a new pressure, rather than deliberate cruelty. The facts once known, attention called,—and reforms began; and they have been going on in behalf of the working people ever since. Much, very much, has been done.

As conditions change, much remains to do. The better adjustment of rights, wages, and taxes will call for the highest intelligence and strongest character. Again, the small tradesman has driven away the little counter where a widow earned her living, the larger tradesman has wiped out the small tradesman, and the department store is now finishing off some of the large tradesmen. It is hard, but it is a part of the great economic movement. It endangers some of the fundamentals of morality, and destroys for the time some of the finer graces.

Ephemeral success sometimes follows deceit, and that breeds a body of commercial frauds; but they cannot endure. A fortune is won by an unscrupulous adventurer; and a hundred fortunes are lost and characters spoiled in trying to follow suit. An ignorant man happens upon wealth or by some mysterious commercial ability wins wealth, and he then thinks himself omniscient. He, not God, is his own creator. He goes to church, but he is Godless. When a nation of people have been seeking for clothes, houses, and comforts in the upbuilding of civilization, is it any wonder that they do not realize that a man's life consisteth not in the abundance of things that he possesseth? There are deceit, hardness, materialism, and vulgarity in the commercial world; and to me the vulgarest of all is not the diamond-studded operator, but the horde of mothers crushing each other around the bargain counter in their endeavor to get something, and that so small, for nothing. The worst of commercialism is that it does not stop at the office, but enters the home, taints the marriage vow, and poisons social life at its springs.

Beyond these rudimentary forms of commercialism, there is another, even more dangerous, because it threatens the liberties and rights of the people. The eye of the public is on it now. I refer to the relation of concentrated masses of wealth to the public service.

I have no time to more than suggest a few of the conditions that have led up to this. Industrial enterprise has drawn many of the strongest and ablest men from political to commercial interests; society and legislation now do for the people what in other days the landlord did; they are concerned more and more with industrial, commercial, and financial questions, from the national tariff to the size of a house-drain. Just at this time, and because of our great industrial development and prosperity, a horde of ignorant voters waiting to be moulded by any strong leader have come to this shore. The wide distribution of wealth has driven merchants and mechanics, widows and trustees of orphans, doctors and ministers, to invest their savings in great enterprises, corporations, and trusts, which, to succeed, must be directed by a few men. We have therefore this situation: a few men responsible for the safekeeping and development of enormous properties, dependent upon legislation, and a great mass of voters, many of them ignorant, represented by their own kind in city or state government, strongly organized by a leader who is in it for what he can get out of it, and who is ever alert with his legislative cohorts to "strike" the great corporations. The people believe that the officers of great corporations so manage that they can get what they want, call it by assessment, bribery, ransom, or what you will, and they brand those otherwise respectable men as cowards and traitors to public liberty.

The Rich Man and the Burglar

A burglar breaks into your house, awakes you, and "strikes" you for $500 which is in your safe downstairs. You expostulate: he answers that he will burn your house. But your children, you cry, will they be safe? He does not know: he wants the money. But if you give it to him, he will try the same on other people. It is against all public duty for you to yield. Again, the threat that he will burn your house; and you, miserable, conscience-stricken that you are doing a cowardly thing, and one against the safety of the public, crawl downstairs, open the safe, and hand over the cash. You have saved your house and children, but how about your duty to the public and your neighbors, as well as to yourself?

This is very much the position of the great trustees of capital, the heads of our great corporations, at the hands of the modern bandit. Shall they jeopardize the income of women and children, merchants and mechanics, and perhaps drive them into poverty? Or shall they accept the situation, yield to the threat, and trust to the authorities to seize the robber, or through an aroused public opinion so to vote, act, and legislate as to change the law and stop this modern brigandage? That some of the promoters and managers of great corporations are unscrupulous is undoubtedly true. The jail is none too good for them, if only the law would touch them. Nor have we a word of apology or justification for any man who yields to or encourages blackmail. The difficulty, however, is not a simple one. It concerns more than the directors and the politicians; it relates to the rights and liberties of the people. I do not have so much fear of the rich man in office, as I do of the poor but weak man in office and the rich man outside. Through the interplay of aroused public opinion, better legislation, and intelligent action, the relief will come. A younger generation, with its eye keen upon that danger-point, is coming to the front.

In some cities of China the houses have no windows on the street, only bare walls and the little door. The families are isolated, narrow, and selfish: there is no public spirit. When the Chinese boy returns home from his Christian Mission School, touched with the spirit of Christian civilization, his first work in bringing civilization to his home is to take a crowbar, knock a hole in the front wall, and make a window, that he may see out and the people see in. He unifies society and creates a public opinion. What is needed as our next step in civilization is to break a hole and make a window that the public may see into the great corporations and trusts and, what is just as important, that the managers may see out and recognize the sentiment of the public.

Light and action—heroic action! There are men to-day waiting and wanting to act, to throw off the shackles of the modern bandit; but they dare not alone: their trusts are too great. What is wanted is a group of men, high in position, great in power, who at great cost, if need be, will stand and say, "Thus far, up to the lines of the nicest honor, shalt thou go, and no farther."

The people have their eye upon the public service. An administration may pay political debts by pushing ignorant and unworthy men into the lower offices, but when it comes to filling positions of great responsibility the President could not, and would not if he could, appoint men less worthy than Wood in Cuba, Allen in Porto Rico, and Taft in the Philippines, men of force, intelligence, and character. Collegiate education does not insure character, but it does sift men and insure intelligence; and, as President Pritchett of the Massachusetts Institute of Technology pointed out in his inaugural address, though less than one per cent of our population are college men, yet from this very small fraction a majority of the legislative, executive, and judicial places of the General Government which have to do in any large way with shaping the policy and determining the character of the government, are chosen.

The Danger from Luxury

One other dark shadow, and I am done. The persistent companion of riches,—luxury and an ability to have what you want. That vice and license are rampant in certain quarters is clear; that vulgar wealth flaunts itself in the face of the people is beyond question; and that the people are rather amused at the spectacle must be confessed. The threatre syndicate will turn on to the boards whatever the people want; and the general tone of the plays speaks not well for the taste and morality of the people. The strain of temptation overwhelms a fraction of our youth. But one has no more right to test the result of prosperity by the small class of the lazy and luxurious than he has to test the result of poverty by the lazy tramp.

With all this said, the great mass of the people are self-restrained and simple. Material prosperity has come apace, and on the whole it uplifts. Responsibility sobers men and nations. We have learned how to win wealth: we are learning how to use and spend it. Every year marks a long step in advance in material prosperity, and character must march in step. Without wealth, character is liable to narrow and harden. Without character, wealth will destroy. Wealth is upon us, increasing wealth. The call of to-day is, then, for the uplift of character,—the support of industry, education, art, and every means of culture; the encouragement of the higher life; and, above all, the deepening of the religious faith of the people; the rekindling of the spirit, that, clothed with her material forces, the great personality of this Nation may fulfil her divine destiny.

I have been clear, I trust, in my opinion that material prosperity is in the long run favorable to morality. Let me be as clear in the statement of that eternal truth, that neither a man's nor a nation's life consists in the abundance of things that he possesseth.

In the investment of wealth in honest enterprise and business, lies our path of character. In the investment of wealth in all that goes towards the uplift of the people in education, art, and religion is another path of character. Above all, and first of all, stands the personal life. The immoral rich man is a traitor to himself, to his material as well as spiritual interests. Material prosperity is upon us; it is marching with us. Character must keep step, ay, character must lead. We want great riches; we want also great men.

3.   Robert Hunter,
Poverty

IN 1904, when Robert Hunter (1874–1942) published his then virtually unique statistical study of poverty in the United States, the nation was in its eighth year of an almost unprecedented economic boom. Its per capita income (about $500 per year) was the highest in the world, and personal wealth was about as well distributed throughout the society as in any large nation in history. Vertical social and economic mobility in America, though probably overestimated by contemporaries, was legendary at home and abroad; although only a small minority of the very rich had followed paths as steep as those of Rockefeller and Carnegie, the fact that there had been even a few such careers suggested an extraordinary incidence of success stories of only slightly less spectacular dimensions. It is not astonishing that such a country should take little stock of its poor; presumably they would take advantage of the manifest opportunities America provided for climbing out of poverty, or else they had little moral substance worth troubling over to begin with. And yet for many that argument no longer sufficed. The severe depression of the 1890's, accompanied as it was by industrial strife and the spectacle of masses of workers on the city streets and along the country roads vainly seeking work, did violence to the comfortable assumption that ample employment awaited the worthy and the willing. Hunter, the son of a carriage manufacturer in Terre Haute, Indiana, was one of those whose comfortable assumptions were exploded by the Panic of 1893. Joining Jane Addams at Hull House in Chicago, he helped organize that city's first free dental clinic for children and one of the country's first municipal lodging houses for vagrants. In 1901 he published Tenement Conditions in Chicago, and in 1902 he went to New York to serve as "head worker" at University Settlement House. Poverty drew heavily on Hunter's own experiences with the poor, on Jacob Riis's How the Other Half Lives (1890), and on published accounts by other settlement-house workers, such as Robert Woods on Boston's South End House. Hunter acknowledged a special debt to R. W. De Forest and Lawrence Veiller's The Tenement House Problem (1903), from which a selection appears in Part III (Document 12). What set Poverty off from the other works was, first, Hunter's astute method of producing statistics with which to measure and define poverty and, second, his insistence that, with the statistics showing poverty to be so much more extensive than most people assumed, one could hardly avoid the conclusion that poverty was a social problem, not a personal or moral one that charity might suffice to handle. For the best general survey of the subject, see Robert H. Bremner's From the Depths: The Discovery of Poverty in the United States (New York, 1956).

SOURCE: Robert Hunter, Poverty (New York: Harper Torchbooks, 1965), pp. xxv–xxviii, 1–64.

Preface

The main objects of this volume are: To define poverty and to estimate its extent at the present time in the United States; to describe some of its evils, not only among the dependent and vicious classes, which constitute the social wreckage in the abysses of our cities, but also among the unskilled, underpaid, underfed, and poorly housed workers; furthermore, to point out certain remedial actions which society may wisely undertake; and, finally, to show that the evils of poverty are not barren, but procreative, and that the workers in poverty are, in spite of themselves, giving to the world a litter of miserables, whose degeneracy is so stubborn and fixed that reclamation is almost impossible, especially when the only process of reclamation must consist in trying to force the pauper, vagrant, and weakling back into that struggle with poverty which is all of the time defeating stronger and better natures than theirs. . . . Especial attention is directed to the larger mass from which the dependent classes are mainly recruited. Although it comprises several million wage-workers, it is, strange to say, almost a forgotten class, confused on the one side with the vicious and dependent and on the other with the more highly paid workers. . . .

The limitations are many. I shall mention but two of those which exist in my description of conditions. The poor of the rural districts have hardly been mentioned, and the working woman and the mother are left almost entirely out of consideration. I have been content to pass over these important problems because I have been less observant of these phases of poverty than of other phases, and I have kept to my original determination not to write of conditions with which I am not personally familiar. Similar limitations may be observed in my dealing with causes and remedies. I have purposely ignored individual causes, and I have mentioned among remedial measures only those for which I have worked or those which have been in certain places and at certain times tried and found of value. The more far-reaching and radical reforms proposed by the socialist, single taxer, and individualist have not been examined here, and therefore not condemned or endorsed. In so far as possible conditions are described as seen; causes which have been watched and studied are mentioned, and remedies which have appealed to me as of immediate importance have been urged. The book as a whole has one aim; namely, to show the grievous need of certain social measures calculated to prevent the ruin and degradation of those working people who are on the verge of poverty. I am at a loss to understand why well-known and generally recognized poverty-breeding conditions, which are both unjust and unnecessary, are tolerated for an instant among a humane, not to say a professedly Christian people. . . .

Chapter I. Poverty

William Dean Howells said to me recently, after I had told him of a visit to Tolstoy: "It is wonderful what Tolstoy has done. He could do no more. For a nobleman, with the most aristocratic ancestry, to refuse to be supported in idleness, to insist upon working with his own hands, and to share as much as possible the hardship and toil of a peasant class, which, but recently, was a slave class, is the greatest thing he could do. But it is impossible for him to share their poverty, for poverty is not the lack of things; it is the fear and the dread of want. That fear Tolstoy could not know." These remarks of Mr. Howells brought to mind the wonderful words of Thomas Carlyle: "It is not to die, or even to die of hunger, that makes a man wretched; many men have died; all men must die. . . . But it is to live miserable we know not why; to work sore and yet gain nothing; to be heart-worn, weary, yet isolated, unrelated, girt in with a cold, universal Laissez-faire." To live miserable we know not why, to have the dread of hunger, to work sore and yet gain nothing,—this is the essence of poverty.

There are many people in the world who believe that the provisions of charity are in the present day so generous and varied that no one need suffer; but, even if this were true, it would not materially lessen the sorrow of the poor. To thousands and thousands of working-men the dread of public pauperism is the agony of their lives. The mass of working-men on the brink of poverty hate charity. Now only their words convey a knowledge of this fact, but their actions, when in distress, make it absolutely undeniable. When the poor face the necessity of becoming paupers, when they must apply for charity if they are to live at all, many desert their families and enter the ranks of vagrancy; others drink themselves insensible; some go insane; and still others commit suicide. . . .

These are the terrible alternatives which the working people in poverty accept in preference to pauperism, and yet it is a curious fact, which psychology alone explains, that the very men who will suffer almost anything rather than become paupers are often the very ones who never care to be anything else when once they have become dependent upon alms. When a family once become dependent, the mental agony which they formerly had disappears. Paupers are not, as a rule, unhappy. They are not ashamed; they are not keen to become independent; they are not bitter or discontented. They have passed over the line which separates poverty from pauperism.

This distinction between the poor and paupers may be seen everywhere. There are in all large cities in America and abroad, streets and courts and alleys where a class of people live who have lost all self-respect and ambition, who rarely, if ever, work, who are aimless and drifting, who like drink, who have no thought for their children, and who live more or less contentedly on rubbish and alms. . . . The lowest level of humanity is reached in these districts. In our American cities Negroes, Whites, Chinese, Mexicans, Half-breeds, Americans, Irish, and others are indiscriminately housed together in the same tenements and even in the same rooms. The blind, the crippled, the consumptive, the aged,—the ragged ends of life; the babies, the children, the half-starved, underclad beginnings in life, all huddled together, waiting, drifting. This is pauperism. There is no mental agony here; they do not work sore; there is no dread; they live miserably, but they do not care.

In the same cities and, indeed, everywhere, there are great districts of people who are up before dawn, who wash, dress, and eat breakfast, kiss wives and children, and hurry away to work or to seek work. The world rests upon their shoulders; it moves by their muscle; everything would stop if, for any reason, they should decide not to go into the fields and factories and mines. But the world is so organized that they gain enough to live upon only when they work; should they cease, they are in destitution and hunger. The more fortunate of the laborers are but a few weeks from actual distress when the machines are stopped. Upon the unskilled masses want is constantly pressing. As soon as employment ceases, suffering stares them in the face. They are the actual producers of wealth, who have no home nor any bit of soil which they may call their own. They are the millions who possess no tools and can work only by permission of another. In the main, they live miserably, they know not why. They work sore, yet gain nothing. They know the meaning of hunger and the dread of want. They love their wives and children. They try to retain their self-respect. They have some ambition. They give to neighbors in need, yet they are themselves the actual children of poverty.

. . . The United States spends more money than any other nation in the world upon statistical investigations, and yet we know less about the poverty of the people than almost any other great nation of the Western world. An immense sum is expended yearly in taking the census and in maintaining the many bureaus in Washington to investigate the conditions of commerce, of labor, of agriculture, of railways, etc. Almost every state has local bureaus existing for the same purpose. After the existence of these bureaus for a period of from twenty to thirty years, no one can tell, or give anything like a fair estimate of, the number of people existing in the community unable to obtain a living wage or its equivalent; or, in other words, unable to obtain the necessaries for maintaining physical efficiency. We cannot now, in any very satisfactory way, tell the number of unemployed, the number of unskilled workers or their wages; we do not know the number of underfed children, or even, and this seems most absurd of all, the number of persons dependent upon the public for support. We do not know the number of men killed by accidents in industry, or injured by dangerous trades. There are immense volumes of wage statistics containing averages so general, and confusing so skilfully all the different classes of labor, that it is next to impossible to make anything specific out of the material. Almost each new publication warns any one from trusting or basing any arguments upon material previously gathered and published. The extent of poverty in the United States is absolutely unknown. Mr. Carroll D. Wright,[1] who of all persons should be able to throw some light on this subject, is unable to quote any statistics whatever when writing on the subject of poverty in his book. His chapter on poverty is in itself a restatement of well-known generalizations of questionable usefulness, and based largely upon the investigations and statements of Professor Amos G. Warner, who, largely as a result of private inquiry, produced an invaluable book upon "American Charities." With no figures whatever to bear out his statement, Mr. Wright takes occasion to speak of the assertion that the "rich

1. *Carroll D. Wright* (1840–1909): famous statistician; one-time lawyer, Massachusetts state senator, chief of Mass. Bureau of Labor (1873), and subsequently first U.S. Commissioner of Labor (1885–1905) and director of the 11th Census (1893).

are growing richer and the poor poorer" as "false in its premises and misleading in its influence." It is unnecessary to say that we might choose to take Mr. Wright's statement or choose to take his opponent's statement. It is largely a matter of temperament which side one takes in the matter, for in either case we have no facts to support our position.

. . . While men in Germany and England have been making exhaustive studies of the poverty and social misery in those countries, and have aroused the people to the grave necessity of social reform, the United States has made almost no progress in obtaining exact knowledge of the condition of the working-classes. . . . There are, however, certain fragments of information which may make us question the prevalent notion that all is well, and that "comparatively speaking," as an economist said to me recently, "we have no poverty." There is a general spirit of optimism, which is not unlike that which existed in England previous to the work of Mr. Booth and Mr. Rountree. It is an optimism which results from ignorance or from the lack of any real concern. Such facts as we have are not sufficient to enable us to make any conclusive estimate, and they are used only for the purpose of serving as indications of the extent of poverty in this country.

. . . Mr. Jacob A. Riis, a few years ago, used some figures which showed that about one-third of the people of New York City were dependent upon charity at some time during the eight years previous to 1890. The report of the United Hebrew Charities for 1901 shows very similar conditions existing among the Jewish population of New York. But even more astonishing than all other facts we have are those furnished by the State Board of Charities. In 1897 the Board endeavored to collect figures of the number of persons assisted by both public and private charities. It was of course impossible to prevent duplications or to get returns from hundreds of the more personal sources of relief-giving, but it was a creditable and most useful piece of public work. Three years later the work was curtailed by decision of the Court of Appeals, and consequently the more complete figures are only available for the three years 1897, 1898, and 1899. . . .

These figures unquestionably contain many duplications. How many, it is impossible to say. It would not be reasonable to believe that 29 per cent of the people of New York found it necessary in the year 1897, or 24 per cent in 1899, to apply for relief. And yet it

should be said that these figures of the State Board do not include
the relief given by the many small clubs, circles, committees, and
Trade Unions; nor is the relief given by many benevolent individuals recorded. There must, of course, be many thousand cases of
distress receiving relief regularly and solely from these personal or
private sources. . . .

Excluding half the number of persons relieved by the dispen-
saries (in order to make some arbitrary allowance for duplications),
even then the number of persons relieved would indicate that the
poverty of New York State is enormous. . . .

The amount of actual distress in the community may be measured also by two additional sets of data. The number of evictions
in any community is a fairly good measure of the minimum
distress. . . . As another indication, the number of pauper burials
should be cited. Every one familiar with the poor knows how
desperately they struggle to give a decent burial to their dead. . . .
And yet one in every ten persons who die in New York is buried at
public expense in Potter's Field. This is, without question, the
lowest limit of misery. If observation counts for anything, I should
say that the number of pauper burials certainly does not represent
half of the actual distress in any community.

The results stated concisely are as follows:

1903	20 percent of the people of Boston in distress.
1897	19 per cent of the people of New York State in distress.
1899	18 per cent of the people of New York State in distress.
1903	14 per cent of the families of Manhattan evicted.
Every year.	10 per cent (about) of those who die in Manhattan have pauper burials.

On the basis of these figures it would seem fair to estimate that
certainly not less than 14 per cent of the people, in prosperous
times (1903), and probably not less than 20 per cent in bad times
(1897), are in distress. The estimate is a conservative one, for
despite all the imperfections which may be found in the data, and
there are many, any allowance for the persons who are given aid by
sources not reporting to the State Board, or for those persons not
aided by the authorities of Boston, or for those persons who,
although in great distress, are not evicted, must counterbalance the

duplications or errors which may exist in the figures either of distress or evictions.

These figures, furthermore, represent only the distress which manifests itself. . . .

From a different point of view,—from figures of the ownership of wealth in this country,—another indication of poverty may be considered. Wealth and poverty seem to be inevitably associated with each other. . . . Here again our figures are deplorably deficient when compared with English ones. There is a general impression that we have a widespread diffusion of property ownership. It is, of course, natural that, with great tracts of land opened within the last century to millions of individuals, there should be an extent of individual ownership of farms in this country far greater than that existing elsewhere. But nevertheless, Mr. George K. Holmes, a cautious and conservative investigator, shows, on the basis of the census figures for 1890, that over 34 per cent of our farmers are renters and an additional 18.6 per cent have their farms mortgaged. All together there are over 52 per cent of the farmers in this country who have only a partial ownership of their farms, or who are propertyless.

The number of persons owning farms is an indication of the ownership of property in the rural districts only; while the figures concerning the ownership of homes give us an indication of the number of persons in cities, towns, and agricultural districts, having no property interests. The census figures for 1900 show that 8,365,739, or considerably over half of the families in the United States, do not own the homes in which they live. In the cities the ownership of homes is much less common than in the smaller towns. Illustrations of this fact are seen in the following percentages of homes hired in various cities:

Boston	81.1
Chicago	74.9
Cincinnati	79.1
Fall River	82.
Holyoke	80.6
New York (Manhattan)	94.1
Philadelphia	77.9

. . . The significant thing in this lack of ownership lies in the fact that a very large majority, probably 90 per cent, of the workmen in the cities and industrial communities, are propertyless, and, fur-thermore, are involved in a weekly indebtedness for rent of from one-fifth to two-fifths of their earnings, regardless of whether they have work or not.

The estimates of wealth and of the distribution of wealth, made by Mr. Holmes, are less reliable than the aforegoing figures of ownership, but they indicate, nevertheless, that there exists in this country "an enormous culture bed for poverty." The entire wealth of the country was estimated by the census of 1890 at $65,000,-000,000. Mr. Holmes concludes, on the basis of his inquiries, that three-tenths of one per cent of the families in this country own one-fifth of this wealth, that is to say, 20 per cent of the wealth of the country. Nine per cent of the families in the country own 71 per cent of the total wealth.

Mr. Charles B. Spahr has estimated, with most painstaking care, the distribution of incomes in the United States. The results of his inquiries are very effectively set forth in the following tables and diagrams:

THE UNITED STATES 1890

ESTATES	NUMBER	AGGREGATE WEALTH	AVERAGE WEALTH
The Wealthy Classes ($50,000 and over)	125,000	$33,000,000,000	$264,000
The Well-to-do Classes ($50,000 to $5,000)	1,375,000	23,000,000,000	16,000
The Middle Classes ($5,000 to $500)	5,500,000	8,200,000,000	1,500
The Poorer Classes (under $500)	5,500,000	800,000,000	150
Total	12,500,000	$65,000,000,000	$5,200

From this table Mr. Spahr concludes that less than half of the families in the United States are propertyless; nevertheless, seven-eighths of the families hold but one-eighth of the national wealth, while but one per cent of the families hold more than the remaining ninety-nine per cent.

Another table, based upon Mr. Spahr's inquiry, and accompanied by a diagram, is taken from Mr. John Graham Brooks' "The Social Unrest."

DISTRIBUTION OF WEALTH IN THE UNITED STATES

CLASS	FAMILIES	PER CENT	AVERAGE WEALTH	AGGREGATE WEALTH	PER CENT
Rich	125,000	1.0	$263,040	$32,880,000,000	54.8
Middle	1,362,500	10.9	14,180	19,320,000,000	32.2
Poor	4,762,500	38.1	1,639	7,800,000,000	13.0
Very Poor	6,250,000	50.0	——	——	——
Total	12,500,000	100.0	$4,800	$60,000,000,000	100.0

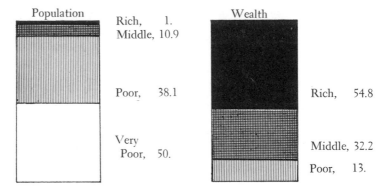

DIAGRAMS SHOWING, BY PERCENTAGES, THE POPULATION AND WEALTH DISTRIBUTION IN THE UNITED STATES

Mr. Brooks says regarding this latter table: "I do not personally believe that trustworthy statistical sources exist that enable one to make tables of this character that are more than mere guesses at the fact. Yet if it were known what the possessions of the one hundred and twenty-six thousand richest families in the United States are, the result would be all that any agitator need ask." How many liberties have been taken with Mr. Spahr's figures in order to construct this latter table I do not know; it can be said, however, that while neither his figures nor those of Mr. Holmes have escaped criticism, the critics have not, thus far, been able to make out a case against them which necessitates any material alteration either of the handling of the data, or of the conclusions finally drawn. Without committing ourselves implicitly to them, we must acknowledge that they indicate an inequality of wealth distribution which should have before now received exhaustive investigation by our official statisticians. . . .

The sins of men should bring their own punishment, and the poverty which punishes the vicious and the sinful is good and necessary. Social or industrial institutions that save men from the painful consequences of vice or folly are not productive of the greatest good. There is unquestionably a poverty which men deserve, and by such poverty men are perhaps taught needful lessons. It would be unwise to legislate out of existence, even were it possible to do so, that poverty which penalizes the voluntarily idle and vicious. In other words, there are individual causes of poverty which should be eradicated by the individual himself, with such help as his family, the teachers, and the preachers may give him. For him society may be able to do little or nothing. The poor which are always to be with us, are, it seems to me, in poverty of their own making.

But as surely as this is true, there are also the poor which we must not have always with us. The poor of this latter class are, it seems to me, the mass of the poor; they are bred of miserable and unjust social conditions, which punish the good and the pure, the faithful and industrious, the slothful and vicious, all alike. We may not, by going into the homes of the poor, be able to determine which ones are in poverty because of individual causes, or which are in poverty because of social wrongs; but we can see, by looking about us, that men are brought into misery by the action of social and economic forces. And the wrongful action of such social and economic forces is a preventable thing.

4.   Herbert Croly,
Marcus Alonzo Hanna, His Life and Work

HERBERT CROLY (1869–1930) is best known as the author of The Promise of American Life (1909), an overlong, but exceptionally discerning, essay that is often credited with having inspired Theodore Roosevelt to adopt the "New Nationalism" program of 1912. Croly was also one of the original editors and a founder in 1914 of the advanced progressive journal, The New Republic. Aside from Roosevelt—whose "New Na-

tionalism" actually traces back several years before he heard of Croly—
the progressive ideas of the serious-minded New Yorker influenced such
important reformers and political leaders as Learned Hand, Felix Frank-
furter, Walter Lippmann, Harold Laski, and Henry Stimson. It may seem
eccentric, then, to focus on a little-known biography that Croly wrote
extolling the virtues of Mark Hanna, one of the Progressive Era's chief
villains, originator of the phrase "stand pat," and notorious "spokesman
for the vested interests"! And yet if one reads carefully the passages presented here, one finds highlighted—even more clearly than in The
Promise's prescriptions for reform—what one leading progressive thinker
really valued. To put it another way, the passages provide us with the
context within which Croly's political remedies must be considered. In
The Promise, Croly had written:

> The American democracy . . . has promised to Americans a sub-
> stantial satisfaction of their economic needs; and it has made that
> promise an essential part of the American national idea. The promise
> has been measurably fulfilled hitherto, because of the prodigious
> natural resources of the continent. . . . But those natural resources
> are now in large measure passed into the possession of individuals,
> and American statesmen can no longer count upon them to satisfy
> the popular hunger for economic independence. . . . The promise
> was made on the strength of what was believed to be an inexhaust-
> ible store of natural opportunities; and it will have to be kept even
> when those natural resources are no longer to be had. . . . If it is
> not kept, the American commonwealth will no longer continue to
> be a democracy.

In Marcus Alonzo Hanna, written three years later, Croly clearly suggests
he has in mind the restoration of a social harmony that would once more
render supreme the attributes possessed by people like the Hannas in the
days of easier affluence. "Whatever the outcome of the attempt now
being made to devise and establish a new system, which will have the
advantages, without the disadvantages, of the old, the traditional system
has ceased, at least for the time being, to be one on which the American
people can unite for the promotion of their joint economic interests."
But, he concludes, "The values inherent in Mark Hanna's example and
life are durable—although they are not likely to be prized at their actual
worth until greater harmony is restored between national traditions and
individual ideals."

The best study of Croly appears in Charles Forcey's The Crossroads
of Liberalism: Croly, Weyl, Lippmann and the Progressive Era, 1900–
1925 (New York, 1961). See also David W. Noble, The Paradox of
Progressive Thought (Minneapolis, Minn., 1958).

SOURCE: Herbert Croly, Marcus Alonzo Hanna, His Life and Work
(Hamden, Conn.: Archon Books, Shoe String Press, 1965), pp.
465–479.

Chapter XXVIII. Conclusion

Inasmuch as Mark Hanna was not a usurper and his career was not a *tour de force*, only one explanation will account for his peculiar success. He must have embodied in his own life and purposes some vital American social and economic tradition, which gave his personality, individual as it was, something more than an individual meaning and impulse; and he must have embodied this tradition all the more effectively because he was not more than half conscious of it. Mark Hanna could not represent anything unless he himself was what he represented. In truth, Mr. Hanna did embody the most vital social and economic tradition in American history—the tradition, that is, of the pioneer. He was an incarnation of the spirit and methods of the men who seized and cleared the public domain, developed its natural resources, started and organized an industrial and commercial system and determined most of our political and social habits and forms. All the salient characteristics of the pioneer are writ clear and large in Mr. Hanna's disposition and achievements. . . .

The foregoing assertions may well strike the average reader as doubtful. How can a man whose successful business career began after the Civil War and who did not become prominent in politics until 1896—how can the life of such a man embody with particular success the spirit and methods of the men who conquered the American wilderness? During the culminating period of his life pioneering in its primitive sense had practically ceased. The wilderness had disappeared. The United States had become more like a European country than like the United States of 1830. The gulf which had been created between the America of 1830 and the America of 1900 would be fairly well measured by the gulf between the manner of life of the lean, hardy frontiersman and that of the affluent Cleveland merchant.

The difficulty is obvious, but it is not conclusive. The men who originate an economic and social impulse and start it off on a career of conquest do not bestow upon it a complete expression. They exhibit its fresh vigor, and they overcome the most serious obstacles in its path; but their expression of it is necessarily crude and partial. The completer revelation must wait on history and experience. Generations must pass before a national social and economic movement develops fully its own latent tendencies and capabilities. The primitive pioneers imposed their social, political and economic ideas upon the country, but by the time their ideas had become part of the national tradition, the conditions in which they originated had changed. After the Civil War the pioneer system had to meet the shock of new economic and social forces. Under the stimulus of these new opportunities and new responsibilities it became in certain respects a new system. The vitality of the movement was depleted by the effort to adapt itself to more complicated social and economic surroundings, but this effort and its results proved to be peculiarly illuminating. Its strength and its weakness became more clearly distinguishable and more fully revealed than ever before, and the hand-writing of its history became far more legible. Inasmuch as only within the past fifteen years has the pioneer been granted his proper place in American economic and social development, it is not unnatural that during the same years there flourished and died the most complete single embodiment of pioneer purposes and methods.

The primary economic task of the pioneer was that of appropriating and developing the land and natural resources of a continent,—a task which combined and confused individual and social profits. The combination and confusion was reflected in the human nature of the period. The early pioneer was an aggressive, energetic, hopeful, grasping individual. He worked and fought primarily for his own advantage, but his individualism did not prevent him from being the maker of a society. In an economic environment which provided opportunities for all, men could fight for themselves without cherishing ill-will or incurring it. As a matter of fact, the pioneer overflowed with good-will and good-fellowship. He and his neighbors were all striving for the same port. Their contests were merely a good-natured race for the quickest voyage and the biggest market.

From the beginning they recognized and acted on the theory that the individual and social profits were indistinguishable. They conceived it to be the business of their government, as the agent of social betterment, to assist them in attaining their personal ends. The public interest, which government was supposed to promote, was conceived chiefly as a collection of individual interests; and the way to promote it was to stimulate individual economic activity. Hence the passion for "public improvements" which possessed the pioneer states and their frequent inability, in making those improvements, to distinguish between the really private and the really public interests involved. It was during these years, long before corporate enterprise had assumed economic importance, that "special interests" established their control over state legislatures. It was during these years that the practice of making American business depend on American politics had its beginning.

In the meantime American business was ceasing to be local and was becoming increasingly national in its operations. As it became national, the successors of the pioneers began to lose their suspicion of the Central Government. They began to understand that the nation could contribute more effectually to the stimulation of economic activity than could the states. . . . Washington became the headquarters from which was directed a comprehensive scheme of state-aided business. The agricultural states obtained the gift of free land to homesteaders. The industrial states secured and kept, as their share of the bargain, among the several localities, a high protective tariff. Other interests were satisfied by free mines, timber and pasture. The railroads claimed land grants as their share of the spoil. Business of all kinds was encouraged by loose corporation laws. In return for all these privileges the various special interests were required only to make use of them. They named their own liquor and drank it when and where and how they pleased. Public and private interests were still conceived to be substantially identical, and the national economic interest a comprehensive collection of special interests.

This Republican economic policy, to the perpetuation of which the public career of Mark Hanna was devoted, is plainly the adaptation to new conditions of the earlier purposes and methods of the pioneer Democrats. The continuity of the tradition is unmistakable. It consisted fundamentally of an attempt to convert the spirit and methods of the pioneer from an agency of local economic development into an agency of national economic development. The pioneer spirit and method, transformed in order to meet larger opportunities and responsibilities, was incorporated into the heart of the national economic system. In one way or another every kind of business was obtaining state aid, and was dependent upon state policy for its prosperity. At the very moment when both business and politics were being modified by specialization and organization, business itself was being fastened irretrievably to politics. And the association, dangerous as it is both for business and politics, lies deep and ineradicable in the American democratic tradition. Democracy has always meant to Americans a political system which contributed, by whatever means, to their individual economic well-being. The pioneer economy, both in its local and national phases, was merely the first attempt to realize this purpose.

To the generation of business men who came to the front after the Civil War and grew up in the midst of this system, it seemed like the order of nature. It assuredly accomplished the purpose for which it was intended, and its success was so considerable that it was accepted as a matter of course by the dominant mass of opinion. Mr. Hanna himself and many others like him was as much of a pioneer in his own region of work as had been the men who with axe and gun pushed their way into the wilderness. He developed mines, discovered or created markets, built furnaces, improved mechanical processes, organized industries and started commercial currents on their course. He watched among his own people the gradual accumulation of social benefits which resulted from the stimulation of individual enterprise, and these benefits seemed to him, not the result of temporary conditions, but the normal and permanent effect of stimulating individual business energy. Neither he nor the men of his generation could understand why the system should not continue of equal benefit to the individual and to society.

Nevertheless, certain parts of this economic system were passing out of the pioneer stage, in which there was a rough approximation of individual and social benefits. The essential character of pioneer economics consisted of an abundance of opportunities due chiefly to a superfluity of accessible natural resources. But even in a country as richly endowed as the United States, natural resources had a limit. As soon as the process of their appropriation had reached a certain stage and had given their proprietors a certain advantage over their future competitors, the machinery began to creak. Under such conditions the state encouragement of private enterprise assumed a different appearance and began to look less like a system of social and more like a system of individual benefits. Society might profit, but not in the same proportion to the profits which the state was showering on the individual. In fact, the balance of the whole system was upset as soon as natural resources became even a little scarce and as soon as the corresponding artificial opportunities, created by state law, became even comparatively inaccessible. Not long after the war public opinion, in those parts of the country which were suffering from local business depression, began to blame the system for their privations, and began to criticise the way in which the appropriated economic power was being exercised. The discontent increased, and thereafter the national policy of state-stimulated enterprise had to bear the burden of hostile political agitation.

The foregoing situation affords the clew to the political contests of the last twenty years. Just in proportion as natural resources and artificial economic opportunities were appropriated and developed, public and private interests did not coincide to the same extent as formerly. The private interests which had received public assistance were driven by the necessities of their position to seek the continuance of this assistance on other than public grounds. Business prosperity was entangled in a system whose assumptions no longer corresponded with the facts of American economic life. Every agitation for economic reform forced voters to choose between alternative evils. They could not withdraw the various privileges which business had been enjoying without disturbing confidence and checking expansion, yet they could not perpetuate the advantages enjoyed by certain kinds of business without making the state increasingly responsible for flagrant economic inequalities. The man who remained true to the traditional system was obliged to countenance and overlook many grave political and economic abuses. The man who attacked the traditional system was obliged to injure many innocent people, disappoint the immediate expectations of many more for a higher standard of living, and launch his fellow-countrymen on a career of dangerous economic and political reorganization.

Mark Hanna proved to be the ablest and most successful supporter of the traditional system developed by the crisis. He supported it, because he had become accustomed to its beneficial effects, without being aware that these benefits might be diminished by the gradual intrusion of scarcity values into the national economy. In his speeches he always assumed that economic opportunities were as abundant and as accessible as ever, and he always refers to the country's natural resources as inexhaustible. He was quite sincere in failing to recognize the change and its consequences, the proof of his sincerity being the harmony between the old tradition and his own business and social habits and practices. Many of his associates reaped their profits from the pioneer system, and supported it by word and deed, but ceased to be the kind of men in which the system originated, and which gave to it its meaning. But Mark Hanna always remained a pioneer, both in his business practice and in his purposes, feelings and ideas. His own life embodied the mixture of individual and social purposes characteristic of the pioneer.

As we have seen, he always remained essentially local in his business enterprises and ambitions and always had the benefit of persistent and familiar social surroundings. While certain of his friends were becoming specialists in financial and business organization, he remained an all-round man, personally competent to manage every aspect of his extensive and complicated business. . . . Above all, he never became that special kind of a man known as a money-maker. As with the pioneer, business was to him the most interesting sort of life provided by his own society. It was an intensely human occupation in which human motives were ever present, and around which he himself gathered a group of essentially human values.

Being every kind of a man demanded by his occupations and interests, he inevitably became a politician as well as a business man. Personal participation in politics was an essential duty and joy of the pioneers. They associated in their own lives public and private motives just as they associated public and private interests in making state policies. His participation in politics was not determined by business motives any more than his participation in business was determined exclusively by business motives. He took it up because it was intrinsically so interesting, and he became more and more absorbed in it because a personal devotion to the careers of certain political friends made it finally much more interesting than business. Of course as a politician he could not help representing business, because business was a part of himself —because business was in his eyes not simply money-making, but the most necessary kind of social labor. . . .

As long as Mr. Hanna lived, the American people, partly because of his influence, remained true to the old system. He carried with him the small traders and proprietors. After his death this class of small traders and proprietors, largely because of Mr. Roosevelt's influence, switched to reform, and they have remained ever since on that same track. Whatever the outcome of the attempt now being made to devise and establish a new system, which will have the advantages, without the disadvantages, of the old, the traditional system has ceased, at least for the time being, to be one on which the American people can unite for the promotion of their joint economic interests. Mark Hanna's public career coincided with the culmination of an epoch, and he himself was unquestionably the hero of this culminating moment of a century of American development. . . .

The conclusion is that Mr. Hanna's personality and career had an essentially social value, which the opponents of his political and economic opinions should be the last to ignore. He gave a highly individual expression both to the practical aspect of pioneer Americanism and to its really underlying tendency. The aggressive and sometimes unscrupulous individualism of the pioneer was redeemed by the conviction that in doing well for himself he was also doing well for society. The pioneer honestly identified and confused individual and social interests, and he was honestly concerned as much for the one as for the other. . . .

The economic and political system advocated by Mr. Hanna may not make for social fair play; but any one who rejects the system should be the more willing to recognize the good faith of the man. . . . If he was lacking, as his critics have declared, in idealism, the deficiency was at least partly due to the very reality of a certain ideal element in his own life. . . .

In any event, the value inherent in Mark Hanna's example and life are durable—although they are not likely to be prized at their actual worth until greater harmony is restored between national traditions and individual ideals. Since Mr. Hanna's death, the trend of American politics has been diverging, not merely from his economic and political system, but from his peculiar emphasis upon the personal aspect of political relations. Politicians are coming to group themselves around principles and to behave as if devotion to principle was a sufficient excuse for a shabby treatment of political friends and for flagrant injustice to political opponents. No doubt some such tendency is natural during a period of changing conditions and fermenting ideas—in which the call of new convictions persuades men to break long-established ties and to repudiate time-honored traditions. But reformers should not accept the change too complacently. Human beings are more real than ideas or principles. Principles divide as well as unite. They inspire doubt as well as faith. If they are destined to conquer, they must have their militant and aggressive phase, yet while they are militant, they are in part untrustworthy. They do not become essentially trustworthy, until they have conquered and are embodied in men to whom candor, fair-play and loyalty in their personal relationships are of as much importance as devotion to principle. They do not become essentially trustworthy, that is, until they have become humanized. Once they have become humanized, their interpreters will place a fairer estimate upon the representatives of an earlier system, like Mark Hanna, whose life realized so much that was characteristic and good in the tradition of his own day and generation.

II

Populism and Progressivism

5. The Omaha Platform

ONE OF the more heedless historiographical clichés concerns the ostensible role played by the Populists as precursors of the Progressive movement. "The real seedbed of progressivism," one of the top specialists has written, "was of course Populism. . . . The progressive program was grounded upon the Populist platform. . . . Almost every plank in that platform was written into law during the progressive years." Most American history textbooks have taken their cue from this kind of presentation.

Urged on by the deprivations they had suffered as a consequence of falling farm prices and the end of the western land boom, many farmers and allied interests called the country's attention in the last decade of the century to the failure of the American promise in that very sector regarded as most fundamental to the national character. That there could be poverty and distress among masses of earnest, God-fearing yeomen was a persuasive argument that privilege, corruption, and chicanery had upset the natural forces conducive to the Good Society. The Populists thus became one of the first major groups to press for a program of national economic and political reform. Specifically, they called upon the federal government to intervene in order to redress certain disadvantages they were suffering at the hands of the industries which serviced their enterprise, that is, controlled the availability of credit, equipment, and access to markets and storage facilities. They argued, moreover, for political reforms to free the lawmaking machinery from the grip of the "vested interests." They addressed a nation, however, that still resisted the proposition that the federal government had legitimate social-policy functions. The fact that they managed to persuade as many voters as they did of the political relevance of monetary, transportation, immigration, and fiscal issues served magnificently to end the shallow partisan gamesmanship of gilded age politics. In this respect, it is undeniable that the Populists helped set the stage for the issue-oriented politics of the Progressive Era.

On the other hand, it is plainly inaccurate to suggest that during the Progressive Era the Populists won the principal reforms they had sought in vain during the nineties. Simple attention to the specific proposals in

45

the Populists' platforms should suffice to demonstrate this. They never won their demand for federal ownership and management of the railroads and the telephone and telegraph systems, or for free silver and a policy of managed inflation. Contrary to the Populists' (and others') demands, the maintenance of large standing armies of industrial mercenaries reached new heights during the Progressive Era; so too did national aid to private corporations for a variety of purposes, including the promotion of foreign policy objectives. Increased benefits for veterans of the Union Army hardly qualified as a Progressive proposal; while the degree to which immigration restriction, when it finally passed, served the demands of labor as against the demands of racists remains a complex issue. Finally, it must be noted that many of the more important planks that proved successful, such as the graduated income tax and a reformed national banking system, had the support of so broad a constituency that it would appear tendentious to credit the Populists with their achievement.

The standard work on this subject remains John D. Hicks, The Populist Revolt (1931). Richard Hofstadter, The Age of Reform (1956) and Walter Nugent, The Tolerant Populists (1963) present more recent, and contrasting, analyses of the problem.

SOURCE: John D. Hicks, *The Populist Revolt* (Lincoln, Nebr.: Bison Books, University of Nebraska Press, 1961), pp. 439–444.

Omaha Platform, July, 1892

Assembled upon the 116th anniversary of the Declaration of Independence, the People's Party of America, in their first national convention, invoking upon their action the blessing of Almighty God, puts forth, in the name and on behalf of the people of this country, the following preamble and declaration of principles:—

The conditions which surround us best justify our cooperation: we meet in the midst of a nation brought to the verge of moral, political, and material ruin. Corruption dominates the ballot-box, the legislatures, the Congress, and touches even the ermine of the bench. The people are demoralized; most of the States have been compelled to isolate the voters at the polling-places to prevent universal intimidation or bribery. The newspapers are largely subsidized or muzzled; public opinion silenced; business prostrated; our homes covered with mortgages; labor impoverished; and the land concentrating in the hands of the capitalists. The urban workmen are denied the right of organization for self-protection; imported pauperized labor beats down their wages; a hireling standing army, unrecognized by our laws, is established to shoot them down, and they are rapidly degenerating into European conditions. The fruits of the toil of millions are boldly stolen to build up colossal fortunes for a few, unprecedented in the history of mankind; and the possessors of these, in turn, despise the republic and endanger liberty. From the same prolific womb of governmental injustice we breed the two great classes—tramps and millionaires.

The national power to create money is appropriated to enrich bondholders; a vast public debt, payable in legal tender currency, has been funded into gold-bearing bonds, thereby adding millions to the burdens of the people. Silver, which has been accepted as coin since the dawn of history, has been demonetized to add to the purchasing power of gold by decreasing the value of all forms of property as well as human labor; and the supply of currency is purposely abridged to fatten usurers, bankrupt enterprise, and enslave industry. A vast conspiracy against mankind has been organized on two continents, and it is rapidly taking possession of the world. If not met and overthrown at once, it forebodes terrible social convulsions, the destruction of civilization, or the establishment of an absolute despotism.

We have witnessed for more than a quarter of a century the struggles of the two great political parties for power and plunder, while grievous wrongs have been inflicted upon the suffering people. We charge that the controlling influences dominating both these parties have permitted the existing dreadful conditions to develop without serious effort to prevent or restrain them. Neither do they now promise us any substantial reform. They have agreed together to ignore in the coming campaign every issue but one. They propose to drown the outcries of a plundered people with the uproar of a sham battle over the tariff, so that capitalists, corporations, national banks, rings, trusts, watered stock, the demonetization of silver, and the oppressions of the usurers may all be lost sight of. They propose to sacrifice our homes, lives and children on the altar of mammon; to destroy the multitude in order to secure corruption funds from the millionaires.

Assembled on the anniversary of the birthday of the nation, and filled with the spirit of the grand general and chieftain who established our independence, we seek to restore the government of the Republic to the hands of "the plain people," with whose class it originated. We assert our purposes to be identical with the purposes of the National Constitution, "to form a more perfect union and establish justice, insure domestic tranquillity, provide for the common defence, promote the general welfare, and secure the blessings of liberty for ourselves and our posterity." We declare that this republic can only endure as a free government while built upon the love of the whole people for each other and for the nation; that it cannot be pinned together by bayonets; that the civil war is over, and that every passion and resentment which grew out of it must die with it; and that we must be in fact, as we are in name, one united brotherhood of freemen.

Our country finds itself confronted by conditions for which there is no precedent in the history of the world; our annual agricultural productions amount to billions of dollars in value, which must, within a few weeks or months, be exchanged for billions of dollars of commodities consumed in their production; the existing currency supply is wholly inadequate to make this exchange; the results are falling prices, the formation of combines and rings, the impoverishment of the producing class. We pledge ourselves, if given power, we will labor to correct these evils by wise and reasonable legislation, in accordance with the terms of our platform. We believe that the powers of government—in other words, of the people—should be expanded (as in the case of the postal service) as rapidly and as far as the good sense of an intelligent people and the teachings of experience shall justify, to the end that oppression, injustice, and poverty shall eventually cease in the land.

While our sympathies as a party of reform are naturally upon the side of every proposition which will tend to make men intelligent, virtuous, and temperate, we nevertheless regard these questions—important as they are—as secondary to the great issues now pressing for solution, and upon which not only our individual prosperity but the very existence of free institutions depends; and we ask all men to first help us to determine whether we are to have a republic to administer before we differ as to the conditions upon which it is to be administered; believing that the forces of reform this day organized will never cease to move forward until every wrong is remedied, and equal rights and equal privileges securely established for all the men and women of this country.

We declare, therefore,—

First. That the union of the labor forces of the United States this day consummated shall be permanent and perpetual; may its spirit enter all hearts for the salvation of the republic and the uplifting of mankind!

Second. Wealth belongs to him who creates it, and every dollar taken from industry without an equivalent is robbery. "If any will not work, neither shall he eat." The interests of rural and civic labor are the same; their enemies are identical.

Third. We believe that the time has come when the railroad corporations will either own the people or the people must own the railroads; and, should the government enter upon the work of owning and managing all railroads, we should favor an amendment to the Constitution by which all persons engaged in the government service shall be placed under a civil service regulation of the most rigid character, so as to prevent the increase of the power of the national administration by the use of such additional government employees.

First, *Money.* We demand a national currency, safe, sound, and flexible, issued by the general government only, a full legal tender for all debts, public and private, and that, without the use of banking corporations, a just, equitable, and efficient means of distribution direct to the people, at a tax not to exceed two per cent per annum, to be provided as set forth in the sub-treasury plan of the Farmers' Alliance, or a better system; also, by payments in discharge of its obligations for public improvements.

(a) We demand free and unlimited coinage of silver and gold at the present legal ratio of sixteen to one.

(b) We demand that the amount of circulating medium be speedily increased to not less than fifty dollars per capita.

(c) We demand a graduated income tax.

(d) We believe that the money of the country should be kept as much as possible in the hands of the people, and hence we demand that all state and national revenues shall be limited to the necessary expenses of the government economically and honestly administered.

(e) We demand that postal savings banks be established by the government for the safe deposit of the earnings of the people and to facilitate exchange.

Second, *Transportation.* Transportation being a means of exchange and a public necessity, the government should own and operate the railroads in the interest of the people.

(a) The telegraph and telephone, like the post-office system, being a necessity for the transmission of news, should be owned and operated by the government in the interest of the people.

Third, *Land.* The land, including all the natural sources of wealth, is the heritage of the people, and should not be monopolized for speculative purposes, and alien ownership of land should be prohibited. All land now held by railroads and other corporations in excess of their actual needs, and all lands now owned by aliens, should be reclaimed by the government and held for actual settlers only.

RESOLUTIONS

Whereas, Other questions have been presented for our consideration, we hereby submit the following, not as a part of the platform of the People's party, but as resolutions expressive of the sentiment of this convention.

1. *Resolved,* That we demand a free ballot and a fair count in all elections, and pledge ourselves to secure it to every legal voter without federal intervention, through the adoption by the States of the unperverted Australian or secret ballot system.

2. *Resolved,* That the revenue derived from a graduated income tax should be applied to the reduction of the burden of taxation now resting upon the domestic industries of this country.

3. *Resolved,* That we pledge our support to fair and liberal pensions to ex-Union soldiers and sailors.

4. *Resolved,* That we condemn the fallacy of protecting American labor under the present system, which opens our ports to the pauper and criminal classes of the world, and crowds out our wage-earners; and we denounce the present ineffective laws against contract labor, and demand the further restriction of undesirable immigration.

5. *Resolved,* That we cordially sympathize with the efforts of organized workingmen to shorten the hours of labor, and demand a rigid enforcement of the existing eight-hour law on government work, and ask that a penalty clause be added to the said law.

6. *Resolved,* That we regard the maintenance of a large standing army of mercenaries, known as the Pinkerton system, as a menace to our liberties, and we demand its abolition; and we condemn the recent invasion of the Territory of Wyoming by the hired assassins of plutocracy, assisted by federal officials.

7. *Resolved,* That we commend to the favorable consideration of the people and the reform press the legislative system known as the initiative and referendum.

8. *Resolved,* That we favor a constitutional provision limiting the office of President and Vice-President to one term, and providing for the election of senators of the United States by a direct vote of the people.

9. *Resolved,* That we oppose any subsidy or national aid to any private corporation for any purpose.

10. *Resolved,* That this convention sympathizes with the Knights of Labor and their righteous contest with the tyrannical combine of clothing manufacturers of Rochester, and declares it to be the duty of all who hate tyranny and oppression to refuse to purchase the goods made by said manufacturers, or to patronize any merchants who sell such goods.

6. William Jennings Bryan, "The Cross of Gold"

WITHIN a year of the promulgation of the Populists' Omaha Platform, what had been wrong with the American political economy became suddenly very much worse. The Panic of 1893 precipitated probably the most severe depression in the country's history up to that time, and the malaise continued for almost four years. Meanwhile, President Grover Cleveland "courageously" stuck by his principles and made one blunder after another in his efforts to cope with the crisis. Standing fast for "sound money" in the face of widely popular demands within his party for an inflationary money policy—including the unlimited restoration of silver to the national currency—the Democratic President aggravated the collapse of (especially farm) prices by securing repeal of the Silver Purchase Act of 1890. Standing firm against "lawlessness," he ordered troops to Chicago to help suppress a massive but peaceful strike against George Pullman's Palace Car Manufacturing Company, despite vehement protests from Illinois's Democratic governor that the state could do without such "federal aid." Cleveland's Administration magnified its one-sided approach to its responsibilities by sending the strike leaders to jail for violating a court injunction of dubious constitutionality; and it devoted its best resources to pressing the case successfully through the Supreme Court (In re Debs, 1895), even as it forfeited by gross mishandling its antitrust prosecution of the so-called Sugar Trust (U.S. v. E. C. Knight,

1895) and its defense of the constitutionality of a federal income tax (Pollock v. Farmers Loan, 1895). By 1896, there was remarkable accumulated evidence to support "conspiracy theories" of the state as the armed agent of the dominant classes for the repression of the masses.

It was in this context that William Jennings Bryan began his bid for the presidency on lecture tours throughout the country. Neither Bryan's candidacy nor his now-famous "Cross of Gold" oration came as a surprise to the Democratic National Convention of 1896. Months before, it had become evident that Bryan, a former one-term Congressman from Nebraska, was the one man who could unite the anti-Cleveland Democrats on the free silver issue, while he spoke the Populist language sufficiently well to win for the Democrats the thousands of voters that had left the GOP in many western states and more that had left the Democrats in the South over the previous four years. The "Cross of Gold" speech— coming at the end of a long debate with the "gold Democrats" over the party platform—epitomized the feelings as well as the arguments against the stand-pat Clevelandites; and in an age when forensics were still assiduously studied in the schools and admired on the hustings, Bryan's oratorical skills earned him the enthusiasm the convention promptly lavished upon him.

Contemporaries and some historians remarked often on the "radical" quality of Bryan's speech. Yet a careful reading shows that far from being an assault on "capitalism," the address clearly includes the small, independent capitalists with the "struggling masses who produce the wealth and pay the taxes of the country." Bryan's principal demand, indeed, seems to have been that the business interests of farmers should be considered at least as carefully as the business interests of the big corporations and Wall Street brokers when government policy was being shaped.

SOURCE: William Jennings Bryan, *The First Battle: The Story of the Campaign of 1896* (Chicago: Conkey, 1896), pp. 199–206.

The Democratic National Convention—July 9, 1896

SPEECH CONCLUDING DEBATE ON THE CHICAGO PLATFORM

Mr. Chairman and Gentlemen of the Convention: I would be presumptuous, indeed, to present myself against the distinguished gentlemen to whom you have listened if this were a mere measuring of abilities; but this is not a contest between persons. The humblest citizen in all the land, when clad in the armor of a righteous cause, is stronger than all the hosts of error. I come to speak to you in defense of a cause as holy as the cause of liberty— the cause of humanity.

When this debate is concluded, a motion will be made to lay

upon the table the resolution offered in commendation of the administration, and also the resolution offered in condemnation of the administration. We object to bringing this question down to the level of persons. The individual is but an atom; he is born, he acts, he dies; but principles are eternal; and this has been a contest over a principle.

Never before in the history of this country has there been witnessed such a contest as that through which we have just passed. Never before in the history of American politics has a great issue been fought out as this issue has been, by the voters of a great party. On the fourth of March, 1895, a few Democrats, most of them members of Congress, issued an address to the Democrats of the nation, asserting that the money question was the paramount issue of the hour; declaring that a majority of the Democratic party had the right to control the action of the party on this paramount issue; and concluding with the request that the believers in the free coinage of silver in the Democratic party should organize, take charge of, and control the policy of the Democratic party. Three months later, at Memphis, an organization was perfected, and the silver Democrats went forth openly and courageously proclaiming their belief, and declaring that, if successful, they would crystallize into a platform the declaration which they had made. Then began the conflict. With a zeal approaching the zeal which inspired the crusaders who followed Peter the Hermit, our silver Democrats went forth from victory unto victory until they are now assembled, not to discuss, not to debate, but to enter up the judgment already rendered by the plain people of this country. In this contest brother has been arrayed against brother, father against son. The warmest ties of love, acquaintance and association have been disregarded; old leaders have been cast aside when they have refused to give expression to the sentiments of those whom they would lead, and new leaders have sprung up to give direction to this cause of truth. Thus has the contest been waged, and we have assembled here under as binding and solemn instructions as were ever imposed upon representatives of the people. . . .

The gentleman who preceded me (ex-Governor [William E.] Russell) spoke of the State of Massachusetts; let me assure him that not one present in all this convention entertains the least hostility to the people of the State of Massachusetts, but we stand here representing people who are the equals, before the law, of the greatest citizens in the State of Massachusetts. When you (turning to the gold delegates) come before us and tell us that we are about to disturb your business interests, we reply that you have disturbed our business interests by your course.

We say to you that you have made the definition of a business man too limited in its application. The man who is employed for wages is as much a business man as his employer; the attorney in a country town is as much a business man as the corporation counsel in a great metropolis; the merchant at the cross-roads store is as much a business man as the merchant of New York; the farmer who goes forth in the morning and toils all day—who begins in the spring and toils all summer—and who by the application of brain and muscle to the natural resources of the country creates wealth, is as much a business man as the man who goes upon the board of trade and bets upon the price of grain; the miners who go down a thousand feet into the earth, or climb two thousand feet upon the cliffs, and bring forth from their hiding places the precious metals to be poured into the channels of trade are as much business men as the few financial magnates who, in a back room, corner the money of the world. We come to speak for this broader class of business men.

Ah, my friends, we say not one word against those who live upon the Atlantic coast, but the hardy pioneers who have braved all the dangers of the wilderness, who have made the desert to blossom as the rose—the pioneers away out there (pointing to the West), who rear their children near to Nature's heart, where they can mingle their voices with the voices of the birds—out there where they have erected schoolhouses for the education of their young, churches where they praise their Creator, and cemeteries where rest the ashes of their dead—these people, we say, are as deserving of the consideration of our party as any people in this country. It is for these that we speak. We do not come as aggressors. Our war is not a war of conquest; we are fighting in the defense of our homes, our families, and posterity. We have petitioned, and our petitions have been scorned; we have entreated, and our entreaties have been disregarded; we have begged, and they have mocked when our calamity came. We beg no longer; we entreat no more; we petition no more. We defy them.

The gentleman from Wisconsin has said that he fears a Robespierre. My friends, in this land of the free you need not fear that a tyrant will spring up from among the people. What we need is an Andrew Jackson to stand, as Jackson stood, against the encroachments of organized wealth.

They tell us that this platform was made to catch votes. We reply to them that changing conditions make new issues; that the principles upon which Democracy rests are as everlasting as the hills, but that they must be applied to new conditions as they arise. Conditions have arisen, and we are here to meet those conditions. They tell us that the income tax ought not to be brought in here; that it is a new idea. They criticise us for our criticism of the Supreme Court of the United States. My friends, we have not criticised; we have simply called attention to what you already know. If you want criticisms, read the dissenting opinions of the court. There you will find criticisms. They say that we passed an unconstitutional law; we deny it. The income tax law was not unconstitutional when it was passed; it was not unconstitutional when it went before the Supreme Court for the first time; it did not become unconstitutional until one of the judges changed his mind, and we cannot be expected to know when a judge will change his mind. The income tax is just. It simply intends to put the burdens of government justly upon the backs of the people. I am in favor of an income tax. When I find a man who is not willing to bear his share of the burdens of the government which protects him, I find a man who is unworthy to enjoy the blessings of a government like ours.

They say that we are opposing national bank currency; it is true. If you will read what Thomas Benton said, you will find he said that, in searching history, he could find but one parallel to Andrew Jackson; that was Cicero, who destroyed the conspiracy of Cataline and saved Rome. Benton said that Cicero only did for Rome what Jackson did for us when he destroyed the bank conspiracy and saved America. We say in our platform that we believe that the right to coin and issue money is a function of government. We believe it. We believe that it is a part of sovereignty, and can no more with safety be delegated to private individuals than we could afford to delegate to private individuals the power to make penal statutes or levy taxes. Mr. Jefferson, who was once regarded as good Democratic authority, seems to have differed in opinion from the gentleman who has addressed us on the part of the minority. Those who are opposed to this proposition tell us that the issue of paper money is a function of the bank, and that the Government ought to go out of the banking business. I stand with Jefferson rather than with them, and tell them, as he did, that the issue of money is a function of government, and that the banks ought to go out of the governing business.

They complain about the plank which declares against life tenure in office. They have tried to strain it to mean that which it does not mean. What we oppose by that plank is the life tenure which is being built up in Washington, and which excludes from participation in official benefits the humbler members of society.

Let me call your attention to two or three important things. The gentleman from New York says that he will propose an amendment to the platform providing that the proposed change in our monetary system shall not affect contracts already made. Let me remind you that there is no intention of affecting those contracts which according to present laws are made payable in gold; but if he means to say that we cannot change our monetary system without protecting those who have loaned money before the change was made, I desire to ask him where, in law or in morals, he can find justification for not protecting the debtors when the act of 1873 was passed, if he now insists that we must protect the creditors.

He says he will also propose an amendment which will provide for the suspension of free coinage if we fail to maintain the parity within a year. We reply that when we advocate a policy which we believe will be successful, we are not compelled to raise a doubt as to our own sincerity by suggesting what we shall do if we fail. I ask him, if he would apply his logic to us, why he does not apply it to himself. He says he wants this country to try to secure an international agreement. Why does he not tell us what he is going to do if he fails to secure an international agreement? There is more reason for him to do that than there is for us to provide against the failure to maintain the parity. Our opponents have tried for twenty years to secure an international agreement, and those are waiting for it most patiently who do not want it at all.

And now, my friends, let me come to the paramount issue. If they ask us why it is that we say more on the money question than we say upon the tariff question, I reply that, if protection has slain its thousands, the gold standard has slain its tens of thousands. If they ask us why we do not embody in our platform all the things that we believe in, we reply that when we have restored the money of the Constitution all other necessary reforms will be possible; but that until this is done there is no other reform that can be accomplished.

Why is it that within three months such a change has come over the country? Three months ago, when it was confidently asserted that those who believe in the gold standard would frame our platform and nominate our candidates, even the advocates of the gold standard did not think that we could elect a president. And they had good reason for their doubt, because there is scarcely a State here today asking for the gold standard which is not in the absolute control of the Republican party. But note the change. Mr. McKinley was nominated at St. Louis upon a platform which declared for the maintenance of the gold standard until it can be changed into bimetallism by international agreement. Mr. McKinley was the most popular man among the Republicans, and three months ago everybody in the Republican party prophesied his election. How is today? Why, the man who was once pleased to think that he looked like Napoleon—that man shudders today when he remembers that he was nominated on the anniversary of the battle of Waterloo. Not only that, but as he listens he can hear with ever-increasing distinctness the sound of the waves as they beat upon the lonely shores of St. Helena.

Why this change? Ah, my friends, is not the reason for the change evident to any one who will look at the matter? No private character, however pure, no personal popularity, however great, can protect from the avenging wrath of an indignant people a man who will declare that he is in favor of fastening the gold standard upon this country, or who is willing to surrender the right of self-government and place the legislative control of our affairs in the hands of foreign potentates and powers.

We go forth confident that we shall win. Why? Because upon the paramount issue of this campaign there is not a spot of ground upon which the enemy will dare to challenge battle. If they tell us that the gold standard is a good thing, we shall point to their platform and tell them that their platform pledges the party to get rid of the gold standard and substitute bimetallism. If the gold standard is a good thing, why try to get rid of it? I call your attention to the fact that some of the very people who are in this convention today and who tell us that we ought to declare in favor of international bimetallism—thereby declaring that the gold standard is wrong and that the principle of bimetallism is better—these very people four months ago were open and avowed advocates of the gold standard, and were then telling us that we could not legislate two metals together, even with the aid of all the world. If the gold standard is a good thing, we ought to declare in favor of its retention and not in favor of abandoning it; and if the gold standard is a bad thing why should we wait until other nations are willing to help us to let go? Here is the line of battle, and we care not upon which issue they force the fight; we are prepared to meet them on either issue or on both. If they tell us that the gold standard is the standard of civilization, we reply to them that this, the most enlightened of all the nations of the earth, has never declared for a gold standard and that both the great parties this year are declaring against it. If the gold standard is the standard of civilization, why, my friends, should we not have it? If they come to meet us on that issue we can present the history of our nation. More than that; we can tell them that they will search the pages of history in vain to find a single instance where the common people of any land have ever declared themselves in favor of the gold standard. They can find where the holders of fixed investments have declared for a gold standard, but not where the masses have.

Mr. Carlisle said in 1878 that this was a struggle between "the idle holders of idle capital" and "the struggling masses, who produce the wealth and pay the taxes of the country;" and, my friends, the question we are to decide is: Upon which side will the Democratic party fight; upon the side of "the idle holders of idle capital" or upon the side of "the struggling masses?" That is the question which the party must answer first, and then it must be answered by each individual hereafter. The sympathies of the Democratic party, as shown by the platform, are on the side of the struggling masses who have ever been the foundation of the Democratic party. There are two ideas of government. There are those who believe that, if you will only legislate to make the well-to-do prosperous, their prosperity will leak through on those below. The Democratic idea, however, has been that if you legislate to make the masses prosperous, their prosperity will find its way up through every class which rests upon them.

You come to us and tell us that the great cities are in favor of the gold standard; we reply that the great cities rest upon our broad and fertile prairies. Burn down your cities and leave our farms, and your cities will spring up again as if by magic; but destroy our farms and the grass will grow in the streets of every city in the country.

My friends, we declare that this nation is able to legislate for its own people on every question, without waiting for the aid or consent of any other nation on earth; and upon that issue we expect to carry every State in the Union. I shall not slander the inhabitants of the fair State of Massachusetts nor the inhabitants of the State of New York by saying that, when they are confronted with the proposition, they will declare that this nation is not able to attend to its own business. It is the issue of 1776 over again. Our ancestors, when but three millions in number, had the courage to declare their political independence of every other nation; shall we, their descendants, when we have grown to seventy millions, declare that we are less independent than our forefathers? No, my friends, that will never be the verdict of our people. Therefore, we care not upon what lines the battle is fought. If they say bimetallism is good, but that we cannot have it until other nations help us, we reply that, instead of having a gold standard because England has, we will restore bimetallism, and then let England have bimetallism because the United States has it. If they dare to come out in the open field and defend the gold standard as a good thing, we will fight them to the uttermost. Having behind us the producing masses of this nation and the world, supported by the commercial interests, the laboring interests, and the toilers everywhere, we will answer their demand for a gold standard by saying to them: You shall not press down upon the brow of labor this crown of thorns, you shall not crucify mankind upon a cross of gold.

7. William Allen White, "What's the Matter with Kansas?"

WILLIAM ALLEN WHITE *was a twenty-eight-year-old editor of a tiny Kansas newspaper—the Emporia Gazette, circulation 500—when he wrote what became one of the most notorious campaign documents of the 1896 presidential campaign. His editorial was written in anger following a brief street incident in which White, short and pudgy and rather dandily attired, was stopped by several lean, shabbily clad farmers (clearly "struggling with poverty," White wrote later) who "hooted,* jeered, and nagged" at him for his earlier editorials on the Populists. "What's the Matter with Kansas?" was quickly spotted by the Republican Party high command, which ordered thousands of copies printed for distribution throughout the country. It marked the beginning of White's long national career as an editor, author, and publicist for political causes.

There is nothing judicious or truly analytical about the editorial. White was always given to excessive expression; he later used the same hyperbolic style on behalf of the Progressive movement (when, for example, he averred, "the voice of the people is the voice of God"). Years afterward, he regretted some of the vitriol here. But it cannot be said he changed his mind about the Populists generally, and in his Autobiography, published half a century later, he tells of having "kept framed in my office over my desk for forty-six years" the letter of praise he received for his editorial from "Czar" Thomas Reed, Republican Speaker of the U.S. House of Representatives. "What's the Matter with Kansas?" is valuable not simply as a a period piece of the Bryan-McKinley campaign, but as a document that tells us much about the differences between those who fought in the Populist cause and those from the same regions who —like White—later became leaders of the Progressive movement. Whatever similarities one may discover in the Populists' and Progressives' platforms, there was a profound difference of (for want of a better word) "class" or "style" between the constituencies of the two reform movements. If this is understood, there is no enigma in the fact that remarkably few of those who became prominently identified with the Progressive movement had earlier shown even a moderate sympathy for the Populists.

SOURCE: The Autobiography of William Allen White (New York: The Macmillan Co., 1946), pp. 280–283.

What's the Matter with Kansas?
August 15, 1896

Today the Kansas Department of Agriculture sent out a statement which indicates that Kansas has gained less than two thousand people in the past year. There are about two hundred and twenty-five thousand families in this state, and there were ten thousand babies born in Kansas, and yet so many people have left the state that the natural increase is cut down to less than two thousand net.

This has been going on for eight years.

If there had been a high brick wall around the state eight years ago, and not a soul had been admitted or permitted to leave,

Kansas would be a half million souls better off than she is today. And yet the nation has increased in population. In five years ten million people have been added to the national population, yet instead of gaining a share of this—say, half a million—Kansas has apparently been a plague spot and, in the very garden of the world, has lost population by ten thousands every year.

Not only has she lost population, but she has lost money. Every moneyed man in the state who could get out without loss has gone. Every month in every community sees someone who has a little money pack up and leave the state. This has been going on for eight years. Money has been drained out all the time. In towns where ten years ago there were three or four or half a dozen money-lending concerns, stimulating industry by furnishing capital, there is now none, or one or two that are looking after the interests and principal already outstanding.

No one brings any money into Kansas any more. What community knows over one or two men who have moved in with more than $5,000 in the past three years? And what community cannot count half a score of men in that time who have left, taking all the money they could scrape together?

Yet the nation has grown rich; other states have increased in population and wealth—other neighboring states. Missouri has gained over two million, while Kansas has been losing half a million. Nebraska has gained in wealth and population while Kansas has gone downhill. Colorado has gained every way, while Kansas has lost every way since 1888.

What's the matter with Kansas?

There is no substantial city in the state. Every big town save one has lost in population. Yet Kansas City, Omaha, Lincoln, St. Louis, Denver, Colorado Springs, Sedalia, the cities of the Dakotas, St. Paul and Minneapolis and Des Moines—all cities and towns in the West—have steadily grown.

Take up the government blue book and you will see that Kansas is virtually off the map. Two or three little scrubby consular places in yellow-fever-stricken communities that do not aggregate ten thousand dollars a year is all the recognition that Kansas has. Nebraska draws about one hundred thousand dollars; little old North Dakota draws about fifty thousand dollars; Oklahoma doubles Kansas; Missouri leaves her a thousand miles behind;

Colorado is almost seven times greater than Kansas—the whole west is ahead of Kansas.

Take it by any standard you please, Kansas is not in it.

Go east and you hear them laugh at Kansas; go west and they sneer at her; go south and they "cuss" her; go north and they have forgotten her. Go into any crowd of intelligent people gathered anywhere on the globe, and you will find the Kansas man on the defensive. The newspaper columns and magazines once devoted to praise of her, to boastful facts and startling figures concerning her resources, are now filled with cartoons, jibes and Pefferian speeches. Kansas just naturally isn't in it. She has traded places with Arkansas and Timbuctoo.

What's the matter with Kansas?

We all know; yet here we are at it again. We have an old mossback Jacksonian who snorts and howls because there is a bathtub in the State House; we are running that old jay for Governor. We have another shabby, wild-eyed, rattle-brained fanatic who has said openly in a dozen speeches that "the rights of the user are paramount to the rights of the owner"; we are running him for Chief Justice, so that capital will come tumbling over itself to get into the state. We have raked the old ash heap of failure in the state and found an old human hoop skirt who has failed as a businessman, who has failed as an editor, who has failed as a preacher, and we are going to run him for Congressman-at-Large. He will help the looks of the Kansas delegation at Washington. Then we have discovered a kid without a law practice and have decided to run him for Attorney General. Then, for fear some hint that the state had become respectable might percolate through the civilized portions of the nation, we have decided to send three or four harpies out lecturing, telling the people that Kansas is raising hell and letting the corn go to weed.

Oh, this is a state to be proud of! We are a people who can hold up our heads! What we need is not more money, but less capital, fewer white shirts and brains, fewer men with business judgment, and more of those fellows who boast that they are "just ordinary clodhoppers, but they know more in a minute about finance than John Sherman"; we need more men who are "posted," who can bellow about the crime of '73, who hate prosperity, and who think, because a man believes in national honor, he is a tool of Wall

Street. We have had a few of them—some hundred fifty thousand —but we need more.

We need several thousand gibbering idiots to scream about the "Great Red Dragon" of Lombard Street. We don't need population, we don't need wealth, we don't need well-dressed men on the streets, we don't need cities on the fertile prairies; you bet we don't! What we are after is the money power. Because we have become poorer and ornerier and meaner than a spavined, distempered mule, we, the people of Kansas, propose to kick; we don't care to build up, we wish to tear down.

"There are two ideas of government," said our noble Bryan at Chicago. "There are those who believe that if you legislate to make the well-to-do prosperous, this prosperity will leak through on those below. The Democratic idea has been that if you legislate to make the masses prosperous their prosperity will find its way up and through every class and rest upon them."

That's the stuff! Give the prosperous man the dickens! Legislate the thriftless man into ease, whack the stuffing out of the creditors and tell the debtors who borrowed the money five years ago when money "per capita" was greater than it is now, that the contraction of currency gives him a right to repudiate.

Whoop it up for the ragged trousers; put the lazy, greasy fizzle, who can't pay his debts, on the altar, and bow down and worship him. Let the state ideal be high. What we need is not the respect of our fellow men, but the chance to get something for nothing.

Oh, yes, Kansas is a great state. Here are people fleeing from it by the score every day, capital going out of the state by the hundreds of dollars; and every industry but farming paralyzed, and that crippled, because its products have to go across the ocean before they can find a laboring man at work who can afford to buy them. Let's don't stop this year. Let's drive all the decent, self-respecting men out of the state. Let's keep the old clodhoppers who know it all. Let's encourage the man who is "posted." He can talk, and what we need is not mill hands to eat our meat, nor factory hands to eat our wheat, nor cities to oppress the farmer by consuming his butter and eggs and chickens and produce. What Kansas needs is men who can talk, who have large leisure to argue the currency question while their wives wait at home for that nickel's worth of bluing.

What's the matter with Kansas?

Nothing under the shining sun. She is losing her wealth, population and standing. She has got her statesmen, and the money power is afraid of her. Kansas is all right. She has started in to raise hell, as Mrs. Lease advised, and she seems to have an over-production. But that doesn't matter. Kansas never did believe in diversified crops. Kansas is all right. There is absolutely nothing wrong with Kansas. "Every prospect pleases and only man is vile."

8. Finley Peter Dunne,
"Reform Administration" and "National Housecleaning"

REFORMERS *tend to be a sober class. Their sometimes single-minded conception of "good" can often shut them off from certain commonplace weaknesses of human beings. They thus present an exposed flank to the weapons of the satirist; and there were few on the American scene who equaled the sharpness of Finley Peter Dunne. As Mark Sullivan once said, Dunne was "not only a popular but a definitely useful institution to a whole generation of American life. . . . Most useful of all, Mr. Dooley supplied the softening solvent of humor to the American atmosphere in times of acute controversy."*

In the two pieces that follow, Dunne treats us to some good-natured criticism of reform, with a lot of hard-nosed and strikingly modern political theory thrown in. He expresses the skepticism of those watching from the sidelines that reform will ever mean anything very useful or permanent. More especially, he presents us with an Irish-American's irony about those who would make over what Anglo-Americans tended to identify with the Irish generally and with Irish-American Democrats in particular! His references to the "rayformers'" promise of "a business administration" and to "laws conthrollin' th' pleasures iv th' poor" point to one of the chief flaws in the progressives' thinking. (Compare Moorfield Storey in Document 11 below.)

SOURCE: Finley Peter Dunne, *Dissertations by Mr. Dooley* (New York: Harper & Brothers, Publishers, 1906), pp. 167–172; 257–262.

Reform Administration

"Why is it," asked Mr. Hennessy, "that a rayform administhration always goes to th' bad?"

"I'll tell ye," said Mr. Dooley. "I tell ye ivrything an' I'll tell ye this. In th' first place 'tis a gr-reat mistake to think that annywan ra-aly wants to rayform. Ye niver heerd iv a man rayformin' himsilf. He'll rayform other people gladly. He likes to do it. But a healthy man'll niver rayform while he has th' strenth. A man doesn't rayform till his will has been impaired so he hasn't power to resist what th' pa-apers calls th' blandishments iv th' timpter. An' that's thruer in politics thin annywhere else.

"But a rayformer don't see it. A rayformer thinks he was ilicted because he was a rayformer, whin th' thruth iv th' matther is he was ilicted because no wan knew him. Ye can always ilict a man in this counthry on that platform. If I was runnin' f'r office, I'd change me name, an' have printed on me cards: 'Give him a chanst; he can't be worse.' He's ilicted because th' people don't know him an' do know th' other la-ad; because Mrs. Casey's oldest boy was clubbed be a polisman, because we cudden't get wather above th' third story wan day, because th' sthreet car didn't stop f'r us, because th' Flannigans bought a pianny, because we was near run over be a mail wagon, because th' saloons are open Sundah night, because they're not open all day, an' because we're tired seein' th' same face at th' window whin we go down to pay th' wather taxes. Th' rayformer don't know this. He thinks you an' me, Hinnissy, has been watchin' his spotless career f'r twinty years, that we've read all he had to say on th' evils iv pop'lar sufferage befure th' Society f'r the Bewildermint iv th' Poor, an' that we're achin' in ivry joint to have him dhrag us be th' hair iv th' head fr'm th' flowin' bowl an' th' short card game, make good citizens iv us an' sind us to th' pinitinchry. So th' minyit he gets into th' job he begins a furyous attimpt to convart us into what we've been thryin' not to be iver since we come into th' wurruld.

"In th' coorse iv th' twinty years that he spint attimptin' to get office, he managed to poke a few warrum laws conthrollin' th' pleasures iv th' poor into th' stachoo book, because no wan cared about thim or because they made business betther f'r th' polis, an' whin he's in office, he calls up th' Cap'n iv the polis an' says he: 'If these laws ar-re bad laws th' way to end thim is to enfoorce thim.' Somebody told him that, Hinnissy. It isn't thrue, d'ye mind. I don't care who said it, not if 'twas Willum Shakespere. It isn't thrue. Laws ar-re made to throuble people an' th' more throuble they make th' longer they stay on th' stachoo book. But th' polis don't ast anny questions. Says they: 'They'll be less money in th' job but we need some recreation,' an' that night a big copper comes down th' sthreet, sees me settin' out on th' front stoop with me countenance dhraped with a tin pail, fans me with his club an' runs me in. Th' woman nex' dure is locked up f'r sthringin' a clothes line on th' roof, Hannigan's boy Tim gets tin days f'r keepin' a goat, th' polis resarves are called out to protict th' vested rights iv property against th' haynyous pushcart man, th' stations is crowded with felons charged with maintainin' a hose conthrary to th' stachoos made an' provided, an' th' tindherline is all over town. A rayformer don't think annything has been accomplished if they'se a vacant bedroom in th' pinitinchry. His motto is 'Arrest that man.'

"Whin a rayformer is ilicted he promises ye a business adminis-thration. Some people want that but I don't. Th' American busi-ness man is too fly. He's all right, d'ye mind. I don't say annything again' him. He is what Hogan calls th' boolwarks iv pro-gress, an' we cudden't get on without him even if his scales are a little too quick on th' dhrop. But he ought to be left to dale with his akels. 'Tis a shame to give him a place where he can put th' comether on millions iv people that has had no business thrainin' beyond occasionally handin' a piece iv debased money to a car conductor on a cold day. A reg'lar pollytician can't give away an alley without blushin', but a business man who is in pollytics jus' to see that th' civil sarvice law gets thurly enfoorced, will give Lincoln Park an' th' public libr'y to th' beef thrust, charge an admission price to th' lake front an' make it a felony f'r annywan to buy stove polish outside iv his store, an' have it all put down to public improvemints with a pitcher iv him in th' corner stone.

"Fortchnitly, Hinnissy, a rayformer is seldom a business man. He thinks he is, but business men know diff'rent. They know what he is. He thinks business an' honesty is th' same thing. He does, indeed. He's got thim mixed because they dhress alike. His idee is that all he has to do to make a business administhration is to have honest men ar-round him. Wrong. I'm not sayin', mind ye, that a man can't do good work an' be honest at th' same time. But whin I'm hirin' a la-ad I find out first whether he is onto his job, an' afther a few years I begin to suspect that he is honest, too. Manny a dishonest man can lay brick sthraight an' manny a man that wudden't steal ye'er spoons will break ye'er furniture. I don't want Father Kelly to hear me, but I'd rather have a competint man who wud steal if I give him a chanst, but I won't, do me plumbin' thin a person that wud scorn to help himsilf but didn't know how to wipe a joint. Ivry man ought to be honest to start with, but to give a man an officc jus' bccause he's honest is like ilictin' him to Congress because he's a pathrite, because he don't bate his wife or because he always wears a right boot on th' right foot. A man ought to be honest to start with an' afther that he ought to be crafty. A pollytician who's on'y honest is jus' th' same as bein' out in a winther storm without anny clothes on.

"Another thing about rayform administhrations is they always think th' on'y man that ought to hold a job is a lawyer. Th' raison is that in th' coorse iv his thrainin' a lawyer larns enough about ivrything to make a good front on anny subject to annybody who doesn't know about it. So whin th' rayform administhration comes in th' mayor says: 'Who'll wc make chief iv polis in place iv th' misguided ruffyan who has held th' job f'r twinty years?' 'Th' man f'r th' place,' says th' mayor's adviser, 'is Arthur Lightout,' he says. 'He's an ixcillent lawyer, Yale, '95, an' is well up on polis matthers. Las' year he read a paper on "The fine polis foorce iv London" befure th' annyal meetin' iv th' S'ciety f'r Ladin' th' Mulligan Fam'ly to a Betther an' Harder Life. Besides,' he says, 'he's been in th' milishy an' th' foorce needs a man who'll be afraid not to shoot in case iv public disturbance.' So Arthur takes hold iv th' constabulary an' in a year th' polis can all read Emerson an' th' burglars begin puttin' up laddhers an' block an' tackles befure eight A.M. An' so it is on ivry side. A lawyer has charge iv the city horseshoein', another wan is clanin' th' sthreets, th' author iv 'Gasamagoo on torts' is thryin' to dispose iv th' ashes be throwin' thim in th' air on a windy day, an' th' bright boy that took th' silver ware f'r th' essay on *ne exeats* an' their relation to life is plannin' a uniform that will be sarviceable an' constitchoochinal f'r th' brave men that wurruks on th' city dumps. An' wan day th' main rayformer goes out expictin' to rayceive th' thanks iv th' community an' th' public that has jus' got out iv jail f'r lettin' th' wather run too long in th' bath tub rises up an' cries: 'Back to th' Univarsity Settlemint.' Th' man with th' di'mon' in his shirt front comes home an' pushes th' honest lawyers down th' steps, an' a dishonest horse shoer shoes th' city's horses well, an' a crooked plumber does th' city's plumbin' securely, an' a rascally polisman that may not be avarse to pickin' up a bet but will always find out whin Pathrolman Scanlan slept on his beat, takes hold iv th' polis foorce, an' we raysume our nachral condition iv illagal merrimint. An' th' rayformer spinds th' rest iv his life tellin' us where we are wrong. He's good at that. On'y he don't undherstand that people wud rather be wrong an' comfortable thin right in jail."

"I don't like a rayformer," said Mr. Hennessy.

"Or anny other raypublican," said Mr. Dooley.

National Housecleaning

"It looks to me," said Mr. Hennessy, "as though this counthry was goin' to th' divvle."

"Put down that magazine," said Mr. Dooley. "Now d'ye feel betther? I thought so. But I can sympathize with ye. I've been readin' thim mesilf. Time was whin I sildom throubled thim. I wanted me fiction th' day it didn't happen, an' I cud buy that f'r a penny fr'm th' newsboy on th' corner. But wanst in a while some homefarin' wandhrer wud jettison wan in me place, an' I'd frequently glance through it an' find it in me lap whin I woke up. Th' magazines in thim days was very ca'ming to th' mind. Angabel an' Alfonso dashin' f'r a marredge license. Prom'nent lady author-essesses makin' pomes at th' moon. Now an' thin a scrap over whether Shakespeare was enthered in his own name or was a ringer, with th' long-shot players always again Shakespeare. But no wan hurt. Th' idee ye got fr'm these here publications was that life was wan glad, sweet song. If annything, ivrybody was too good to ivrybody else. Ye don't need to lock th' dure at night. Hang ye'er watch on th' knob. Why do polismen carry clubs? Answer, to knock th' roses off th' throlley-poles. They were good readin'. I liked thim th' way I like a bottle iv white pop now an' thin.

"But now whin I pick me fav'rite magazine off th' flure, what do I find? Ivrything has gone wrong. Th' wurruld is little betther thin a convict's camp. Angabel an' Alfonso ar-re about to get marrid whin it is discovered that she has a husband in Ioway an' he has a wife in Wisconsin. All th' pomes be th' lady authoressesses that used to begin: 'Oh, moon, how fair!' now begin: 'Oh, Ogden Armour, how awful!' Shakespeare's on'y mintioned as a crook. Here ye ar-re. Last edition. Just out. Full account iv th' Crimes iv Incalculated. Did ye read Larsen last month on 'Th' use iv Burglars as Burglar Alarums'? Good, was it? Thin read th' horrible disclosures about th' way Jawn C. Higgins got th' right to build a bay-window on his barber-shop at iliven forty-two Kosciusko Avnoo,

South Bennington, Arkansaw. Read Wash'n'ton Bliffens's dhread-ful assault on th' board iv education iv Baraboo. Read Idarem on Jawn D.; she's a lady, but she's got th' punch. Graft ivrywhere. 'Graft in th' Insurance Comp'nies,' 'Graft in Congress,' 'Graft in th' Supreem Coort,' 'Graft be an Old Grafter,' 'Graft in Lithra-choor,' be Hinnery James; 'Graft in Its Relations to th' Higher Life,' be Dock Eliot; 'Th' Homeeric Legend an' Graft; Its Cause an' Effect; Are They th' Same? Yes and No,' be Norman Slapgood.

"An' so it goes, Hinnissy, till I'm that blue, discouraged, an' broken-hearted I cud go to th' edge iv th' wurruld an' jump off. It's a wicked, wicked, horrible, place, an' this here counthry is about th' toughest spot in it. Is there an honest man among us? If there is throw him out. He's a spy. Is there an institution that isn't corrupt to its very foundations? Don't ye believe it. It on'y looks that way because our graft iditor hasn't got there on his rounds yet. Why, if Canada iver wants to increase her popylation all she has to do is to sind a man in a balloon over th' United States to yell: 'Stop thief!' At th' sound iv th' wurruds sivinty millyon men, women, an' little scoundhrelly childher wud skedaddle f'r th' frontier, an' lave Jerome, Folk, an' Bob La Follette to pull down th' blinds, close th' dure, an' hang out a sign: 'United States to rent.' I don't thrust anny man anny more. I niver did much, but now if I hear th' stealthy step iv me dearest frind at th' dure I lock th' cash dhrawer. I used to be nervous about burglars, but now I'm afraid iv a night call fr'm th' Chief Justice iv th' Supreem Coort or th' prisidint iv th' First National Bank.

"It's slowly killin' me, Hinnissy, or it wud if I thought about it. I'm sorry George Wash'n'ton iver lived. Thomas Jefferson I hate. An' as f'r Adam, well, if that joker iver come into this place I'd— but I mustn't go on.

"Do I think it's all as bad as that? Well, Hinnissy, now that ye ask me, an' seein' that Chris'mas is comin' on, I've got to tell ye that this counthry, while wan iv th' worst in th' wurruld, is about as good as th' next if it ain't a shade betther. But we're wan iv th' gr-reatest people in th' wurruld to clean house, an' th' way we like best to clean th' house is to burn it down. We come home at night an' find that th' dure has been left open an' a few mosquitoes or life-insurance prisidints have got in, an' we say: 'This is turr'ble. We must get rid iv these here pests.' An' we take an axe to thim. We desthroy a lot iv furniture an' kill th' canary bird, th' cat, th'

cuckoo clock, an' a lot iv other harmless insects, but we'll fin'lly
land th' mosquitoes. If an Englishman found mosquitoes in his
house he'd first thry to kill thim, an' whin he didn't succeed he'd
say: 'What pleasant little humming-bur-rds they ar-re. Life wud be
very lonesome without thim,' an he'd domesticate thim, larn thim
to sing 'Gawd Save th' King,' an' call his house Mosquito Lodge. If
these here inthrestin' life-insurance scandals had come up in Merry
ol' England we'd niver hear iv thim, because all th' boys wud be in
th' House iv Lords be this time, an' Lord Tontine wud sit hard on
anny scheme to have him searched be a lawyer fr'm Brooklyn. But
with this here nation iv ours somebody scents something wrong
with th' scales at th' grocery-store an' whips out his gun, another
man turns in a fire alarm, a third fellow sets fire to th' Presbyterian
Church, a vigilance comity is formed an' hangs ivry foorth man; an'
havin' started with Rockyfellar, who's tough an' don't mind bein'
lynched, they fin'lly wind up with desthroyin' me because th' steam
laundhry has sint me home somebody else's collars.

"It reminds me, Hinnissy, iv th' time I lived at a boardin'-house
kept be a lady be th' name iv Doherty. She was a good woman, but
her idee iv life was a combination iv pneumony an' love. She was
niver still. Th' sight iv a spot on th' wall where a gintleman boorder
had laid his head afther dinner would give her nervous prostration.
She was always polishin', scrubbin', sweepin', airin'. She had a
plumber in to look at th' dhrains twice a week. Fifty-two times a
year there was a rivolution in th' house that wud've made th' Czar
iv Rooshya want to go home to rest. An' yet th' house was niver
really clean. It looked as if it was to us. It was so clean that I always
was ashamed to go into it onless I'd shaved. But Mrs. Doherty said
no; it was like a pig-pen. 'I don't know what to do,' says she. 'I'm
worn out, an' it seems impossible to keep this house clean.' 'What
is th' trouble with it?' says he. 'Madam,' says me frind Gallagher,
'wud ye have me tell ye?' he says. 'I wud,' says she. 'Well,' says he,
'th' throuble with this house is that it is occupied entirely be
human bein's,' he says. 'If 'twas a vacant house,' he says, 'it cud
aisily be kept clean,' he says.

"An' there ye ar-re, Hinnissy. Th' noise ye hear is not th' first
gun iv a rivolution. It's on'y th' people iv th' United States batin' a
carpet. Ye object to th' smell? That's nawthin'. We use sthrong
disinfectants here. A Frinchman or an Englishman cleans house be
sprinklin' th' walls with cologne; we chop a hole in th' flure an'

pour in a kag iv chloride iv lime. Both are good ways. It depinds on how long ye intind to live in th' house. What were those shots? That's th' housekeeper killin' a couple iv cockroaches with a Hotchkiss gun. Who is that yellin'? That's our ol' frind High Finance bein' compelled to take his annual bath. Th' housecleanin' season is in full swing, an' there's a good deal iv dust in th' air; but I want to say to thim neighbors iv ours, who're peekin' in an' makin' remarks about th' amount iv rubbish, that over in our part iv th' wurruld we don't sweep things undher th' sofa. Let thim put that in their pipes an' smoke it."

"I think th' counthry is goin' to th' divvle," said Mr. Hinnissy, sadly.

"Hinnissy," said Mr. Dooley, "if that's so I congratylate th' wurruld."

"How's that?" asked Mr. Hennessy.

"Well," said Mr. Dooley, "f'r nearly forty years I've seen this counthry goin' to th' divvle, an' I got aboord late. An' if it's been goin' that long an' at that rate, an' has got no nearer thin it is this pleasant Chris'mas, thin th' divvle is a divvle iv a ways further off thin I feared."

9. Congressman Samuel W. McCall, On the Hepburn Railroad Regulation Act (1906)

GOVERNMENT regulation of industry was probably the outstanding national issue of the Populist and Progressive eras. Although most historiography tends to deal with the issue as one of "intervention" versus "nonintervention" (or, "socialism" versus "laissez faire"), it has become increasingly clear that what contemporaries were most often disputing was what kind of regulation and for what specific purposes. Most railroad managers, for example, wanted Interstate Commerce Commission assistance in averting rate wars by facilitating certain kinds of traffic arrangements; many railroad stockholders wanted government protection against directors who depreciated securities through financial manipulations; most of all, diverse shippers and producers, especially in the West and South, wanted the government to protect them against discriminatory rate and service policies. Each group tended to portray its demands as part of the contemporary quest for social justice. On the other hand, on each specific issue, opponents of government intervention enjoyed a pragmatic base for argument. These interest groups tended to have won reasonably advantageous terms in market-place bargaining, and state intervention could only mean—and was often pointedly designed for—a reduction of those advantages. Understandably, such interests preferred to take their chances with the vagaries of the economic order rather than with those of the political order.

Samuel W. McCall was a Republican Congressman from Massachusetts, a state whose economic ascendency had long been threatened by the westward movement of population and the distant location of industrial resources. It had nevertheless maintained a strong economy because its early strength had earned it advantageous arrangements with major financial and transportation interests. Now, in the Progressive Era, many southern and western states sought those advantages by using political leverage to reshape the railroad rate structure. McCall's argument against "political rate making" stands as a classic defense of the conservative position on the regulation issue. It should provide perspective to the well-known reform proposals.

SOURCE: Congressional Record, 59th Cong., 1st Sess. (February 2, 1906), pp. 1969–1973.

Mr. Chairman . . . What is demanded to meet the real evil . . . is legislation making clear beyond question the right of every man to equal treatment and giving him the amplest remedy for every violation of his right. The private car, refrigerated car, the industrial [rail] switch, receiving a part of the through rate as if it were an independent line, every instrument of favoritism and injustice had justly received public condemnation. . . . Rebates and discrimination in all their protean forms were the real evil. . . . [But there is] no possible relation between the giving of rebates and the fixing of rates by a commission. . . . [A] railroad could as easily give a criminal rebate from a rate fixed by a commission as from one fixed by itself. . . .

Do we want rate making by a Government board? . . . It is upon the advocates of this bill to show that we should set aside the American system of fixing freight rates which has given us rates hardly half as high as are paid by the other great countries of the world, although our railroads pay their labor twice the wages paid in the other countries. . . . Magnificent platitudes about eminent domain and our duty to exercise the great commerce powers of the Constitution will not sustain the burden. . . .

Take first the experience of Germany, which for more than a

quarter of a century has had rates fixed by the Government. In the case of Germany . . . the Government owns the railroads. . . . The state is merely managing its own property and manfully paying the bills. In that country [in order to avoid "discrimination"] the rates were made upon a mileage basis, and this difficulty was at once encountered. If the rates were high enough per mile so that traffic hauled for a short distance would yield a net revenue, they would be so high for a long haul as to be practically prohibitive of long-distance traffic; and on the other hand, if the mileage rate were so low that merchandize could be carried a great distance profitably, the short-distance traffic would be carried at a loss. The German Government made repeated attempts to [taper the rates, so that it, for example] . . . would permit the wheat of eastern Germany to find its way by rail to the great manufacturing centers along the Rhine. Saxony, in the center of Germany, also produces wheat and the Saxon millers and landowners contended that they had a "natural right" to the market in their neighborhood, and that it was a discrimination for the Government to bring the wheat of eastern Germany at an exceptionally low rate to western Germany in competition with the wheat and flour of Saxony. The German Government is a reasonably autocratic government, and yet, resist as it would, it was finally compelled to yield and to reestablish the mileage rate; . . . [so that] 125 miles was the maximum distance at which wheat could be carried by rail in Germany for domestic consumption . . . [and] for most purposes of trade eastern Germany and the Rhine country were farther apart than Germany and New York or Germany and Buenos Aires.

The same thing was illustrated in the raising of sugar. . . . [To encourage sugar growing in Germany] the state railroads would sell tickets to the [sugar] laborer for less than the regular rates; but the landowners of other portions of Germany claimed that these special rates had the result of inducing the labor, which they would naturally employ, to leave them unless they paid higher wages—in effect these landowners claimed that the excursion tickets operated to take away their natural rights. . . .

This insistence upon the right to a market which proximity gives, this resistance to discrimination and favoritism shown by hauling at a low rate the merchandize of a community at a great distance so that it may compete in the same market with the nearby community, is also seen in the manufacture of iron and steel. And the effect of the recognition of the natural-right theory, the mileage theory, in Germany, resisted in vain by the Government, has been undeniably toward establishing a zone system of commerce, toward preventing Germany from becoming a common market, and to break it up into little principalities for the purpose of trade. . . .

You will find a similar condition in France to that which exists in Germany. [There the Government also owns the railroads, and a commission of thirty-three highly trained experts sets rates.] . . . The French experts find it necessary to deviate from their ordinary rates, and in a single year 80 per cent of the traffic was carried at special rates. What would be the effect upon public opinion in this country if our national railroad Commission should yield to fair economic demands and permit, if they could do so under this bill, such a deviation from the regular rates?

In England the railroads are not owned by the nation. . . . However, the Government established parliamentary rates. . . . They were maximum rates such as you propose to have created under this bill. The tendency has been for the railroads to adhere to the maximum rate or to approach it closely. The establishment of rates materially lower would be a confession that the maximum rates were unreasonably high and might lead to action by the Government reducing the maximum rate. . . .

In this country the interstate rates have been made by the railroads with practically no check. . . . It has been the prime policy of the railroads to develop a vast continental traffic drawn at low rates and between the most remote sections of the country. It has been to make America a common market. The "natural right" theory has more than once been involved. The low long-distance rate brought the agricultural products of the West in competition with the farms of New York, New England, and Pennsylvania, in markets which, on the "natural right" theory, belonged to farmers of the last named States. And while your lands have gone up enormously in value the farms of New England and the East have greatly declined in value. Yet on the whole the East has benefitted because it concentrated its energies upon manufactures and trade and the railroads took its products to the West at low rates in the cars which bore your produce East, and which would otherwise have returned empty. . . .

The Interstate Commerce Commission has more than once affirmed the "natural right" theory, and if it is to pass upon the conflicting claims of sections it cannot escape from that theory. The elevator and dock owners and great merchants of New York protest against a rate from the West to New York on wheat for internal consumption. The low rate for the export of wheat was directly for the benefit of the farmer, but it took from the men of New York certain profits that they claimed the "natural right" to have . . . and the Interstate Commerce Commission ordered that the rate on the wheat destined for export should be the same as that for New York. . . . [But the Supreme Court ultimately overturned the decision.]

The striking feature in the American railroad system, then, has been the remarkable development of the low long-distance rate which has made of the country a common market and has stimulated trade between its most remote parts. . . . They are self-made rates, resulting from the free play of commercial and industrial forces. . . .

Suppose we had a governmental commission [during the years of the depression following 1873] . . . when the East was politically the strongest section and held the dominant power. Is it not almost a certainty that they would have listened to the protest of the latter section against the disturbance of their domestic market . . . and that those now mighty and stable Commonwealths that lie beyond the Mississippi would have waited for that great development which the railroads forced upon them? Why, those great States are the very daughters of the economic American system [sic] of making freight rates. They would not have come into being under the system established by this bill, and yet they are now blindly clasping hands to strangle the mother who bore them. . . .

The most effective [railroad] competition is not between two or more parallel railroads serving the same points, but between railroads connecting different sources of supply with the same market. The competition between markets has done more to reduce freight rates permanently in this country than the competition between parallel roads, including the injurious and spasmodic "cutting" in rate wars. . . . The primary instinct of self-preservation will inspire railroads to protect the markets of the territory they serve. Every interest of private property impels them not merely to preserve, but to build up their communities. But here you propose to have a governmental agency step in and set aside the primary edicts of commerce and trade. It may be for this agency to say not that the railroad shall serve its own interests by serving the interests of its territory, but to say that the natural advantages of its community are not equal to those of a competing community a thousand miles distant served by another railroad, and that the latter community should have a relatively better rate. And it will doubtless be claimed that it has power, in order to prevent what may be called discrimination between communities to readjust the rates.

Suppose the farmers of Vermont should contend before the Commission that they were only 200 miles from Boston and that it was a destruction of their natural market for the agricultural products of the West to be brought 1000 miles into Boston as cheaply as their own produce, and that their rate to Boston should be relatively reduced. What will your Government commission say to that? Or suppose some iron-manufacturing locality in Pennsylvania should assert that the low rates on coal and pig-iron to Worcester, in New England, was a discrimination against the rights of the former locality, what will your railroad commission say to that? It is inevitable that sooner or later, struggle as you may, you will repeat the experience of Germany and have a distance tariff. . . .

The Commission may by an order destroy the prosperity of a section of the country and may, in effect, impose restrictions upon commerce between States which it was the prime purpose of the Constitution to prevent. With the Government fixing rates, constituencies would inevitably carry their grievances into politics. I believe it will be contended that your bill in substance confers the power to impose a rate for one section in its relation to the rate of another section. You will therefore have the different parts of the country knocking at the door of the National Government for favors, and intrigue and politics will rekindle the sectional jealousies that have now been happily allayed. . . .

You propose to confer upon a mere human agency a practical task that would be superhuman. It is made their duty upon complaint to revise any and all the thousand millions or more freight rates in the country and an untold number of passenger rates. . . . We are to have a Commission made up of prodigies. . . . The President . . . last April . . . gave his notion—and a lofty one it was—of the character of the men who should constitute the Commission. "They should not," he said, "be swayed by any influence whatever—social, political, or any other—to show improper favoritism to the railroads," and, "on the other hand, if the rate is unjustly attacked, no matter if that attack has behind it the feeling or prejudice of 99 per cent of the people," they will stand up against the attack. This is a noble ideal, but where are these paragons to be found? Even far higher officers than commissioners are not always found to be unresponsive to public sentiment. . . .

But the difficulty will be not so much with the men as with the system. They will be unable to perform those impossible duties, and then their work is near the political line, across which they will inevitably drift, and, as has been attempted already in some of the most enlightened States in the Union, some day, acting under pressure or under the spur of ambition or of a desire to "do things," some great [rate] schedule is liable to be broken into atoms, and the commerce and industry of one section may be arbitrarily transferred to another. I believe that it is vastly better for the interests of the country, so long as rates can be fixed under the operation of economic laws to reject the artificial methods proposed by this bill, which makes of a commission a sort of Providence with power to create one city and destroy another. . . .

As representing some of the people of New England upon this floor, I say to you that I believe they do not care to offer up supplications to any statutory deity at Washington for the right to continue to exist, but that they will bravely take their chances with those economic forces which . . . have hitherto ruled. . . . New England can more safely reckon with the constant or slowly changing economic forces than have her domestic commerce subject to the "theories of progress" of a commission, possibly of martinets and almost certainly of politicians. The prosperity of her people is vital to the exitence of the great railroads which now serve them, but if that should be entirely disregarded, if the railroads should attempt to destroy themselves by destroying the communities which support them, the people of New England still have the courts. . . .

10.   Charles McCarthy,
The Wisconsin Idea

No STATE reform movement gained greater renown in the Progressive Era than that of Wisconsin. Aside from the specific reforms identified with the governorship of Robert M. LaFollette, what especially distinguished "the Wisconsin Idea," as it was popularly known by contemporaries, was the coordination of the legislative process with the professional expertise embodied in the Wisconsin Legislative Reference Service. Charles Mc-Carthy (1873–1921) was chief of the service. In that capacity he helped prepare hundreds of major bills for legislators of all political parties, and in addition he assisted in legislative research projects concerned with various social and economic problems.

Wisconsin progressivism, although indeed "agrarian" (as one might expect in a chiefly agricultural state), placed a distinct emphasis upon reason, intelligence, and "science" for the shaping of reform, in contrast to the emphasis that the Populists generally placed upon "grass roots democracy" and "popular government." In McCarthy's explication of the "Wisconsin Idea" there is no hostility to industry or to commerce, but indeed an expression of desire to improve the environment in which business generally might thrive. McCarthy's emphatic disavowal of pro-gressivism's alleged link with socialism is similarly instructive. Conserva-tive contemporaries and some historians have confused the progressive objectives with those of the socialists. McCarthy indicates—mostly by implication, since he could hardly have been concerned with matters that were to become historiographical issues later—that, although pro-gressives often secured the support of socialists in legislative proposals, the partnership was not much more than coincidental; on the whole, progres-sives included among their principal objectives the thwarting of socialist pressure and the revitalization of individualism in its stead.

SOURCE: Charles McCarthy, The Wisconsin Idea (New York: The Macmillan Co., 1912), pp. 273, 286–289, 294–303.

Chapter X. Conclusion

The legislation discussed thus far in this little book has been selected because it shows most clearly the fundamentals of the Wisconsin idea. . . .

Ten years ago what an uproar capital would have caused, had

such an array of bills been proposed to any legislature, yet no capital has been driven out of this state—in fact everything is advancing with great strides. It is rapidly becoming a manufacturing state. It ranks seventh in the table showing the amount of corporation taxes collected by the United States government from the various states. . . .

Granting that this prosperity may not be the result of this legis· lation, it may be good evidence that the Wisconsin legislature has proceeded with great caution and made its laws only after the most careful scrutiny of the delicate machinery of industry. It may be said that these conditions might have existed if none of these laws had been passed but the fact that prosperity has increased at a rate as great as, if not greater than, any state in the country, is evidence that if *laws are made carefully* and are made to fit into the harmony of industrial conditions, greater advances can be made than by following the wild shouts of reformers who would destroy without constructing. . . .

Is all of this socialism? Quite the opposite; it strives to give the individual a better opportunity to possess property—the very antithesis of socialism. . . .

. . . The fact is, most of the legislation which the socialists have introduced has had nothing to do with socialistic propaganda but in many cases has proposed the very things advocated by thoughtful men in every country of the world save America. It will be remembered that the socialists in Germany for many years were opposed to the whole plan of industrial insurance and only recently have accepted it. So far does this plan of expediency go, that one time when the writer happened to remark to a socialist member that a proposed plan to extend credit, by means of a well known European device so that workingmen might possess a little property, was not really socialism, the member replied with a smile, "It is an excellent bill and good enough socialism for us."

The socialists are looking abroad and putting forth well tried experiments, mixed in many cases it is true with their peculiar propagandist ideals, which because of their source, excite a blind and unreasoning opposition. If our people would give more study to great economic movements in other lands they would realize this truth.

So marked have been the changes throughout the world and so astonishing the fact that they have actually seemed to have increased prosperity, that the conservative Boston *Transcript* is compelled to remark in a recent editorial on England:

> Take all together, this makes an astounding program of social improvement, all the more astounding in the fact that it should have been undertaken by the staidest of all governments. This marks a really stupendous innovation in governmental procedure. Our friends, the socialists, have always been ridiculed for their pet claim that it is the business of the government to spread happiness and plenty among the people. Yet here, in a country the very quickest of all to foam at the very word "Socialism," is a string of acts each having as its tacit side-issue the partial redistribution of wealth and the spread of happiness!
>
> Thus far these measures, too, seem to have worked. The Old-Age Pensions act has undoubtedly mitigated a great deal of want and misery. And the so-called "revolutionary" budget, of which so much disaster was predicted, has left behind it the unmistakable effect of improved business conditions and greater prosperity. This latter effect may have arisen simply from the ending of a business suspense. Still, a very bad measure would have permitted only a halfway recuperation. On the surface there seems nothing impractical about these ventures of government into the sphere of humanitarianism. There may be later and hidden costs to pay, but they are not now apparent. But the point of all this is the speculation which it warrants.
>
> May it not be that the time has come for us, after all, to frame slightly larger conceptions of government that we have been holding? Is the chief end of government any longer to be the collection of taxes, the maintenance of order, and the other material duties that have long been held to constitute its entire responsibility? Half unconsciously the men who have framed a network of paternalistic measures in Germany, even wider than that in England, seem to have assumed for government a new moral obligation. And this has been found not to involve any serious disturbances to property and vested rights. Are we perhaps going down a new path? Have these other countries beaten us by a decade to a now old and settled New Nationalism?

After a careful study of socialism in Germany the writer has come to the conclusion that many of the reforms advocated by that party will eventually lead to the destruction of its main thesis. The individual initiative and the efficiency of the individual caused by the breaking up of class distinctions, the establishment of merit and ability in the place of family or title, the equitable distribution of taxation and the very equality of opportunity resulting, will lead to an individuality which will cause men to press forward in the acquisition of private property. Those who have seen the land hunger of the American immigrant can well testify to that. Provide the ladder, make free the way and human beings will climb and no plan ever made by Karl Marx or any other man, of whatever party or sect, will prevent the acquisition of private property. . . . Says Jane Addams:

> Is it because our modern industrialism is so new that we have been slow to connect it with the poverty all about us? The socialists talk constantly of the relation of economic wrong to destitution, and point out the connection between industrial maladjustment and individual poverty, but the study of social conditions, the obligation to eradicate poverty, cannot belong to one political party nor to one economic school, and after all it was not a socialist, but that ancient friend of the poor, St. Augustine, who said, "Thou givest bread to the hungry, but better were it, that none hungered and thou had'st none to give to him."

Is it good policy or good politics to allow the socialists to become the champions of women in industry, the defender of the child from exploitation, friend of the poor and downtrodden and yet expect to defeat them at the polls in a period characterized by growing humane feeling? Can we wrap in a parcel everything which Christianity has approved since the time of the Great Founder and label it, "Socialism, don't touch"? When it comes to the attainment of any reasonable legislation for the true betterment of human beings, the only way to beat the Socialists "is to beat them to it." . . .

The best there is of our sturdy individualism must be preserved. In Wisconsin, the wise leaders have foreseen this and are determined to keep intact every bit of the spirit of the men who made the "Iron Brigade" and hence are building slowly and surely the beginnings of a new individualism. . . .

If you were responsible for the business of government, would you not apply the common rules of efficiency, Mr. Business Man? Do you not believe it would pay well to make a heavy investment in hope, health, happiness and justice? Do you not think you would get enormous dividends in national wealth? Isn't there something worth while, something which will pay in the strong ideal of this New Individualism of Wisconsin?

III

Progressivism and
the Problem of the Cities

11. Moorfield Storey,
"The Government of Cities"

THIS ARTICLE, which first appeared in the New England Magazine for
June 1892, helps reveal the roots of the most common progressive proposals for reform of city government. Progressive reform in the cities had
two principal impetuses. One emanated from the settlement-house and
social-worker movements, which urged the need for certain city services
for the poor, including soup kitchens, vagrants' lodgings, playgrounds,
parks, tenement-inspection agencies, and the like. The other and more
powerful impetus originated in boards of trade, merchants' associations,
and chambers of commerce, which urged honesty, efficiency, and economy in the administration of the police, fire, public works, and sanitation
departments, and in the allocation of franchises, contracts, and licenses
to the private businesses of the community. Although the interests of the
two groups coincided often enough for them to join in campaigns against
"the bosses," their mutual incompatibility quickly became evident once
the vested interests were displaced. Whereas the services urged by the
social reformers required increased city expenditures, the reforms demanded by the "good government" groups implied tax cuts and reduced
spending. Although Moorfield Storey probably ought not to be included
among the progressives (during the Progressive Era he generally fought
most of the reform measures that even the business associations supported), his analysis of what was wrong with city government is a clear
and candid presentation of the typical civic reformer's view. Storey was
a Boston Brahmin who had participated in the old mugwump campaigns
for civil service reform and whose special brand of idealism carried him
to positions of leadership with the Anti-Imperialist League in 1900 and
the NAACP at its inception in 1910. With an eye more to the national
scene than the specific predicaments of city living, Storey could argue
that the "really vital" issues that confronted the American commonwealth concerned "financial honesty" (by which he meant holding the

*line against free silver and other inflationary proposals) and the tariff.
The cities' problems, he argued, simply were not political problems at
all. A successful corporation lawyer, Storey manifested a commonplace
optimism in the application of "business principles" to the conduct of
most social activities. "The government of a city," he claimed, "is a mere
matter of business." A man of genuine humanistic ideals, Storey nevertheless—like so many of his type in his day—was innocently blind to the
political relevance of demands for government attention by the many
underprivileged groups within the cities.*

SOURCE: Moorfield Storey, "The Government of Cities," New
England Magazine, VI, No. 4 (June 1892), pp. 432–441.

Every American is brought up to believe two things: First, that
we are par excellence a business people, pre-eminently endowed
with what we are pleased to call "sound business sense"; and
second, that we invented and understand better than any other
nation the art of self-government. These are fundamental articles
in our national creed, comfortable household beliefs that are
handed down from father to son, and we cling to them with
unquestioning faith. Yet how shall we reconcile them with the fact
that our large cities are, with scarcely an exception, badly governed,
and in many instances disgracefully governed! When we are applying the principles of self-government most directly, where the
people are nearest to their agents and feel their neglect or misman-
agement most keenly, our "sound business sense" deserts us and
we fail lamentably.

What are the causes of this failure? How can we secure good
municipal government? No more important questions confront the
American people to-day, and they must be answered.

These questions concern not merely the dwellers in the cities,
who suffer the immediate effects of bad government, but every
citizen of this country; for a city which is governed by corrupt men
is a plague spot that infects the whole body politic. Baltimore
dominates the State of Maryland, New Orleans exercises a baleful
influence over Louisiana. Nor is the evil stayed by State lines; a
corrupt city government may poison the politics of the whole
country. Tammany Hall rules the city of New York. It claims the
power to elect and defeat presidents, and so to shape the policy of
the country. . . . It is mortifying to think how many months and
years of honest and earnest labor to educate the people upon such

vital issues as tariff reform and financial honesty may be brought to
naught by a miserable bargain made in the city of New York. It is
humiliating to reflect that the national conventions of great parties
may be governed in their choice of a candidate for the highest
office in this country by the supposed necessity of conciliating men
like Tweed and John Kelly. Indeed, the very existence of Republican government may almost be said to be at stake. . . .

The officials who administer the government of a city deal with
pure business questions. It is their duty to see that the air which we
breathe is unpolluted; that the water which we drink is pure; that
our sewers do not fill our houses with poison; that the streets upon
which we walk are well paved and clean; that their use is properly
regulated so as to preserve the respective rights of pedestrians and
those who ride in public or private conveyances; that our lives and
property are protected by efficient police; that fires are prevented
and extinguished; that the new uses of electricity for light, power,
and the transmission of intelligence are carefully guarded so as to
give the public the service which it needs without undue risk to the
citizen; that our schools are well conducted; that the spread of infectious diseases is checked; that we are not injured by unwholesome food and drink; that our feet are not obstructed by snow on
the sidewalks, nor our heads crushed by ice from the roofs. From
birth to death, at home, at school, in the street, in the theatre, in
church, eating, drinking, breathing, sleeping, walking, sick or well,—
at every moment of our lives, our health, our safety, and our property depend very largely on the excellence of our city government.
Not merely the necessaries, but the luxuries of life, libraries, art
museums, parks, music, architecture, painting, and sculpture are
within the sphere of municipal government. If that government is
inefficient and corrupt, we feel it at every turn in our daily life; if it
is efficient and honest, all our lives are made easier. If we give the
subject a moment's thought, we cannot but see how large a part of
the business which concerns us all most nearly is intrusted to our
municipal governments.

There is nothing in the nature of things which makes it impossible to govern a city well. If we cross the ocean and examine what
some of us like to call "the effete monarchies of the old world," we
shall find that the business of ruling a city is well understood. The
streets of London and Paris, and even Liverpool, seem surprisingly
clean to any one who is familiar with the streets of an American

city. The sewers of Paris are models, and the efficiency of the French police is proverbial. The disastrous conflagrations which so constantly lay waste large sections of our cities and towns are almost unknown on the continent of Europe. Illustrations might be multiplied, but Glasgow and Birmingham deserve more than a passing mention, for they are conspicuous examples of the successful application to municipal affairs of that "sound business sense" upon which we so unreasonably plume ourselves. . . .

This is a brief résumé which shows what can be done by the intelligent application of business principles to the conduct of municipal affairs. . . . One of the greatest dangers which beset our system arises from the existence in our cities and states of large aggregations of capital, whose owners have interests at variance with those of the general public. A street railway monopoly or a great gas or water company is naturally anxious to make as much money as possible, and to secure whatever privileges will aid in the accomplishment of this object. The public, on the other hand, which gives such a corporation its franchises, which permits it to use the streets and grants it various rights, is anxious in return to get the best possible accommodation at the lowest possible price. The attempts of the corporation to secure new privileges, and the use of those already granted should be carefully watched in the public interest, so that the fulfilment of its obligations may be secured. On the other hand, there are always demagogues or honest fanatics or venal politicians who suggest unreasonable demands on the corporation, which the persons interested in the latter consider attacks upon their vested rights. There is inevitably a conflict of interest, and out of this grows the danger that the corporations will feel themselves obliged to gain their ends defensive or offensive by corruption, and that dishonest men will seek municipal office in order to be corrupted. When legislation is for sale, no man and no private or public right are safe; and it is important, therefore, to have as few great corporations which may be tempted to corrupt as possible. [As some omitted paragraphs would show, Storey here clearly suggests municipal ownership of certain public service companies.]

Both Glasgow and Birmingham are governed by a council consisting of a large number of members who serve without pay, and as the best citizens are elected to these offices it is considered an honor to serve the city. These cities succeed in getting able and honest men to manage their business and in consequence it is managed well.

What do we do?

. . . Everywhere, with rare exceptions, inferior men are elected to municipal office, and any man, however little his education or his previous training may have fitted him for the work, is considered competent to deal with the complicated problems of municipal government. A succession of men more or less incompetent follow each other at brief intervals over the stage, and as a result there is no consistent economical administration of a city's business. Of Boston, a year ago, a gentleman who had been studying the operation of the various departments said, "The methods are such that no business house could adopt them and keep out of bankruptcy six months."

We are badly governed because we choose incompetent, dishonest, or at best inexperienced men to govern us. We will admit the fact. We all lament it. What is the remedy? Is it possible that a great business people like ourselves is powerless to change this stage of things? Must we look forward to an indefinite future of tame submission to saloon-keepers and actual or probable convicts? Is there no chance of a new anti-slavery movement in which we, the slaves, shall rise against such masters? . . .

It is not that Americans do not know what good government is or do not want it. It is not that they are content with their rulers, but they find it easier to pay a little more in taxes, to swallow a little dust, to breathe a little foul air, and to treat disease as inevitable, than to spend in working for the public time and money for which no one thanks them, and which are taken from lucrative business, or from rest and recreation. . . .

There are three motives which may induce good men to take public office: The desire for money, the desire for honor, and public spirit, or the sense of duty. We appeal to neither. Our salaries are inadequate even if we could promise a tenure of office during good behavior. Municipal office has ceased to be regarded as especially honorable; and however keen may be his sense of duty, it is difficult to persuade a public-spirited citizen that he ought to seek municipal office and engineer his own campaign. Until the people whose business is to be done are sufficiently interested in having it done well to select good officers, elect them, and keep them in office by proper support, our citizens will continue to be governed by incompetent men and persons who make office profit-able in illegitimate ways.

There is another thing which cannot be neglected in enumerating the causes which contribute to misrule in our cities. They contain a large number of ignorant voters, mainly of foreign birth or descent, many of whom know nothing of our government or even of our language, and who are easily led by a few men whose influence is for sale, and whose prejudices are easily inflamed. These men are ignorant, not wicked. They can be influenced for good as well as for bad. They do not want bad water, bad air, and squalid abodes. They do not wish to see their families die of infectious disorders, and if they could be made to understand the facts they would be ready to vote for everything which will improve their condition. Their numbers make them an element in the situation which must be considered. . . .

There is a close parallel between the business of a great railroad corporation and the business of a great city. Both require great administrative and financial ability; skill in the selection of men, power of organization, and strength of will. The ability to organize a force which will run trains for freight and passengers economically and efficiently is not in kind different from the ability to organize a force which will clean or pave streets regularly and well. The ability to secure the best results from a given expenditure of money in well built railroads and strong bridges is of the same character as the ability to get like results from a similar expenditure in well-constructed sewers or water works. The man who can deal successfully with rival companies competing for his business, can meet with equal success the demands of street railway companies or gas companies competing with each other to obtain franchises from the city. The same financial skill which preserves the proper ratio between the income and expenses of a business corporation will find ample opportunity to display itself in dealing with the finances of a municipal corporation. . . .

Should we not all rejoice if our municipal business was in the hands of men trained to do it well, and have we not energy and sense enough to secure so desirable a result? Let us simply, as members of a great business corporation, apply the same rules to the selection of our president and directors that are followed by stockholders in smaller business corporations. Instead of letting a number of politicians associated with the national parties meet and nominate some of themselves as candidates for the offices of the city, why should not we have an entirely new departure? Why should not the business men of the city, irrespective of their political or religious opinions, form a municipal party for the simple purpose of electing competent municipal officers, and keeping them in office as long as they do their work well? . . .

The next step is to make positions in the city employ attractive to such men as we need, men of ability and character. To fill the higher offices in a city government requires a great deal of time and hard work, and we cannot organize our government upon the theory that a considerable number of the most capable citizens will sacrifice themselves for the benefit of the rest. In the long run we must pay for good work if we expect to get it. We cannot compete with private employers unless we are willing to pay as much. The work of governing a city is not especially agreeable, and the city can well afford to pay for the best talent that can be had. Large salaries are not so expensive as large stealings and poor work. The men who now pretend to serve our cities without compensation are often better paid than the men who receive the largest salaries that private corporations offer. . . . If we have not time to govern ourselves, we must pay some one else to do our work.

Money alone will not get such men as we need. There must be some assurance of permanence, some hope of promotion. We must offer a career, if we would tempt into our service the able young men who every year are choosing their professions. . . . Is it impossible in America to create such a profession? Are we forever bound to our present unbusiness-like method of selecting our officers at random, and turning them out as soon as they begin to know their business?

With citizens organized to insure good municipal government, it would be comparatively easy by proper effort to reach and influence the mass of ignorant voters, who now help the vicious bosses to govern our cities, but it is the part of prudence not to take too many chances against ourselves. We are struggling with a great many complicated questions, which it takes intelligence to understand. They are to be settled by gradually educating the people. Public opinion is the ultimate force in this country, if not, indeed, everywhere, but it takes time and effort to create and direct it. A colony of Italians, Scandinavians, Germans, or Irish, preserving their national language and their national ideas, and living as foreigners among us is very difficult to reach, but their votes count just as much as the votes of the most highly educated men among us. We must make our naturalization laws more stringent. It is not consistent with business principles to admit men as equal partners in a prosperous firm, who bring neither experience nor capital, who know nothing of the business, and do not even speak the same language with the other partners. . . .

Once persuade the people that the government of a city is a mere matter of business and induce them to treat it as such, and municipal reform is assured.

12. Robert W. De Forest and Lawrence Veiller, *The Tenement House Problem*

REFORMERS *are sometimes compelled to persuade the public of the need to modify certain conventions or to give priority to certain values. In the long run, this was implicit in the progressive reform movement. But at the outset of the era, reformers thought it necessary merely to persuade the public of the existence of conditions that contravened already prevailing conventions. In 1900, while Theodore Roosevelt was still governor of New York, the legislature established a State Tenement Commission under the direction of Robert De Forest, then president of the New York Charity Organization Society, and Lawrence Veiller, the society's secretary. The Tenement House Problem derived from the Commission's report, which evoked from the legislature a remarkable number of reform laws. The rapid disappearance of the most onerous conditions described in the report testifies to how quickly law sometimes can change living conditions. Before the laws of 1903, for example, air shafts, privies, and "school sinks" were commonplace, and thus accepted as "inevitable"; after the laws, they became virtually unimaginable in American apartment-house construction.*

Apart from the remarkably graphic descriptions of living conditions suffered by the poor in the crowded housing of the cities, the report tells us much about the motives of the reformers. Note, for example, how the editors appeal to the profit motive on behalf of reform. Note also how they (and some of those who testified before their commission) focus on the moral improvements that housing reform would bring.

For the best coverage of the New York tenement situation, see Roy Lubove, The Progressives and the Slums (Cambridge, Mass., 1962).

SOURCE: Robert W. De Forest and Lawrence Veiller (eds.), *The Tenement House Problem* (New York: The Macmillan Company, 1903), pp. 385–388, 421–442.

Tenement Evils as Seen by the Tenants

Life on the East Side

The following was written by a young woman of twenty, a tenement dweller all her life:—

Being born and bred on the East Side, I am somewhat in a position to judge the various discomforts that exist in the modern tenements. The greatest evil is the lack of light and air.

The air shaft is so narrow that the kitchen windows in two houses adjoin one another. In most houses the air shafts are the only means of light and air for at least two out of every three rooms, and the only means of lighting the staircases.

The first thing that awakens one in the morning is the loud voices of the various tenants, intermingled with the odors that arise from the kitchen windows. It is, indeed, wonderful that you can distinguish any one voice among them all. If we are to give the reason for the people's loud voices, let us first consider how difficult it is for one to make himself understood in this medley and confusion; in this congested living House of Babel, it becomes habitual for us to raise our voices.

After the children are sent to school, the various mothers commence their house-cleaning, then comes the question, What is to be done with the garbage of the day? Most women solve it by throwing it into the street and air shaft. It is much easier than climbing the dark stairs and running the risk of breaking one's legs. In some cases it is almost a necessity to throw it out, the premium on space is so high in their tiny kitchens, which hold wash-tubs, water-sink, and chairs, and just room enough to turn about. In this room the cooking, the washing of clothes, the daily ablutions of the various members of the family, take place.

The cooking is generally abbreviated to one meal a day, the other meals consisting of tea or coffee, with bread and butter.

On washing and ironing days the children are sent to school with a cent to buy candy, instead of lunch.

After the principal meal of the day is over, the kitchen changes its appearance into a study room; the older children sit at the table doing their arithmetic, while the younger ones sit on the floor or any available space, with a large book on their laps for a desk.

The public schools are beginning to realize the East Side needs by opening their playgrounds for quiet study and play, which is a dire necessity; where every inch of space is utilized in their houses, it is a relief to get into a large, airy room.

The law forbids putting pots or pans outside of windows on fire-escapes, but the rooms are not supplied with enough closets or refrigerators, hence the only means of getting rid of them.

Another step in tenement house reform would be compulsory bath-rooms and lavatories. How can the children be taught decency where male and female intermingle without the slightest regard to sex or common decency? Bath-rooms would not only help to keep the people healthier, but would elevate the standard of morality.

E. B.

A woman who is the housekeeper of a five-story tenement house, and who for twenty years has lived in tenement houses, when asked in what way she would like them changed, exclaimed without a moment's hesitation and very emphatically:—

"No air shafts!" she then added, "I sweep mine every two days, but sometimes it smells so it makes me sick to my stomach. In summer I've got to sweep it every day, or I can't stand it. You see it's damp down there, and the families, they throw out garbage and dirty papers and the insides of chickens, and other unmentionable filth. The housekeeper before me wasn't so particular, and I just vomited when I first cleaned up the air shaft. Then it's so hard to get into, you know. I have to crawl through the window, and in that other air shaft I have to climb down a ladder, and me with the rheumatism, it aches me. That other housekeeper before me wasn't so strict. I found the cellar full of mattresses and old things when I came. Now my cellar's just as clean as my halls, and my agent says it would do for Fifth Avenue. You know they call my house a flat, and the next one, just like it, a tenement. The house across the street is awful dirty, and so all kinds of people live there together, Italians and Jews and Christians, and they quarrel terrible.

"You must please excuse these clothes drying in my room, but I can't climb the stairs to the roof, it makes my heart beat so, and other bad feelings. That's what all the other women says, too; and I don't dare to hang a fine wash in the air shaft, because some one else might put out a red wash or a blue wash above it, and it drips down and makes you do your wash all over again."

During the conversation the housekeeper was interrupted twice by men who wanted to see the apartment. "It's on the stoop in the rear," she explained. "Three rooms and ten dollars a month; two on the air shaft, and one at the back. The gas costs too much; I have to burn kerosene oil myself, and them rooms is very dark; mine's light. The ladies that have lived in them rooms always complained of headache and dizziness. When I used to live in dark rooms on —— street I used to have headache and get dizzy, but now I'm all right. And then when you get up on top where it's sunny, the stairs near kills you. A friend of mine has had her top floor empty three months. My husband when he was alive, never could live up top. He always said it made him sick to go through the halls with the smells of so many different families. He used to say air shafts ought to have wires across the windows to keep people from throwing things out. But the noise hurts me. It comes down the air shaft so that sometimes I can't sleep all night." . . .

Tenement Evils as Seen by An
Inspector

I worked for the Tenement House Commission from about the middle of July till November 1, 1900, as follows: Inspecting back to back rear tenements; inspecting existing tenements in each borough; inspecting fire-escapes in Brooklyn; inspecting a list of sixty-four houses declared to be the worst in the city in 1894 by the Board of Health.

During three and a half months, while I visited every borough except the Bronx, I did not fail in any instance to gain admission to any house or place where I wished to enter, nor to secure any reasonable information. In general, people did not know what the Tenement House Commission was; but they knew that a visit to their cellars, water-closets, roofs, and rooms was a relief from their masters,—the housekeeper and the "agent,"—and won their interest, sympathy, and coöperation (if the housekeeper was not in sight). The attitude of owners, agents, and some housekeepers is— in some instances—artfully, almost mockingly, servile, just as if they took for granted that there was something unreal about inspecting a house. In some cases after the inspection, a member of the family would be sent after me to say that "the boss" had sent for me to come to his rooms, or sometimes I was very urgently invited to come into the saloon to drink or to smoke; one agent stood in front of me talking, with the bills hanging out of his vest pocket, and one frightened man led me into a rear dark passage and offered to give me a tip, to keep him out of trouble. I did not make any attempt to draw out any one, so that the foregoing examples may be regarded as indicating the free habit of lessees and property holders.

During three and a half months of inspection in Manhattan, Brooklyn, Long Island City, Williamsburg, Greenpoint, and Richmond, I never met a single representative of the Board of Health. I never found a place, where such an official was known to have been around recently. . . .

BACK TO BACK TENEMENTS IN MANHATTAN

These houses stand back to back, or the rear house abuts on the side of another house. The space left between the rear walls of abutting houses varies from nothing to 40 inches, or, at a few houses, more. When a rear house is surrounded on three sides by walls it is hopeless, unless the whole apartment is converted into one room, which even does not afford cross ventilation. As it is, almost all of these houses are very short, being two rooms deep, allowing two rooms to an apartment. In some houses, where practicable, these bedrooms have windows at the sides. In some, where it would be practicable, walls have not been opened. In the majority of rear houses these bedrooms vary from pitch-black to somewhat dark, with little or no ventilation.

Although this rear space is so narrow, yet there are the same number of windows to it as if these opened to free space. The result is that people will throw anything out of the windows; rubbish, dirt, garbage, contents of the chamber-pot, etc. It is the favorite resort for cats, both dead and alive. There is no place that affords more occasion for neighborhood friction, because neighborhoods of different ranks of cleanliness and different nationalities come into contact in a very tight place. One street is clean and has American tenants. The landlord furnishes a well-equipped rear house, and has every window covered on the outside by wire netting. Another street is occupied by the latest arrival from Sicily or Riga, and the houses are dilapidated. The people pour the things named above into this rear space; there are no wire nettings. The result is great friction, quarrels, and notice to the Board of Health, which ignores the summons. Such a place in kind is on Chrystie Street, where dirt is dripping from those rear walls and adheres to the walls. This is the general character of such rear walls. . . .

One very objectionable nuisance is the use of roofs instead of water-closets by children and also by adults. This is especially characteristic of the "East Side." This condition and practice exist because the instinct of cleanliness is not strong enough to overcome the fatigue of climbing the stairs from the yard or cellar. For instance, the people on the top floor of No. — Monroe Street have to climb five flights of stairs from the closet to their apartment. The location of closets ought to be regulated according to the perpendicular distance from the apartments.

Some housekeepers, to prevent this nuisance, have locked the roof doors, which adds still another danger.

HALLS

The most barbarous parts of buildings are the halls. A person coming in from the sunlight outside, plunges into these halls just like a car filled with men plunges and disappears in the black mouth of a mine shaft. If he is fortunate in not running against anybody, he stumbles along, finding his way with his feet. At this, the tenants throw open the doors to ask who is wanted, but he hurries forward as rapidly as possible and rushes out upon the roof or into some open room, because the air is so dense and stifling that he wishes to escape quickly. The only light and ventilated halls are in the oldest houses, of little depth, with a window to the yard.

Long, deep houses, with two or four families on the floor, have dark or pitch-black halls, and the air in the halls is more or less stifling.

"Double-deckers" have one window at the middle, lighting and ventilating the stairway, not the halls. This light and air comes from the air shaft; hence even the stairway of the lower two or three stories is dark. Even if, as in a few, there is another window instead of the water-closet opposite, giving two opposite windows to the middle or neck of the hall, yet the air does not circulate into the halls, which can be noticed at once by breathing. In "double-deckers" the hall passages are pitch-black and unventilated.

Where there ought to be a light burning on each hall, or two lights because of the thick, stuffy air in which a light turns red like the sun hid by the smoke, there is only one on the second floor, or none at all.

Now, why are most of these halls so densely filled with poisonous air? Imagine running through one of the Lake Shore tunnels, then fancy again such a tunnel in a tenement house, and as much air entering at either end as it is possible where there can be no draught, and supposing dense fumes of frying fat and boiling vegetables are produced inside the ends of the tunnel. Fancy that these are blown inward until they meet another body of dead air left by two or four adults or eight or ten adults, eight to sixteen children (two or four apartments, remember) who have slept there for eight hours. The damp, foul bedclothes are also waiting for a chance to catch the least particle of fresh air. This combined current, blown in from either end, meets in the middle and has to seek a counter-current back to the openings of our tunnel (out into the yard and street). In the middle it accumulates and fills up the halls, where it stagnantly remains. Now, imagine somebody clenching his teeth, his fists in his pockets, keeping the middle of the stairs to avoid touching the greasy sides, holding his breath and bravely dashing through this poisonous mass,—and you have somewhat of an idea of a tenement hall.

One of the greatest pleasures enjoyed is to get out on the roof and catch the first whiff of good air. . . .

BASEMENTS

. . . In Brooklyn and Williamsburg the garbage barrels (wooden casks) stand in the cellar one week before the contents are removed. The smell is so foul that people represent that it has made them sick, and the smell was found nauseating to me.

On the East Side, at Mulberry Street and in Williamsburg, "Kosher" butchers confine poultry in close cellars. The torture should not be permitted, and the stink is intolerable.

On Staten Island there are less cellars along the line of the Bay, on account of tide water and the sewer. Wherever they are, however, they are dirty like those of Brooklyn.

In Long Island City I went through about ten blocks in the new suburbs, and saw only one dirty cellar.

YARDS

The 10-foot yard behind double-deckers is clean only if swept daily, for there is a perfect rain of refuse from the windows of the ten to fourteen apartments above. These yards are usually not open to access. . . .

WATER CLOSETS

The School Sinks.—These are in the yard; they are in one group in a common building for one, two, three, or four houses. . . .

The scrubbing and cleanliness of the closet chamber is so irregular that no general statement will cover a majority of cases. There are many closets that have deposits of offal on the seat or the floor, or are on both, and outside on the yard floor. . . .

I find that wherever there is a saloon without an inside water-closet—or sometimes where there is—some or all of the closets of the school sink are wet or covered with offal or defiled beyond description. The customers of the saloon spoil one closet, then they abandon it, to try another, until they have ruined all as far as they can go. This is so general that a person could tell that there was a saloon near by as soon as he observed the closets. Urinating closets are a source of great impurity, because they are thickly coated with foulness, and give a keen stench to the atmosphere in the yard where children play and come in contact with them. They are generally abandoned to foulness.

Every saloon ought to be absolutely prohibited from using a school sink or water-closets used at the same time by families, and a complete closet ought to be provided inside the saloon. . . .

THE VAULT

I found a great deal of the most reprehensible neglect of the closet vaults during the summer. Such a vault ought to be flushed out with fresh water twice during a summer's day. All such closets fill the yard with a foul smell, and even the house as far as the street, sometimes to the degree of making the tenants sick. As mentioned before, sometimes the reason is in saving or stinting water by the direction of a sordid landlord. Often people said that they flushed out the sink at 10 o'clock P.M. to prevent the exhausting of the domestic supply, which was a ready excuse when closets were found improperly flushed. At others, people did not know how often they flushed them. Some said, "Oh! about two or three times a week," others said, "Once a week." One woman said, "About once every two weeks," with an air of satisfied ignorance, while at one place the sink had remained unflushed for three weeks and the stink was terrible. My general impression is, that in a great many districts these sinks were indifferently neglected.

The Water Closets

These are of two kinds, with a tank and chain, or with a circular pipe around the bowl and a self-regulating pipe. The latter closet takes the place of the school sink in the Borough of Brooklyn. There are also some in Manhattan. It does not afford enough current pressure to wash out the inside of the bowl, which is usually coated, and when the pipe is itself attacked by the coating, the water supply is gradually reduced. . . . On the East Side I found things that ought to be photographed—trap water-closets heaped over the top, running over, and the stench such as to pervade the halls and apartments, and to make any civilized person ill.

In many places, all over New York, patent-medicine men have a printed placard, framed, covered with a glass, and fastened on the wall, ostensibly warning those who use the closets not to wet the seats, but under this warning the advertisement of medicines for private diseases of men. These are put up in family closets. At one place I found five such placards.

The results of the inspections, I believe, will show about three apartments to one closet, and if we could ascertain accurately the whole number of families where there is overcrowding, the number would exceed even that. At many places there is no order about the closets, and no one knows how many families use the same closet. The tendency is when a closet is spoiled by pollution to concentrate on the cleaner ones, and abandon the others. In such cases they may have been abandoned for such a long period that the outside offal is dried and hard. I have seen all the closets in one yard so bad that the tenants of that house went across to the yard of the next house to use those closets. . . .

Baths

My chance for observation was very limited. I do not recall a single tenement in Manhattan with a bath of any kind. Only five houses can be recalled where I saw baths, and these were in Brooklyn. They would not have been there, had not the houses lapsed from a much higher rank than they hold at present. . . . There was no coal in any one of them (which, by the way, is a favorite current figure of speech in this age of florid rhetoric), although the tenants were of the lowest, dirtiest class. Nor was there anything else in the tubs. The tubs, like all the rest of the building, were dilapidated and could not be expected to be used. If used, the fact would throw extraordinary credit upon the tenants. . . . The alleged charge made by a sweeping generalization that the tenement house population would use the bath-tubs for storing coal or anything else is unjust and untrue. . . . Bathing facilities are a family convenience. The tenement house system is one of artificial conditions forced by economic causes. Unrestrained greed has gradually drawn together the dimensions of the tenements, until they have become so narrowed that the family life has become dissolved, and the members have been thrust out and scattered. The father is in the saloon; the youth teem in procession up and down the lighted streets past concert halls and licensed dens of infamy; the boys rove in hordes in the alley, the girls in the rear yards; the women are on the fire-escapes making clothing in the gloom, and the family cat sits on the refuse in the narrow spaces between back to back rear houses. The redemption of the tenement classes lies partly in the restoration of the family, the most conservative unit in civilization, to its proper share of space, natural light, and air, and the cultivation of the domestic arts, one of which is personal cleanliness. Bathing is a necessity in the crowded city; in the country it is not. The enhancement of land values and the necessity of artificial cleanliness or bathing lead back to the same common root as their cause; namely, the forced, artificial, anti-natural concentration of population. Public conveniences for private utilities crystallize class distinctions and eliminate family functions. . . .

There is one class of people, with more anxiety for gain than philanthropy, which maintains that the industrial class are what they are and are to remain so; that they are unworthy of conveniences, since their passion is for ruining houses, and that their honeycombed houses must not be provided with these conveniences for fear of their wearing out. There is another class, composed of abstract enthusiasts, who fancy that the raw, undeveloped classes have entirely the same intelligent sense of the fitness of things as they consciously have themselves, and who attribute to the masses of immigrated population the same delicate sensitiveness, the same knowledge and character, which they themselves have only by virtue of education and the hereditary accumulation of good breeding. . . . Both these classes take a narrowed view of things and stop short of an acquainting distance from reality. There are large bodies of acquired population to whom ignorance, uncleanliness, and rawness, and a mean standard of living are born in the blood, bred to the bone. Society is bringing up their children in the public schools, and just so must society elevate them to a higher standard of wants and their satisfaction, and a higher or American sanitary level. . . .

There is no better synonym for it than the term organized discipline. The whole city can be speedily thrown into organized vice; who doubts that? It can be lifted the other way, by patient, enduring application. . . .

There is no other sane expedient. If high legal requirements be imposed upon owners, who are often represented by petty agents or incompetent lessees, it would merely lead to a mocking evasion or blackmail. The property owner, too, must be protected against the ignorance of the tenant. Italians are said, when told to whitewash, to take cold slack of lime, and daub windows, ceilings, woodwork, and floors; or, if told to wash the floors, they are said to draw bucketful after bucketful of water from the sink and empty it upon the floor. What are the causes for the universal decayed and soiled marks on ceilings, under the sinks and wash-tubs, but ignorance and neglect to use the sinks properly? Tenants on the East Side do not draw the chains in water-closets, which are stopped up in consequence.

The tenants must also be protected against their own ignorance. If there is a little window that admits air into the dark, unventilated bedroom, the tenant will frequently hang a picture in front. It became my custom to look behind pictures for windows, when I wished to make record of them. More often they will obstruct this only means of ventilation by draperies, curtains, or laces. They will fill up a rear wall space with rubbish and empty the chamber vessel out of the rear window.

13.   Adna Ferrin Weber,
The Growth of Cities in the Nineteenth Century

It is impossible to write about American history without reference to the so-called urban-rural conflict. Such conflict of course is not peculiar to the United States, nor to industrial societies. But it is possible that the intensity of the American myth about its agrarian foundations did combine with the particularly jarring features of the country's rapid industrialization to exacerbate the problem and to cause Americans generally to exaggerate the baleful influence of urban growth on American civilization. Urban and agrarian reformers were often in agreement on this. Occasionally someone like Frederic C. Howe can refer to the city—as in the title of his 1905 book—as "The Hope of Democracy." More often, though, urban progressives focused automatically on how to deal with the destructive qualities of city life. Frequently they expressed the hope that the spectacular concentration of population in urban centers over the previous quarter century might be reversed and industry and commerce decentralized in the old-fashioned, self-contained towns. As Woodrow Wilson declared in his 1912 campaign: "In all that I may have to do in public affairs in the United States I am going to think of towns such as I have seen in Indiana, towns of the old American pattern, that own and operate their own industries, hopefully and happily."

Adna Weber, a Columbia University economist and deputy commissioner of labor statistics for New York State, confronted the anticity prejudices of his day head on. In a scholarly statistical study that covers European as well as American cities, Weber disposed of the myths about the deleterious mental, moral, and physical effects of city life. He then proceeded to argue the positive value of urban living, not least the advantages to individual liberty and enlightenment available in the urban environment. His study suggests that, among other things, the evils Americans conventionally attributed to the cities were only more easily visible there.

SOURCE: Adna Ferrin Weber, *The Growth of Cities in the Nineteenth Century* (New York: Longmans, 1899), pp. 388–441.

All of our investigations in the course of the present chapter point to the conclusion that the townsman is on the average a more efficient industrial unit than the rural immigrant. The city proletariat . . . appears to be recruited from the country-born rather than from the real city dwellers. In fact, the countryman coming to the city begins a slow ascent, rather than a descent; his children, instead of being men of "lower physique with less power of persistent work" advance to a higher rank on the industrial and social ladder, while the third generation, instead of dying out, is still more capable and efficient. . . .

As a class, the country immigrants do not at once assume the higher positions in the economic organism, but enter the unskilled occupations where muscular strength and vigor are in demand. Among the rural immigrants there are indeed some few skilled artisans, but there are very few cases of country laborers becoming artisans in the cities. The immigrants at first take up with such menial occupations as domestic and personal service, work in hotels and restaurants, postmen, cab-drivers and truckmen, and, in some cases, with the building trades. It is only gradually that they work their way into the skilled industries, in which the city-born have a far larger representation. . . .

Notwithstanding such facts, it is commonly held that city life produces dwarfed, stunted men and degenerates; fortunately, statistics of physical infirmities exist which dispel such fears about the effects of city life. It is now generally recognized that a connection exists between congenital blindness, congenital deaf-mutism and congenital imbecility or feeble-mindedness, i.e., they are all results of impaired constitutional vigor. Now recent statistics show that these infirmities are rather more prevalent in rural districts and small towns than in the cities, while insanity, which is rather a nervous than a bodily failing, prevails chiefly in the cities. From the exceedingly valuable report by Dr. John S. Billings on the Insane, Feeble-minded, Deaf and Dumb, and Blind, in the United States at the Eleventh Census, the following figures are derived, showing the ratio of the specified classes to 100,000 of the population:

	UNITED STATES	CITIES OF 50,000+	AUTHORITY
Insane	170.0	242.9	Tables 151, 153
Feeble-minded	152.7	74.3	" 172, 174
Deaf Mutes	64.8	48.7	" 189, 191
Blind	80.8	53.5	" 223, 225

These results are confirmed by European statistics. . . .

It is clear then that while city life produces, or at least maintains fewer of the severer physical infirmities, like blindness, deaf-mutism and idiocy, than does the country, it does favor the increase of insanity.

The average height and girth of chest are significant criteria of physical vigor; and of the two, the latter is the more important, since it is indisputable that the strongest individuals and races are those that have the greatest chest capacity and lung power.

As regards stature, the preponderance of opinion in the past has been that city life exerts a depressing effect upon the individual. . . .

From Cato's time down, statesmen have declared that the bravest men and most daring soldiers have come from the land. . . .

Now it is to be observed that the believers in town degeneracy base their arguments on antiquated statistics. There can be no doubt that down to very recent times the health and vigor of urbanites compared unfavorably with that of men who worked in the open air, just as their death-rates did. But in the last quarter century the evidence in both cases has changed. In 1874 a French authority declared that fitness for army service depends less on density of population than on wealth, climate, daily life. Health and vigor may always be preserved if men in cities will make proper provision for open-air exercise, cleanliness and a pure food supply. Professor Marshall, who is not afraid of looking the evils of town life in the face, is right when he says that "it is not to be concluded that the race is degenerating physically, nor even that its nervous strength is, on the whole, decaying. On the contrary, the opposite is plainly true of those boys and girls who are able to enter fully into modern outdoor amusements, who frequently spend holidays in the country, and whose food, clothing and medical care are abundant and governed by the best knowledge."

But after all, progress depends less on purely physical strength than on moral resolution or nervous strength. In the words of the writer just quoted, "the power of sustaining great muscular exertion depends on force of will and strength of character as well as on constitutional strength. This energy (strength of man, not of body) is moral rather than physical; but yet it depends on the physical conditions of the nervous strength. This strength of the man himself, this resolution, energy, and self-mastery, or in short this 'vigor' is the source of all progress: it shows itself in great deeds, in great thoughts, and in the capacity for true religious feeling."

Now, it is precisely the high nervous organization of city-bred soldiers that has enabled them to last through long campaigns as well as or better than countrymen with their rude physical health. It made the students of Berlin University able to bear fatigue better than the average soldier in the war of 1870–1, and rendered the New England store-clerks equal to all the strain of Sherman's march to the sea in 1864. When to nervous strength is joined the muscular development to be found among the athletic middle-class youth in American and English suburban towns, one is justified in hailing them as world conquerors. Seven years ago an English writer, referring to the young men of Wimbledom and Battersea, near London, had the foolhardiness to eulogize them as future victors of Marathons; but yesterday, and he saw his prediction fulfilled as American city lads marched to victory on Cuban soil, side by side with the rough cowboys of the western plains.

Having dealt with the subject of physical health and vigor, it now remains to consider the influence of city life upon intelligence and morals.

Education.—As regards education, it must be obvious that the agglomeration of population is more favorable than its dispersion can be. In fact, one would naturally turn to the cities and towns for the best schools, since they alone can afford to provide the expensive advantages incident to the grading of pupils and the division of labor educationally. It is not surprising, therefore, that the urban schools of the United States have 190 class days per annum, and the rural schools only 115; and that the attendance in the city is 70 per cent of the enrolment, while in the country it is 62 per cent. Moreover, the statistics of illiteracy in the United States are favorable to the cities, notwithstanding the reception by the cities of the bulk of illiterate foreigners. . . .

With very few exceptions (New York City, Pittsburg, Cleveland, Detroit), the cities have a better educated population than the rest of the State in which they are situated. The difference in favor of the cities is in many instances very marked, although in the case of Baltimore, New Orleans and Louisville, it is explicable by the different proportions of negroes in the population. There can be no doubt about the superiority of the city schools, both primary and secondary. Educators in fact now recognize the inferiority of rural schools as one of their most pressing problems, and the National Educational Association is even now discussing the ample report on rural schools presented at its 1897 meeting by its Committee of Twelve.

But the education of the schools forms only a part of a man's education. Their discipline must be supplemented by outside reading and experience; alone it too often promotes superficiality. And this is the peculiar danger of urban habits of life. The city boy is taught to read, but not to think; the result is seen in the immense constituency of "yellow journalism." Country newspapers are trivial enough, but they do not descend to the depths of moral degradation of sensational metropolitan journals, manufactured for city readers.

Town education has been so well described by Mr. Hobson[1] that it would be a loss not to quote his words:

> That town life, as distinguished from town work, is educative of certain intellectual and moral qualities, is evident. Setting aside that picked intelligence which flows to the town to compete successfully for intellectual employment, there can be no question but that the townsman has a larger superficial knowledge of the world and human nature. He is shrewd, alert, versatile, quicker and more resourceful than the countryman. In thought, speech, action, this superiority shows itself. The townsman has a more developed consciousness, his intelligence is constantly stimulated in a thousand ways by larger and more varied society, and by a more diversified and complex economic environment. While there is reason to believe that town work is on the average less educative than country work, town life more than turns the scale. The social intercourse of the club, the trade society, the church, the home, the public-house, the music-hall, the street, supply innumerable educative influences, to say nothing of the ampler opportunities of consciously organized intellectual education which are available in large towns. If, however, we examine a little deeper the character of town education and intelligence, certain tolerably definite limitations show themselves. School instruction, slightly more advanced than in the country, is commonly utilized to sharpen industrial competition and to feed that sensational interest in sport and crime which absorbs the attention of the masses in their non-working hours; it seldom forms the foundation of an intellectual life in which knowledge and taste are reckoned in themselves desirable. The power to read and write is employed by the great majority of all classes in ways which evoke a minimum of thought and wholesome feeling. Social, political and religious preju-

1. *The Evolution of Modern Capitalism*, pp. 338–9.

dices are made to do the work which should be done by careful thought and scientific investigation. Scattered and unrelated fragments of half-baked information form a stock of "knowledge" with which the townsman's glib tongue enables him to present a showy intellectual shop-front. Business smartness pays better in the town, and the low intellectual qualities which are contained in it are educated by town life. The knowledge of human nature thus evoked is in no sense science; it is a mere rule-of-thumb affair, a thin mechanical empiricism. The capable business man who is said to understand the "world" and his fellow-men, has commonly no knowledge of human nature in the larger sense, but merely known from observation how the average man of a certain limited class is likely to act within a narrow prescribed sphere of self-seeking. Town life, then, strongly favors the education of certain shallow forms of intelligence.

The only statistical measure of morality, as distinguished from religion, is negative, being in fact a measure of immorality,—the amount of vice and crime recorded by the police authorities. . . . Criminal statistics undoubtedly put the cities in a bad light. In England, for example, the cities have double or even quadruple the amount of crime that the rural communities have. . . .

The vast majority of crimes are against property, having numbered 53,621 in a total of 56,281, and these are largely larcenies. As regards the graver offenses against the person, London occupies a middle rank (murder) and a low rank in sexual crimes (rape).

But it does not appear that crime is increasing disproportionately in the cities. . . .

Our statistics of vice are mainly restricted to the subject of illegitimacy. . . . Violations of the person are less frequent in the English cities than in the rural counties. Illegitimacy, on the other hand, appears to center in the cities. . . .

Judging from the statistics, the cities must be hot-beds of immorality. But their case is not so bad as it seems. It must be remembered that maternity hospitals are always located in cities, and many of the women who enter these are countrywomen who come to the city to conceal their shame. Levasseur is the authority for the statement that over one-fourth (4,405) of the illegitimate births in 1884 (16,137, or 26.7 per cent. of all births) were such cases. He says that nearly one-half were the fruits of *liaisons*, which in Paris are regarded as a form of marriage, leaving something over one-fourth the alleged number as the real product of Parisian immorality. With these deductions, the Paris rate would be somewhat less than twice that of the rural populations.

But there is still another factor in the problem, namely, the larger proportion of young unmarried women in the cities. This factor, taken into consideration, will account for much of the city illegitimacy. . . . On the whole, it is to be doubted if the cities are much worse than the rural districts as regards illegitimacy; the question cannot be determined definitely until other countries furnish the refined rate. In this country, unfortunately, no distinction between rural and urban populations has been made in the matter of illegitimacy.

Infanticide, as the European criminal statistics have shown, is more prevalent in the country than in the city, while abortion seems to be less prevalent there.

Prostitution, regarded as a profession, is certainly a city institution, but many social workers doubt whether the sexual morality of the country is on a higher plane, from their knowledge of the large proportion of prostitutes who were first corrupted in country homes. The morals of "wicked Paris" have frequently been impeached, but sociologists who know the facts declare that a very large part of the Parisian vice is supported by travellers and foreign sojourners. . . . Similarly with other cities: they have a great deal of vice, to be sure, but it is the property of a distinct class of the population. . . .

The amount of viciousness and criminality in cities is probably exaggerated in popular estimation from the fact that the cities have long been under the blaze of an Argus-eyed press, so that the worst is known about them. They have hitherto overshadowed the evils in the moral life of villages, but several recent rural crimes of unwonted atrocity have awakened in the nation a truer realization of the actual facts. Many sociologists have also realized that the rural centre is not so "idyllic" as has been imagined.

But if there is actually a larger criminal and vicious class in the cities, as would be a priori expected from the fact that the cities are the foci of attraction, it does not follow that the danger of contamination is greater. The fact is that in the city the crime is localized; it is confined to particular classes and the remaining social classes are so much the cleaner. There are perhaps relatively more offenses committed in the city than in the village,[2] but not so

2. In using statistics of offenses to compare the moral conditions of different places, care must be taken to exclude such offenses as consist merely in a violation of a local ordinance, e.g., neglect to clean a sidewalk of snow.

many more offenders. And most people will admit that there is considerable difference between a society where the same man comes before [the] magistrate six times, and another society where six men come before the judge once.

The cities, moreover, have the benefit of an educated public opinion on moral questions which is often effective to suppress the beginnings of vice. The power of social opinion, supported by legislation, has been abundantly demonstrated in the transformation of factory labor. There was a time when factories were actual "men-consumers," producing a morally and physically dwarfed and stunted race. That time is forever past in America and England, while to-day the worst conditions are found in the home ("sweating") industries. The same strong social opinion that wiped out factory abuses by the Factory Acts must now be concentrated on the evils of city life.

Finally, the fact must not be overlooked that the city affords more opportunities for the exhibition of virtues as well as of vices, and "if our annals of virtue were kept as carefully as our annals of vice, we might find that town life stood higher in the one than in the other." Every day the city witnesses the performance not merely of acts of generosity and self-denial, but of heroic self-sacrifice. Over against the professional criminal is to be put the policeman; against the roué, the fireman who uncomplainingly faces danger and death day after day. The records of city charitable societies would reveal innumerable deeds of kindness, but would still leave unrevealed the thousand and one generous acts of service performed by the poor themselves for the relief of the unfortunate in their midst.

Amidst the discouragements incited by a contemplation of the failure of our city governments to achieve anything like the success of American rural local government, we may derive some small consolation from the fact that things are not now so bad as they used to be. Let us read De Tocqueville's description of our cities in the thirties, and take fresh courage to renew the struggle for municipal reform. Says the illustrious author of Democracy in America (Reeve's trans. 2d Am. ed., p. 270):

> The United States have no metropolis; but they already contain several very large cities. Philadelphia reckoned 161,000 inhabitants, and New York 202,000 in 1830. The lower orders which inhabit

these cities constitute a rabble even more formidable than the populace of European towns. They consist of freed Blacks in the first place, who are condemned by the laws and by public opinion to an hereditary state of misery and degradation. They also contain a multitude of Europeans who have been driven to the shores of the New World by their misfortunes or their misconduct, and these men inoculate the United States with all their vices, without bringing with them any of those interests which counteract their baneful influence. As inhabitants of a country where they have no civil rights, they are ready to turn all the passions which agitate the community to their own advantage; thus, within the last few months serious riots have broken out in Philadelphia and New York. Disturbances of this kind are unknown in the rest of the country, which is nowise alarmed by them because the population of the cities has hitherto exercised neither power nor influence over the rural districts.

Nevertheless, I look upon the size of certain American cities, and especially on the nature of their population, as a real danger which threatens the future security of the democratic republic of the New World; and I venture to predict that they will perish from the circumstance, unless the Government succeeds in creating an armed force, which, whilst it remains under the control of the majority of the nation, will be independent of the town population and able to repress its excesses.

Social Effects

Good government and even social solidarity are threatened by class antagonisms. The actual cause of such social antipathies will be found in an exaggerated individualism, which has been developed by an era of industrialism, out of mediaeval militarism. The new industrial forces which transformed the solidified Age of Authority into a liquefied Age of Freedom, have naturally been more predominant in the cities than elsewhere, for the close contact of man with man in a dense population removes prejudices and engenders liberalism. The cities have always been the cradles of liberty, just as they are to-day the centres of radicalism. Every man of the world knows that isolation and solitude are found in a much higher degree in the crowded city than in a country village, where one individual's concerns are the concern of all. The cities, then, are favorable to free thought and the sense of individual responsibility.

But it is a question whether the loosening of the ties of individual responsibility has not gone too far. "The great danger to morality and good government," says Roscher, "is that the individual is lost in the multitude of atoms,—a condition that may abolish the sense of duty and make the great city as insecure as the opposite extreme, the wilderness." Now this extreme individualism of the cities is merely one manifestation of the—shall we say excessive—fluidity of modern society, and its cause is chiefly industrial. Cities vary in their lack of social feeling (*i.e.*, individualism), and those cities have the least portion of it which are most given to industrial enterprises in which the competitive system has obtained full sway.

It may be said, indeed, that it is our industrial system, and not city life, which engenders the essentially egoistic, self-seeking and materialistic attitude; but so long as the cities remain the results of the competitive industrial regime, they must share the blame. No one can view with equanimity the continual drift of population to the cities where it will be subject to such demoralizing influences. . . .

This separation of classes which has so nearly destroyed social solidarity in all large cities, is especially dangerous in the United States (where, under democratic forms, solidarity is especially indispensable) on account of differences in race and religion, as well as social rank and condition. In American cities the "upper" social ranks—the commercial and professional classes—are predominantly American and Protestant; the "lower" ranks—the hewers of wood and drawers of water—are on the contrary chiefly of foreign origin and of the Roman Catholic faith. The danger of class antagonism is therefore peculiarly great in our cities. . . .

Now, it is perfectly natural that the most noticeable traces of the humanitarian movement should be found in the cities, where the greatest abuses of industrialism and materialism existed. Men cannot live long in close contact without acquiring a painful sense of the separateness of individual interests, of the absurdity of identifying the individual's interest with the interest of society and the consequent policy of *laissez-faire*. I may enjoy playing a cornet during the cool summer evenings; but that is not to the interest of my neighbor who has to go to work early in the morning and so needs early sleep. It may be greatly to my interest to build a tannery on a vacant city lot that comes to me cheap; but it is not the interest of people who have fine residences on adjoining property. It may be to my interest to employ poverty-stricken families, living amidst filth and contagious diseases, to make cheap shirts and clothing; but it is not to the interest of my fellow-citizens. In short, there arise a thousand and one conflicts between individual interests and social interests, and in their adjustment selfishness is curbed and a social feeling excited. . . .

Concerning the effects of the movement toward the cities upon the rural population, we have already said something from the economic point of view. Socially regarded, it is a misfortune *for the villages* that their most enterprising and choice youth should be drawn away. This must certainly lower the tone of town and village life and even produce a local stagnation. . . .

Henry George puts the case against city growth in its worst light when he says that "just as the wen or tumor, drawing the wholesome juice of the body into its vortex, impoverishes all other parts of the frame, so does the crowding of human beings in the city impoverish human life in the country. The unnatural life of the great cities means an equally unnatural life in the country."

What, if any, are the benefits secured to the entire social body in compensation for these evil effects of concentration of population upon the life of the non-urban population? And is there no advantage to the villages themselves?

Economically, as we have learned, the concentration of large masses of people upon small areas at once multiplies human wants and furnishes the means of their satisfaction; and the benefits are communicated to the surrounding country, which finds in the cities a market for its production and a stimulus to the diversification of the same.

Socially, the influence of the cities is similarly exerted in favor of liberal and progressive thought. The variety of occupation, interests and opinions in the city produces an intellectual friction, which leads to a broader and freer judgment and a great inclination to and appreciation of new thoughts, manners, and ideals. City life may not have produced genius, but it has brought thinkers into touch with one another, and has stimulated the divine impulse to originate by sympathy or antagonism. As the seat of political power, as the nursery of the arts and sciences, as the centre of industry and commerce, the city represents the highest achievements of political, intellectual and industrial life. The rural population is not merely conservative; it is full of error and prejudice; it receives what enlightenment it possesses from the city. Nor is the small city free from the same reproach; while it performs the useful function of an intermediary between the progressiveness, liberalism, radicalism of the great city, and the conservatism, bigotry, of the country, it is the chief seat of the pseudo-bourgeois Philistine. . . .

It is at least ground for encouragement that the leading nations of the modern world are those which have the largest city populations. That cities are both cause and consequence of a high *Cultur* can hardly be doubted.

14. Lincoln Steffens,
"Philadelphia: Corrupt and Contented"

CERTAINLY *the most famous Progressive Era document on the cities is Lincoln Steffens's* The Shame of the Cities *(1904), a collection of his articles on city corruption originally written for* McClure's Magazine. *What Steffens found most wrong with the cities was neither the diseconomy of their administration, as conventional analysts like Moorfield Storey contended, nor the absence of heart for the poor, of which social workers like Robert Hunter complained. The shame of the cities lay in what their best citizens acquiesced in and even regarded as normal. Philadelphia for example, he says, was not merely corrupt; it was corrupted. Bribery and graft had become part of the mechanism for getting things done in a society grown too complex for its formal institutions. A few years later, Steffens was to come to the conclusion he maintained on and off until his death in 1936; namely, that the problem of government corruption was insoluble as long as the cities relied on private enterprise and the profit motive to provide essential public services.*

SOURCE: Lincoln Steffens, "Philadelphia: Corrupt and Contented," *McClure's Magazine,* X (July 1903), reprinted in *The Shame of Cities* (New York: McClure, Phillips & Co., 1904), pp. 193–229.

July 1903
Other American cities, no matter how bad their own condition may be, all point with scorn to Philadelphia as worse—"the worst-governed city in the country." St. Louis, Minneapolis, Pittsburg submit with some patience to the jibes of any other community; the most friendly suggestion from Philadelphia is rejected with contempt. The Philadelphians are "supine," "asleep"; hopelessly

ring-ruled, they are "complacent." "Politically benighted," Philadelphia is supposed to have no light to throw upon a state of things that is almost universal.

This is not fair. Philadelphia is, indeed, corrupt; but it is not without significance. Every city and town in the country can learn something from the typical political experience of this great representative city. New York is excused for many of its ills because it is the metropolis, Chicago because of its forced development; Philadelphia is our "third largest" city and its growth has been gradual and natural. Immigration has been blamed for our municipal conditions; Philadelphia, with 47 per cent. of its population native-born of native-born parents, is the most American of our greater cities. It is "good," too, and intelligent. I don't know just how to measure the intelligence of a community, but a Pennsylvania college professor who declared to me his belief in education for the masses as a way out of political corruption, himself justified the "rake-off" of preferred contractors on public works on the ground of a "fair business profit." Another plea we have made is that we are too busy to attend to public business, and we have promised, when we come to wealth and leisure, to do better. Philadelphia has long enjoyed great and widely distributed prosperity; it is the city of homes; there is a dwelling house for every five persons,—men, women, and children,—of the population; and the people give one a sense of more leisure and repose than any community I ever dwelt in. Some Philadelphians account for their political state on the ground of their ease and comfort. There is another class of optimists whose hope is in an "aristocracy" that is to come by and by; Philadelphia is surer that it has a "real aristocracy" than any other place in the world, but its aristocrats, with few exceptions, are in the ring, with it, or of no political use. Then we hear that we are a young people and that when we are older and "have traditions," like some of the old countries, we also will be honest. Philadelphia is one of the oldest of our cities and treasures for us scenes and relics of some of the noblest traditions of "our fair land." Yet I was told how once, "for a joke," a party of boodlers counted out the "divvy" of their graft in unison with the ancient chime of Independence Hall.

Philadelphia is representative. This very "joke," told, as it was, with a laugh, is typical. All our municipal governments are more or less bad, and all our people are optimists. Philadelphia is simply the most corrupt and the most contented. Minneapolis has cleaned up, Pittsburg has tried to, New York fights every other election, Chicago fights all the time. Even St. Louis has begun to stir (since the elections are over), and at the worst was only shameless. Philadelphia is proud; good people there defend corruption and boast of their machine. My college professor, with his philosophic view of "rake-offs," is one Philadelphia type. Another is the man, who, driven to bay with his local pride, says: "At least you must admit that our machine is the best you have ever seen." . . .

The Philadelphia organization is upside down. It has its root in the air, or, rather, like the banyan tree, it sends its roots from the center out both up and down and all around, and there lies its peculiar strength. For when I said it was dependent and not sound, I did not mean that it was weak. It is dependent as a municipal machine, but the organization that rules Philadelphia is, as we have seen, not a mere municipal machine, but a city, State, and national organization. The people of Philadelphia are Republicans in a Republican city in a Republican State in a Republican nation, and they are bound ring on ring on ring. The President of the United States and his patronage; the National Cabinet and their patronage; the Congress and the patronage of the Senators and the Congressmen from Pennsylvania; the Governor of the State and the State Legislature with their powers and patronage; and all that the mayor and city councils have of power and patronage—all these bear down upon Philadelphia to keep it in the control of Quay's boss and his little ring. This is the ideal of party organization, and, possibly, is the end toward which our democratic republic is tending. If it is, the end is absolutism. Nothing but a revolution could overthrow this oligarchy, and there is its danger. With no outlet at the polls for public feeling, the machine cannot be taught anything it does not know except at the cost of annihilation.

But the Philadelphia machine-leaders know their business. As I said in "Tweed Days in St. Louis," the politicians will learn, if the people won't, from exposure and reform. The Pennsylvania bosses learned the "uses of reform"; we have seen Quay applying it to discipline McManes, and he since has turned reformer himself, to punish local bosses. The bosses have learned also the danger of combination between citizens and the Democrats. To prevent this, Quay and his friends have spread sedulously the doctrine of "reform within the party," and, from the Committee of One Hundred on, the reformers have stuck pretty faithfully to this principle. But lest the citizens should commit such a sin against their party, Martin formed a permanent combination of the Democratic with the Republican organization, using to that end a goodly share of the Federal and county patronage. Thus the people of Philadelphia were "fixed" so that they couldn't vote if they wanted to, and if they should want to, they couldn't vote for a Democrat, except of Republican or independent choosing. . . .

But the greatest lesson learned and applied was that of conciliation and "good government." The people must not want to vote or rebel against the ring. . . . The people had been taught to expect but little from their rulers: good water, good light, clean streets well paved, fair transportation, the decent repression of vice, public order and public safety, and no scandalous or open corruption, would more than satisfy them. It would be good business and good politics to give them these things. Like Chris Magee, who studied out the problem with him, Martin took away from the rank and file of the party and from the ward leaders and office holders the privilege of theft, and he formed companies and groups to handle the legitimate public business of the city. It was all graft, but it was to be all lawful, and, in the main, it was. Public franchises, public works, and public contracts were the principal branches of the business, and Martin adopted the dual boss idea, which we have seen worked out by Magee and Flinn in Pittsburg. In Philadelphia it was Martin and Porter, and just as Flinn had a firm, Booth & Flinn, Ltd., so Porter was Filbert and Porter.

Filbert and Porter got all the public contracts they could handle, and the rest went to other contractors friendly to them and to the ring. Sometimes the preferred contractor was the lowest bidder, but he did not have to be. The law allowed awards to be the "lowest and best," and the courts held that this gave the officials discretion. But since public criticism was to be considered, the ring, to keep up appearances, resorted to many tricks. One was to have fake bids made above the favorite. Another was to have the favorite bid high, but set an impossible time limit; the department of the city councils could extend the time afterwards. Still another was to arrange for specifications which would make outsiders bid high, then either openly alter the plans or let the ring firm perform work not up to requirements. . . .

There was a limit to the "rake-off," and some insiders have told me that it had been laid down as a principle with the ring that the people should have in value (that is, in work or benefit, including a fair profit) ninety-five cents out of every dollar. In some of the deals I have investigated, the "rake-off" over and above profit was as high as twenty-five per cent. Still, even at this, there was "a limit," and the public was getting, as one of the leaders told me, "a run for its money." Cynical as it all sounds, this view is taken by many Philadelphians almost if not quite as intelligent as my college professor.

But there was another element in the policy of conciliation which is a potent factor in the contentment of Philadelphia, and I regard it as the key to that "apathy" which has made the community notorious. We have seen how Quay had with him the Federal resources and those of the State, and the State ring, and we have seen how Martin, having the city, mayor, and councils, won over the Democratic city leaders. Here they had under pay in office at least 15,000 men and women. But each of these 15,000 persons was selected for office because he could deliver votes, either by organizations, by parties, or by families. These must represent pretty near a majority of the city's voters. But this is by no means the end of the ring's reach. In the State ring are the great corporations, the Standard Oil Company, Cramp's Shipyard, and the steel companies, with the Pennsylvania Railroad at their head, and all the local transportation and other public utility companies following after. They get franchises, privileges, exemptions, etc.; they have helped finance Quay through deals: the Pennsylvania paid Martin, Quay said once, a large yearly salary; the Cramps get contracts to build United States ships, and for years have been begging for a subsidy on home-made ships. The officers, directors, and stockholders of these companies, with their friends, their bankers, and their employees, are of the organization. Better still, one of the local bosses of Philadelphia told me he could always give a worker a job with these companies, just as he could in a city department, or in the mint, or post-office. Then there are the bankers who enjoy, or may some day enjoy, public deposits; those that profit on loans to finance political financial deals; the promoting capitalists who share with the bosses on franchises; and the brokers who deal in ring securities and speculation on ring tips. Through the exchange the ring financiers reach the investing public, which is a large and influential body. The traction companies, which bought their way from beginning to end by corruption, which have always been in the ring, and whose financiers have usually shared in other big ring deals, adopted early the policy of bribing the people with "small blocks of stock." Dr. Frederick Speirs, in his "The Street Railway System of Philadelphia," came upon transactions which "indicate clearly that it is the policy of the Union Company to get the securities into the hands of a large number of small holders, the plain inference being that a wide distribution of securities will fortify the company against possible attacks by the public." In 1895 he found a director saying: "Our critics have engaged the Academy of Music, and are to call an assemblage of people opposed to the street railways as now managed. It would take eight Academies of Music to hold the stockholders of the Union Traction Company."

But we are not yet through. Quay has made a specialty all his life of reformers, and he and his local bosses have won over so many that the list of former reformers is very, very long. Martin drove down his roots through race and religion, too. Philadelphia was one of the hot-beds of "know-nothingism." Martin recognized the Catholic, and the Irish-Irish, and so drew off into the Republican party the great natural supply of the Democrats; and his successors have given high places to representative Jews. "Surely this isn't corruption!" No, and neither is that corruption which makes the heads of great educational and charity institutions "go along," as they say in Pennsylvania, in order to get appropriations for their institutions from the State and land from the city. They know what is going on, but they do not join reform movements. The provost of the University of Pennsylvania declined to join in a revolt because, he said, it might impair his usefulness to the University. And so it is with others, and with clergymen who have favorite charities; with Sabbath associations and City Beautiful clubs; with lawyers who want briefs; with real estate dealers who like to know in advance about public improvements, and real estate owners who appreciate light assessments; with shopkeepers who don't want to be bothered with strict inspections. . . .

Such, then, are the ramifications of this machine, such is its strength. No wonder Martin could break his own rules, as he did, and commit excesses. Philadelphia is not merely corrupt, it is corrupted. . . .

That corruption had reached the public schools and was spreading rapidly through the system, was discovered by the exposure and conviction of three school directors of the twenty-eighth ward. It was known before that teachers and principals, like any other office holders, had to have a "pull" and pay assessments for election expenses. "Voluntary contributions" was the term used, but over the notices in blue pencil was written "2 per cent.," and teachers who asked directors and ward bosses what to do, were advised that they would "better pay." Those that sent less than the amount suggested, got receipts: "check received; shall we hold for balance or enter on account?" But the exposure in the twenty-eighth ward brought it home to the parents of the children that the teachers were not chosen for fitness, but for political reasons, and that the political reasons had become cash.

Miss Rena A. Haydock testified as follows: "I went to see Mr. Travis, who was a friend of mine, in reference to getting a teacher's certificate. He advised me to see all of the directors, especially Mr. Brown. They told me that it would be necessary for me to pay $120 to get the place. They told me of one girl who had offered $250, and her application had been rejected. That was before they broached the subject of money to me. I said that I didn't have $120 to pay, and they replied that it was customary for teachers to pay $40 a month out of their first three months' salary. The salary was $47. They told me they didn't want the money for themselves, but that it was necessary to buy the other faction. Finally I agreed to the proposition, and they told me that I must be careful not to mention it to anybody or it would injure my reputation. I went with my brother to pay the money to Mr. Johnson. He held out a hat, and when my brother handed the money to him he took it behind the hat."

The regular business of the ring was like that of Pittsburg, but more extensive. I have space only for one incident of one phase of it: Widener and Elkins, the national franchise buyers, are Philadelphians, and they were in the old Martin ring. They had combined all the street railways of the city before 1900, and they were withdrawing from politics, with their traction system. But the Pennsylvania rings will not let corporations that have risen in corruption reform and retire . . . plans were laid to "mace" the street railways.

"Macing" is a form of high blackmail. When they have sold out all they have, the politicians form a competing company and compel the old concern to buy out or sell out. While Widener and Elkins were at sea, bound for Europe, in 1901, the Philadelphia ring went to the Legislature and had introduced there two bills, granting a charter to practically all the streets and alleys not covered by tracks in Philadelphia, and to run short stretches of the old companies' tracks to make connections. . . .

The charters were granted on June 5, and that same day a special meeting of the Philadelphia Select Council was called for Monday. There the citizens of Philadelphia met the oncoming charters, but their hearing was brief. The charters went through without a hitch, and were sent to Mayor Ashbridge on June 13.

The mayor's secretary stated authoritatively in the morning that the mayor would not sign that day. But he did. An unexpected incident forced his hand. John Wanamaker sent him an offer of $2,500,000 for the franchises about to be given away. Ashbridge threw the letter into the street unread. Mr. Wanamaker had deposited $250,000 as a guarantee of good faith and his action was becoming known. The ordinances were signed by midnight, and the city lost at least two and one-half millions of dollars; but the ring made it and much more. When Mr. Wanamaker's letter was published, Congressman Foerderer, an incorporator of the company, answered for the machine. He said the offer was an advertisement; that it was late, and that they were sorry they hadn't had a chance to "call the bluff." Mr. Wanamaker responded with a renewal of the offer of $2,500,000 to the city, and, he said, "I will add $500,000 as a bonus to yourself and your associates personally for the conveyance of the grants and corporate privileges you now possess." That ended the controversy.

But the deal went on. Two more bills, called "Trolley Chasers," were put through, to finish off the legislation, too hurriedly done to be perfect. One was to give the company the right to build either elevated or underground, or both; the second to forbid all further such grants without a hearing before a board consisting of the Governor, the Secretary of the Commonwealth, and the Attorney-General. With all these franchises and exclusive privileges, the new company made the old one lease their plant in operation to the company which had nothing but "rights," or, in Pennsylvania slang, a "good, husky mace."

Ashbridgeism put Philadelphia and the Philadelphia machine to a test which candid ring leaders did not think it would stand. What did the Philadelphians do? Nothing. They have their reformers: they have men like Francis B. Reeves, who fought with every straight reform movement from the days of the Committee of One Hundred; they have men like Rudolph Blankenburg, who have fought with every reform that promised any kind of relief; there are the Municipal League, with an organization by wards, the Citizens' Municipal League, the Allied Reform League, and the Law and Order Society; there are young men and veterans; there are disappointed politicians and ambitious men who are not advanced fast enough by the machine. There is discontent in a good many hearts, and some men are ashamed. But "the people" won't follow. One would think the Philadelphians would follow any leader; what should they care whether he is pure white or only gray? But they do care. "The people" seem to prefer to be ruled by a known thief than an ambitious reformer. They will make you convict their Tweeds, McManeses, Butlers, and Shepherds, and even then they may forgive them and talk of monuments to their precious memory, but they take delight in the defeat of John Wanamaker because they suspect that he is a hypocrite and wants to go to the United States Senate. . . .

Is there no hope for Philadelphia? Yes, the Philadelphians have a very present hope. It is in their new mayor, John Weaver. There is nothing in his record to inspire faith in an outsider. He speaks himself of two notorious "miscarriages of justice" during his term as District Attorney; he was the nominee of the ring; and the ring men have confidence in him. But so have the people, and Mr. Weaver makes fair promises. So did Ashbridge. There is this difference, however: Mr. Weaver has made a good start. He compromised with the machine on his appointments, but he declared against the protection of vice, for free voting, and he stopped some "wholesale grabs" or "maces" that appeared in the Legislature, just before he took office. . . .

It looks as if the Philadelphians were right about Mr. Weaver, but what if they are? Think of a city putting its whole faith in one man, in the *hope* that John Weaver, an Englishman by birth, will give them good government! And why should he do that? Why should he serve the people and not the ring? The ring can make or break him; the people of Philadelphia can neither reward nor punish him. For even if he restores to them their ballots and proves himself a good mayor, he cannot succeed himself; the good charter forbids more than one term.

IV

Changing Business Conditions

15. Andrew Carnegie,
"Business"

It must be a jarring experience today to see the word "communism" used, as Andrew Carnegie used it in 1896, in a description of the business corporation. To be sure, communism had as yet no connection with Russian Bolshevism, but it was nevertheless associated with international working-class revolution and had in most American discourse a decidedly opprobrious meaning. To gain an understanding of Carnegie's use of the word is to acquire a sense of the magnitude of the transformation of business enterprise at the end of the nineteenth century and to understand also some of the major anxieties of the Progressive Era. Five years before he was to retire by selling out his giant steel-manufacturing interests (prior to their merger into the first billion-dollar corporation in history, the United States Steel Corporation), Carnegie gave an address at Cornell University on January 11, 1896. In it he outlined the central tenets of traditional, proprietary business enterprise. In the main, the speech commended a business career to the bright youth of the day, urging its constructive, even idealistic, qualities; but it is worth noting that Carnegie referred to a kind of business career that it had already become difficult to enter, because the great corporations had pre-empted the major opportunities.

Carnegie was already too old and too inflexible to become a progressive reformer, although after his retirement he did devote much of his energy to world-peace campaigns. But it is striking how closely he followed the lines of some later progressive assaults upon modern corporate practices—his attack on speculation, for example, and his acknowledgment that corporate enterprise had reduced individual options for young men intent on a business career. Carnegie's point that "a man can thoroughly master only one business" anticipates remarkably Louis Brandeis's point about banker management and interlocking directorates in his Other People's Money (1913), the popular exposé of the "Money Trust."

source: Andrew Carnegie, "Business," lecture delivered at Cornell University, January 11, 1896; reprinted in The Empire of Business (New York: Doubleday, Page & Co., 1902).

Choice of a Career

There is no great fortune to come from salary, however high, and the business man pursues fortune. If he be wise he puts all his eggs in one basket, and then watches the basket. . . . If he mine coal and sell it, he attends to the black diamonds; if he owns and sails ships, he attends to shipping, and he ceases to insure his own ships just as soon as he has surplus capital and can stand the loss of one without imperilling solvency; if he manufacture steel, he sticks to steel, and severely lets copper alone. . . . This is because a man can thoroughly master only one business, and only an able man can do this. I have never yet met the man who fully understood two different kinds of business; you cannot find him any sooner than you can find a man who thinks in two languages equally and does not invariably think only in one.

Subdivision, specialization, is the order of the day. . . .

We often hear in our day that it is impossible for young men to become owners, because business is conducted upon so great a scale that the capital necessary reaches millions, and, therefore, the young man is doomed to a salaried life. Now there is something in that view only so far as the great corporations are concerned, because an interest in these is only attainable by capital; you can buy so many shares for so many dollars, and as the class of young men I address are not willing to remain forever salaried men, but are determined sooner or later, to become business men upon their own account, as masters, I do not believe that employment in a great corporation is as favorable for them as with private owners. . . .

But there are many corporations which are not corporations, many instances of partnership in which the corporate form has been adopted, and yet the business continued substantially as a partnership, and comparing such institutions with the great corporations whose ownership is here, there, and everywhere, we find a most notable difference. Take, for instance, the great steamship lines of the world. Most of these, as those of you who read well know, fail to make returns to their shareholders. The shares of some of the greatest companies have been selling at half and sometimes one third their cost. These are corporations, pure and simple, but if we look at other lines engaged upon the same ocean, which are managed by their owners and in which, generally, one great business man is deeply interested and at the head, we find large dividends each year and amounts placed to the reserve fund. It is the difference between individualism and communism applied to business, between the owners managing their own business as partners, and a joint stock concern of a thousand shifting owners ignorant of the business. . . .

Do not be fastidious; take what the gods offer. Begin, if necessary, with a corporation, always keeping your eye open for a chance to become interested in a business of your own. . . .

Business Men and Speculators

All pure coins have their counterfeits; the counterfeit of business is speculation. A man in business always gives value in return for his revenue, and thus performs a useful function. His services are necessary and benefit the community; besides, he labours steadily in developing the resources of the country, and thus contributes to the advancements of the race. This is genuine coin. Speculation, on the contrary, is a parasite fastened upon the labour of the business men. . . .

You can never be an honest man of business and a speculator. The modes and aims of the one career are fatal to the other. No business man can honestly speculate, for those who trust him have a right to expect strict adherence to business methods. . . .

The old prejudice against trade has gone even from the strongholds of Europe. This change has come because trade itself has changed. In old days every branch of business was conducted upon the smallest retail scale, and small dealings in small affairs breed small men; besides, every man had to be acquainted with the details, and, indeed, each man manufactured or traded for himself. The higher qualities of organization and of enterprise, of broad views and of executive ability, were not brought into play. In our day, business in all branches is conducted upon so gigantic a scale that partners of a huge concern are rulers over a domain. The large employer of labour sometimes has more men in his industrial army than the petty German kings had under their banners.

It was said of old that two of a trade never agree; to-day the warmest friendships are formed in every department of human effort among those in the same business; each visits the other's counting-house, factory, warehouse; and are shown the different methods; all the improvements; new inventions and freely adapt them to their own business.

Affairs are now too great to breed petty jealousies, and there is now allied with the desire for gain the desire for progress, invention, improved methods, scientific development, and pride of success in these important matters; so that the dividend which the business man seeks and receives today, is not alone in dollars . . . [but rather] in the shape of satisfaction in being instrumental in carrying forward to higher stages of development the business which he makes his life-work. . . .

The business career is thus a stern school of all the virtues, and there is one supreme reward which it often yields which no other career can promise; I point to noble benefactions which it renders possible. It is to business men following business careers that we chiefly owe our universities, colleges, libraries, and educational institutions as witness Girard, Lehigh, Chicago, Harvard, Yale, Cornell, and many others.

What monument can a man leave behind him productive of so much good, and so certain to hand his name down to succeeding generations, hallowed with the blessings of thousands in each decade who have within its walls received that most precious possession, as a sound and liberal education? These are the works of men who recognized that surplus wealth was a sacred trust, to be administered during the life of its possessor for the highest good of his fellows.

If, then, some business men may fall subject to the reproach of grasping, we can justly claim for them as a class what honest Thomas Cromwell claimed for the great cardinal, and say: "If they have a greed of getting, yet in bestowing they are most princely, as witness these seats of learning."

16.   The Rule of Reason,
Standard Oil v. the United States

THE UNITED STATES SUPREME COURT *played a vital role in the rise to dominance of the corporate form of business enterprise. By declaring the corporation a "legal person" (Santa Clara decision, 1886), it granted to the business corporation constitutional privileges previously reserved* solely for individual human beings. It thereby made it possible for the courts to negate efforts by state legislatures to constrain corporate behavior. The Supreme Court then proceeded to cripple the Federal Antitrust Act of 1890 by declaring that manufacturing was not governable by Congress under the commerce clause, even if all the raw materials and most of the finished products necessarily crossed state and national boundaries (E. C. Knight decision, 1895). For the proponents of large-scale modern corporate enterprise, however, there were still some serious problems. In a few antitrust cases during the McKinley Administration involving the price-fixing efforts of interstate railroad and oil pipeline companies (Trans-Missouri Freight Association, 1897; Joint Traffic Association, 1898; Addyston Pipe, 1899), the Court conceded the legitimate application of the Sherman Act. In the majority opinion in the Trans-Missouri case, moreover, the Court explicitly rejected the defense argument that the Sherman Act had intended to outlaw only unreasonable restraints of trade, since—the defense had argued—all contracts constitute in some measure a restraint on trade. The Court turned the argument around: since all contracts in some measure restrain trade, and since common law already limited contracts that unreasonably restrain trade, clearly then Congress had intended something else, namely, that all restraints of trade were to be regarded as unlawful; that the test of lawfulness should be in the fact of the agreement for restraint, not in the ostensible reasonableness of the restraint.

Corporate leaders found further cause to worry when, in 1905, with Justice Oliver Wendell Holmes speaking for the majority, the Court appeared to reverse the E. C. Knight decision by enunciating the "stream of commerce" doctrine (Swift & Co. v. the U.S.), whereby manufacturing was to fall within the regulatory province of Congress whenever it could be viewed as one stage of an essentially interstate or international flow of goods from producers to consumers. Corporate leaders now worried anew that the courts would henceforth have to enforce Congress's apparent policy in support of small-unit, proprietary forms of business enterprise. But in 1911, Chief Justice White allayed some of the more extreme fears. Choosing a case in which the Court sustained federal prosecutions against the unpopular Standard Oil and American Tobacco companies, White delivered an obiter dictum in which he presented, virtually verbatim, the contentions of the defense in the fifteen-year-old Trans-Missouri case.

Included below are White's declaration of what came to be dubbed the "Rule of Reason" and Justice John Marshall Harlan's opinion concurring in the decision but dissenting from the reasoning of the Court's majority. (Compare Harlan's dissent in Plessy v. Ferguson below—Document 22—where he earlier warned of the hazards implicit in the Court undertaking to decide on the "reasonableness" of social behavior.)

SOURCE: *Standard Oil Company of New Jersey, et al. v. the United States*, 221 U.S. 1 (1911).

Chief Justice White

In view of the common law and the law in this country as to restraint of trade, which we have reviewed, and the illuminating effect which that history must have under the rule to which we have referred, we think it results:

(a) That the context manifests that the statute was drawn in the light of the existing practical conception of the law of restraint of trade, because it groups as within that class, not only contracts which were in restraint of trade in the subjective sense, but all contracts or acts which theoretically were attempts to monopolize, yet which in practice had come to be considered as in restraint of trade in a broad sense.

(b) That in view of the many new forms of contracts and combinations which were being evolved from existing economic conditions, it was deemed essential by an all-embracing enumeration to make sure that no form of contract or combination by which an undue restraint of interstate or foreign commerce was brought about could save such restraint from condemnation. The statute under this view evidenced the intent not to restrain the right to make and enforce contracts, whether resulting from combination or otherwise, which did not unduly restrain interstate or foreign commerce, but to protect that commerce from being restrained by methods, whether old or new, which would constitute an interference that is an undue restraint.

(c) And as the contracts or acts embraced in the provision were not expressly defined, since the enumeration addressed itself simply to classes of acts, those classes being broad enough to embrace every conceivable contract or combination which could be made concerning trade or commerce or the subjects of such commerce, and thus caused any act done by any of the enumerated methods anywhere in the whole field of human activity to be illegal if in restraint, it inevitably follows that the provision necessarily called for the exercise of judgment which required that some standard should be resorted to for the purpose of determining whether the prohibitions contained in the statute had or had not in any given case been violated. Thus not specifying, but indubitably contemplating and requiring a standard, it follows that it was intended that the standard of reason which had been applied at the common law and in this country in dealing with subjects of the character embraced by the statute, was intended to be the measure used for the purpose of determining whether in a given case a particular act had or had not brought about the wrong against which the statute provided. . . .

Mr. Justice Harlan Concurring in Part, and Dissenting in Part

A sense of duty constrains me to express the objections which I have to certain declarations in the opinion just delivered on behalf of the court.

I concur in holding that the Standard Oil Company of New Jersey and its subsidiary companies constitute a combination in restraint of interstate commerce, and that they have attempted to monopolize and have monopolized parts of such commerce—all in violation of what is known as the Anti-trust Act of 1890. 26 Stat. 209, c. 647. The evidence in this case overwhelmingly sustained that view and led the Circuit Court, by its final decree, to order the dissolution of the New Jersey corporation and the discontinuance of the illegal combination between that corporation and its subsidiary companies.

In my judgment, the decree below should have been affirmed without qualification. But the court, while affirming the decree, directs some modifications in respect of what it characterizes as "minor matters." It is to be apprehended that those modifications may prove to be mischievous. In saying this, I have particularly in view the statement in the opinion that "it does not necessarily follow that because an illegal restraint of trade or an attempt to monopolize or a monopolization resulted from the combination and the transfer of the stocks of the subsidiary corporations to the New Jersey corporation, that a like restraint of trade or attempt to monopolize or monopolization would necessarily arise from agreements between one or more of the subsidiary corporations after the transfer of the stock by the New Jersey corporation." Taking this language, in connection with other parts of the opinion, the subsidiary companies are thus, in effect, informed—unwisely, I think —that although the New Jersey corporation, being an illegal combination, must go out of existence, they may join in an agreement to *restrain commerce* among the States if such restraint be not "undue."

In order that my objections to certain parts of the court's opinion may distinctly appear, I must state the circumstances under which Congress passed the Anti-trust Act, and trace the course of judicial decisions as to its meaning and scope. This is the more necessary because the court by its decision, when interpreted by the language of its opinion, has not only upset the long-settled interpretation of the act, but has usurped the constitutional functions of the legislative branch of the Government. With all due respect for the opinions of others, I feel bound to say that what the court has said may well cause some alarm for the integrity of our institutions. Let us see how the matter stands.

All who recall the condition of the country in 1890 will remember that there was everywhere, among the people generally, a deep feeling of unrest. The Nation had been rid of human slavery—fortunately, as all now feel—but the conviction was universal that the country was in real danger from another kind of slavery sought to be fastened on the American people, namely, the slavery that would result from aggregations of capital in the hands of a few individuals and corporations controlling, for their own profit and advantage exclusively, the entire business of the country, including the production and sale of the necessaries of life. . . .

Guided by these considerations, and to the end that the people, *so far as interstate commerce* was concerned, might not be dominated by vast combinations and monopolies, having power to advance their own selfish ends, regardless of the general interests and welfare, Congress passed the Anti-trust Act of 1890 in these words (the italics here and elsewhere in this opinion are mine):

"Sec. 1. *Every* contract, combination in the form of trust or otherwise, or conspiracy, in restraint of trade or commerce among the several States, or with foreign nations, is hereby declared to be illegal. Every person who shall make *any such contract or engage in any such combination or conspiracy*, shall be deemed guilty of a misdemeanor, and, on conviction thereof, shall be punished by fine not exceeding five thousand dollars, or by imprisonment not exceeding one year, or by both said punishments, in the discretion of the court. § 2. Every person who shall monopolize, or attempt to monopolize, or combine or conspire with any other person or persons, to monopolize *any part* of the trade or commerce among the several States, or with foreign nations, shall be deemed guilty of a misdemeanor, and, on conviction thereof, shall be punished by fine not exceeding five thousand dollars, or by imprisonment not exceeding one year, or by both said punishments, in the discretion of the court. § 3. *Every* contract, combination in form of trust or *otherwise*, or conspiracy, in restraint of trade or commerce in any Territory of the United States or in the District of Columbia, or in restraint of trade or commerce between any such Territory and another, or between any such Territory or Territories and any State or States or the District of Columbia, or with foreign nations, or between the District of Columbia and any State or States or foreign nations, is hereby declared illegal. Every person who shall make any *such* contract or engage in any *such* combination or conspiracy, shall be deemed guilty of a misdemeanor, and, on conviction thereof, shall be punished by fine not exceeding five thousand dollars, or by imprisonment not exceeding one year, or by both said punishments, in the discretion of the court." 26 Stat. 209, c. 647.

The important inquiry in the present case is as to the meaning and scope of that act in its application to interstate commerce.

In 1896 this court had occasion to determine the meaning and scope of the act in an important case known as the *Trans-Missouri Freight Case*. 166 U.S. 290. The question there was as to the validity under the Anti-trust Act of a certain agreement between numerous railroad companies, whereby they formed an association for the purpose of establishing and maintaining rates, rules and regulations in respect of freight traffic over specified routes. Two questions were involved: first, whether the act applied to railroad carriers; second, whether the agreement the annulment of which as illegal was the basis of the suit which the United States brought. The court held that railroad carriers were embraced by the act. In determining that question, the court, among other things, said:

"The language of the act includes *every* contract, combination in the form of trust or otherwise, or conspiracy, in restraint of trade or commerce among the several States or with foreign nations. So far as the very terms of the statute go, they apply to *any* contract of the nature described. . . ."

The court then proceeded to consider the second of the above questions, saying: " . . . What is the meaning of the language as used in the statute, that 'every contract, combination in the form

of trust or otherwise, or conspiracy in restraint of trade or commerce among the several States or with foreign nations, is hereby
declared to be illegal?' Is it confined to a contract or combination
which is only in unreasonable restraint of trade or commerce, or
does it include what the language of the act plainly and in terms
covers, all contracts of that nature? It is now with much amplifica-
tion of argument urged that the statute, in declaring illegal every
combination in the form of trust or otherwise, or conspiracy in
restraint of trade or commerce, does not mean what the language
used therein plainly imports, but that it only means to declare
illegal any such contract which is in *unreasonable* restraint of trade,
while leaving all others unaffected by the provisions of the act; that
the common law meaning of the term 'contract in restraint of
trade' includes only such contracts as are in *unreasonable* restraint
of trade, and when that term is used in the Federal statute it is not
intended to include all contracts in restraint of trade, but only
those which are in unreasonable restraint thereof. . . . By the
simple use of the term 'contract in restraint of trade,' *all* contracts
of that nature, whether valid or otherwise, would be included, and
*not alone that kind of contract which was invalid and unenforce-
able as being in unreasonable restraint of trade.* When, therefore,
the body of an act pronounces as illegal every contract or combination in restraint of trade or commerce among the several States,
etc., the plain and ordinary meaning of such language is not limited
to that kind of contract alone which is in unreasonable restraint of
trade, but *all* contracts are included in such language, and no
exception or limitation can be added without placing in the act
that which has been omitted by Congress. . . ."

I have made these extended extracts from the opinion of the
court in the *Trans-Missouri Freight Case* in order to show beyond
question, that the point was there urged by counsel that the Anti-
trust Act condemned *only* contracts, combinations, trusts and
conspiracies that were in *unreasonable* restraint of interstate commerce, and that the court in clear and decisive language met that
point. . . . With full knowledge of the then condition of the
country and of its business, Congress determined to meet, and did
meet, the situation by an absolute, statutory prohibition of "*every*
contract, combination in the form of trust or otherwise, in restraint
of trade or commerce." Still more; in response to the suggestion by
able counsel that Congress intended only to strike down such

contracts, combinations and monopolies as unreasonably restrained interstate commerce, this court, in words too clear to be misunderstood, said that to so hold was "to read into the act by way of *judicial legislation,* an exception not placed there by the lawmaking branch of the Government." "This," the court said, as we have seen, "*we cannot* and *ought not* to do."

. . . It may be stated here that the country at large accepted this view of the act, and the Federal courts throughout the entire country enforced its provisions according to the interpretation given in the *Freight Association Case.* What, then, was to be done by those who questioned the soundness of the interpretation placed on the act by this court in that case? As the court had decided that to insert the word "unreasonable" in the act would be "judicial legislation" on its part, the only alternative left to those who opposed the decision in that case was to induce Congress to so *amend* the act as to recognize the right to restrain interstate commerce to a *reasonable* extent. The public press, magazines and law journals, the debates in Congress, speeches and addresses by public men and jurists, all contain abundant evidence of the general understanding that the meaning, extent and scope of the Anti-trust Act had been judicially determined by this court, and that the only question remaining open for discussion was the wisdom of the policy declared by the act—a matter that was exclusively within the cognizance of Congress. But at every session of Congress since the decision of 1896, the lawmaking branch of the Government, with full knowledge of that decision, has refused to change the policy it had declared or to so amend the act of 1890 as to except from its operation contracts, combinations and trusts that *reasonably* restrain interstate commerce.

But those who were in combinations that were illegal did not despair. They at once set up the baseless claim that the decision of 1896 disturbed the "business interests of the country," and let it be known that they would never be content until the rule was established that would permit interstate commerce to be subjected to *reasonable* restraints. Finally, an opportunity came again to raise the same question which this court had, upon full consideration, determined in 1896. I now allude to the case of *United States* v. *Joint Traffic Association,* 171 U.S. 505, decided in 1898. . . .

". . . Learned counsel in the *Joint Traffic Case* urged a reconsideration of the question decided in the *Trans-Missouri Case* contending that "the decision in that case [the *Trans-Missouri Freight Case*] is quite plainly erroneous, and the consequences of such error are far reaching and disastrous, and clearly at war with justice and sound policy, and the construction placed upon the Anti-trust statute has been received by the public with surprise and alarm." . . .

The question whether the court should again consider the point decided in the *Trans-Missouri Case*, 171 U.S. 573, was disposed of in the most decisive language, as follows: " . . . The court is asked to reconsider a question but just decided after a careful investigation of the matter involved. There have heretofore been in effect two arguments of precisely the same questions now before the court, and the same arguments were addressed to us on both those occasions. The report of the *Trans-Missouri Case* shows a dissenting opinion delivered in that case, and that the opinion was concurred in by three other members of the court. That opinion, it will be seen, gives with great force and ability the arguments against the decision which was finally arrived at by the court. It was after a full discussion of the questions involved and with the knowledge of the views entertained by the minority as expressed in the dissenting opinion, that the majority of the court came to the conclusion it did. . . . This court, *with care and deliberation* and also with a full appreciation of their importance, again considered the questions involved in its former decision. A majority of the court once more arrived at the conclusion it had first announced, and accordingly it denied the application. And now *for the third time* the same arguments are employed, and the court is again asked to recant its former opinion, and to decide the same question in direct opposition to the conclusion arrived at in the *Trans-Missouri Case*. The learned counsel while making the application frankly confess that the argument in opposition to the decision in the case above named has been so fully, so clearly and so forcibly presented in the dissenting opinion of Mr. Justice White [in the *Freight Case*] that it is hardly possible to add to it, nor is it necessary to repeat it. The fact that there was so close a division of opinion in this court when the matter was first under advisement, together with the different views taken by some of the judges of the lower courts, led us to the most careful and scrutinizing examination of the arguments advanced by both sides, and it was after such an examination that the majority of the court came to the conclusion it did. It is not now alleged that the court on the former occasion overlooked any argument for the respondents or misapplied any controlling authority. It is simply insisted that the court, notwithstanding the arguments for an opposite view, arrived at an erroneous result, which, for reasons already stated, ought to be reconsidered and reversed. *As we have twice already deliberately and earnestly considered the same arguments which are now for a third time pressed upon our attention,* it could hardly be expected that our opinion should now change from that already expressed."

These utterances, taken in connection with what was previously said in the *Trans-Missouri Freight Case,* show so clearly and affirmatively as to admit of no doubt that this court, many years ago, upon the fullest consideration, interpreted the Anti-trust Act as prohibiting and making illegal not only every contract or combination, in whatever form, which was in restraint of interstate commerce, without regard to its reasonableness or unreasonableness, but all monopolies or attempts to monopolize "any part" of such trade or commerce. Let me refer to a few other cases in which the scope of the decision in the *Freight Association Case* was referred to: In *Bement v. National Harrow Co.,* 186 U.S. 70, 92, the court said: "It is true that it has been held by this court that the act (Anti-trust Act) included any restraint of commerce, whether *reasonable or unreasonable*"—citing *United States v. Trans-Missouri Freight Asso.,* 166 U.S. 290; *United States v. Joint Traffic Association,* 171 U.S. 505; *Addyston Pipe &c. Co. v. United States,* 175 U.S. 211. In *Montague v. Lowry,* 193 U.S. 38, 46, which involved the validity, under the Anti-trust Act, of a certain association formed for the sale of tiles, mantels, and grates, the court referring to the contention that the sale of tiles in San Francisco was so small "as to be a negligible quantity," held that the association was nevertheless a combination in restraint of interstate trade or commerce in violation of the Anti-trust Act. In *Loewe v. Lawlor,* 208 U.S. 274, 297, all the members of this court concurred in saying that the *Trans-Missouri, Joint Traffic* and *Northern Securities cases* "hold in effect that the Anti-trust Law has a broader application than the prohibition of restraints of trade unlawful at common law." In *Shawnee Compress Co. v. Anderson* (1907), 209 U.S. 423, 432, 434, all the members of the court again concurred in declaring that "it has been decided that not only unreasonable, but all direct restraints of trade are prohibited, the law being thereby distinguished from the common law." In *United States* v. *Addyston Pipe Company*, 85 Fed. Rep. 271, 278, Judge Taft, speaking for the Circuit Court of Appeals for the Sixth Circuit, said that according to the decision of this court in the *Freight Association Case*, "contracts in restraint of interstate transportation were within the statute, whether the restraints could be regarded as reasonable at common law or not." In *Chesapeake & Ohio Fuel Co.* v. *United States* (1902), 115 Fed. Rep. 610, 619, the Circuit Court of Appeals for the Sixth Circuit, after referring to the right of Congress to regulate interstate commerce, thus interpreted the prior decisions of this court in the *Trans-Missouri,* the *Joint Traffic* and the *Addyston Pipe and Steel Co. cases:* "In the exercise of this right, Congress has seen fit to prohibit *all* contracts in restraint of trade. It has not left to the courts the consideration of the question whether such restraint is reasonable or unreasonable, or whether the contract would have been illegal at the common law or not. The act leaves for consideration by judicial authority no question of this character, but *all* contracts and combinations are declared illegal if in restraint of trade or commerce among the States." . . .

In the opinion delivered on behalf of the minority in the *Northern Securities Case*, 193 U.S. 197, our present Chief Justice referred to the contentions made by the defendants in the *Freight Association Case*, one of which was that the agreement there involved did not unreasonably restrain interstate commerce, and said: "Both these contentions were decided against the association, the court holding that the Anti-trust Act did embrace interstate carriage by railroad corporations, and as that act prohibited *any* contract in restraint of interstate commerce, *it hence embraced all contracts of that character, whether they were reasonable or unreasonable.*" One of the Justices who dissented in the *Northern Securities Case* in a separate opinion, concurred in by the minority, thus referred to the *Freight* and *Joint Traffic* cases: "For it cannot be too carefully remembered that that clause applies to 'every' contract of the forbidden kind—a consideration which was the turning point of the *Trans-Missouri Freight Association* case. . . . Size has nothing to do with the matter. A monopoly of 'any part' of commerce among the States is unlawful."

In this connection it may be well to refer to the adverse report made in 1909, by Senator Nelson, on behalf of the Senate Judiciary

Committee, in reference to a certain bill offered in the Senate and which proposed to amend the Anti-trust Act in various particulars. That report contains a full, careful and able analysis of judicial decisions relating to combinations and monopolies in restraint of trade and commerce. Among other things said in it which bear on the questions involved in the present case are these: "The Anti-trust Act makes it a criminal offense to violate the law, and provides a punishment both by fine and imprisonment. To inject into the act the question of whether an agreement or combination is *reasonable* or *unreasonable* would render the act as a criminal or penal statute indefinite and uncertain, and hence, to that extent, utterly nugatory and void, and would practically amount to a repeal of that part of the act. . . . And while the same technical objection does not apply to civil prosecutions, *the injection of the rule of reasonableness or unreasonableness would lead to the greatest variableness and uncertainty in the enforcement of the law. The defense of reasonable restraint would be made in every case and there would be as many different rules of reasonableness as cases, courts and juries.* What one court or jury might deem unreasonable another court or jury might deem reasonable. A court or jury in Ohio might find a given agreement or combination reasonable, while a court and jury in Wisconsin might find the same agreement and combination unreasonable. . . . To amend the Anti-trust Act, as suggested by this bill, would be to entirely emasculate it, and for all practical purposes render it nugatory as a remedial statute. Criminal prosecutions would not lie and civil remedies would labor under the greatest doubt and uncertainty. The act as it exists is clear, comprehensive, certain and highly remedial. It practically covers the field of Federal jurisdiction, and is in every respect a model law. To destroy or undermine it at the present juncture, when combinations are on the increase, and appear to be as oblivious as ever of the rights of the public, would be a calamity." The result was the indefinite postponement by the Senate of any further consideration of the proposed amendments of the Anti-trust Act.

After what has been adjudged, upon full consideration, as to the meaning and scope of the Anti-trust Act, and in view of the usages of this court when attorneys for litigants have attempted to reopen questions that have been deliberately decided, I confess to no little surprise as to what has occurred in the present case. . . .

My brethren, in their wisdom, have deemed it best to pursue a different course. They have now said to those who condemn our former decisions and who object to all legislative prohibitions of contracts, combinations and trusts in restraint of interstate commerce, "You may now restrain such commerce, provided you are reasonable about it; only take care that the restraint i[s] not undue." The disposition of the case under consideration, according to the views of the defendants, will, it is claimed, quiet and give rest to "the business of the country." On the contrary, I have a strong conviction that it will throw the business of the country into confusion and invite widely-extended and harassing litigation, the injurious effects of which will be felt for many years to come. When Congress prohibited *every* contract, combination or monopoly, in restraint of commerce, it prescribed a simple, definite rule that all could understand, and which could be easily applied by everyone wishing to obey the law, and not to conduct their business in violation of law. But now, it is to be feared, we are to have, in cases without number, the constantly recurring inquiry—difficult to solve by proof—whether the particular contract, combination, or trust involved in each case is or is not an "unreasonable" or "undue" restraint of trade. Congress, in effect, said that there should be *no* restraint of trade, *in any form*, and this court solemnly adjudged many years ago that Congress meant what it thus said in clear and explicit words, and that it *could not* add to the words of the act. But those who condemn the action of Congress are now, in effect, informed that the courts will allow such restraints of interstate commerce as are shown not to be unreasonable or undue.

It remains for me to refer, more fully than I have heretofore done, to another, and, in my judgment—if we look to the future—the most important aspect of this case. That aspect concerns the usurpation by the judicial branch of the Government of the functions of the legislative department. . . .

I said at the outset that the action of the court in this case might well alarm thoughtful men who revered the Constitution. I meant by this that many things are intimated and said in the court's opinion which will not be regarded otherwise than as sanctioning an invasion by the judiciary of the constitutional domain of Congress—an attempt by interpretation to soften or modify what some regard as a harsh public policy. . . . The courts have nothing to do with the wisdom or policy of an act of Congress. Their duty is to ascertain the will of Congress, and if the statute embodying the expression of that will is constitutional, the courts must respect it. They have no function to declare a public policy, nor to amend legislative enactments. . . . Nevertheless, if I do not misapprehend its opinion, the court has now read into the act of Congress words which are not to be found there, and has thereby done that which it adjudged in 1896 and 1898 could not be done without violating the Constitution, namely, by interpretation of a statute, changed a public policy declared by the legislative department.

After many years of public service at the National Capital, and after a somewhat close observation of the conduct of public affairs, I am impelled to say that there is abroad, in our land, a most harmful tendency to bring about the amending of constitutions and legislative enactments by means alone of judicial construction. As a public policy has been declared by the legislative department in respect of interstate commerce, over which Congress has entire control, under the Constitution, all concerned must patiently submit to what has been lawfully done, until the People of the United States—the source of all National power—shall, in their own time, upon reflection and through the legislative department of the Government, require a change of that policy. There are some who say that it is a part of one's liberty to conduct commerce among the States without being subject to governmental authority. But that would not be liberty, regulated by law, and liberty, which cannot be regulated by law, is not to be desired. The Supreme Law of the Land—which is binding alike upon all—upon Presidents, Congresses, the Courts and the People—gives to Congress, and to Congress alone, authority to regulate interstate commerce, and when Congress forbids any restraint of such commerce, in any form, all must obey its mandate. To overreach the action of Congress merely by judicial construction, that is, by indirection, is a blow at the integrity of our governmental system, and in the end will prove most dangerous to all. Mr. Justice Bradley wisely said, when on this Bench, that illegitimate and unconstitutional practices get their first footing by silent approaches and slight deviations from legal modes of legal procedure. *Boyd v. United States*, 116 U.S. 616, 635. We shall do well to heed the warnings of that great jurist.

17.   Frederick W. Taylor,
The Principles of Scientific Management

THE "gospel of efficiency" was one of the chief activating principles of the Progressive Era. It signified the effort of Americans to reduce waste and to make more economical use of resources that the nation could no longer regard as unlimited. No individual was more closely identified with the movement for "efficiency" than Frederick W. Taylor (1856–1915). A personally compulsive man who suffered throughout his life from insomnia, Taylor was the champion of the caliper and the stop-watch as instruments for ordering personal behavior. In 1899, Taylor gained renown for instructing an unskilled Bethlehem Steel Company laborer in how to shovel 47 tons of pig iron a day, 35 tons more than the average. Taylor achieved this feat by carefully prescribing the exact length and weight of the shovel, the precise posture of the worker, the bite of each thrust, the arc of the swing, and the rest interludes at each specified number of shovel loads. Like many progressive theorists, Taylor contended that in "science" man could find solutions to the problems of scarcity. Labor critics thought that "scientific management" was but another phrase for the loathed speed-up and piece-work systems, but Taylor argued that increased productivity would lead to higher wages more surely than constricting the labor market through unionization. For a time, scientific management attained the dimensions of a movement, which left many permanent changes in American society—in education, for example, as well as in business and industrial labor relations. But although generally identified with progressivism, it tended to heighten the impersonal qualities of modern life and to increase the social alienation that underlay much of contemporary protest and reform politics.

SOURCE: Frederick Winslow Taylor, "Principles of Scientific Management," from *Scientific Management* (New York: Harper & Row, 1947), pp. 48–65. Copyright 1911 by F. W. Taylor; renewed 1939 by Louise M. S. Taylor. Reprinted by permission of Harper & Row, Publishers.

I ordinarily begin with a description of the pig-iron handler. For some reason, I don't know exactly why, this illustration has been talked about a great deal, so much, in fact, that some people seem to think that the whole of scientific management consists in handling pig-iron. The only reason that I ever gave this illustration, however, was that pig-iron handling is the simplest kind of human effort; I know of nothing that is quite so simple as handling pig-iron. A man simply stoops down and with his hands picks up a piece of iron, and then walks a short distance and drops it on the ground. Now, it doesn't look as if there was very much room for the development of a science; it doesn't seem as if there was much room here for the scientific selection of the man neither by progressive training, nor for cooperation between the two sides; but, I can say, without the slightest hesitation, that the science of handling pig-iron is so great that the man who is fit to handle pig-iron as his daily work cannot possibly understand that science; the man who is physically able to handle pig-iron and is sufficiently phlegmatic and stupid to choose this for his occupation is rarely able to comprehend the science of handling pig-iron; and this inability of the man who is fit to do the work to understand the science of doing his work becomes more and more evident as the work becomes more complicated, all the way up the scale. I assert, without the slightest hesitation, that the high class mechanic has a far smaller chance of ever thoroughly understanding the science of his work than the pig-iron handler has of understanding the science of his work, and I am going to try and prove to your satisfaction, gentlemen, that the law is almost universal—not entirely so, but nearly so—that the man who is fit to work at any particular trade is unable to understand the science of that trade without the kindly help and cooperation of men of a totally different type of education, men whose education is not necessarily higher but a different type from his own.

I dare say most of you gentlemen are familiar with pig-iron handling and with the illustration I have used in connection with it, so I won't take up any of your time with that. But I want to show you how these principles may be applied to some one of the lower classes of work. You may think I am a little highfalutin when I speak about what may be called the atmosphere of scientific management, the relations that ought to exist between both sides, the intimate and friendly relations that should exist between employee and employer. I want, however, to emphasize this as one of the most important features of scientific management, and I can hardly do so without going into detail, without explaining minutely the duties of both sides, and for this reason I want to take some of your time in explaining the application of these four principles of scientific management to one of the cheaper kinds of work, for instance, to shoveling. This is one of the simplest kinds of work, and I want to give you an illustration of the application of these principles to it.

Now, gentlemen, shoveling is a great science compared with pig-iron handling. I dare say that most of you gentlemen know that a good many pig-iron handlers can never learn to shovel right; the ordinary pig-iron handler is not the type of man well suited to shoveling. He is too stupid; there is too much mental strain, too much knack required of a shoveler for the pig-iron handler to take kindly to shoveling.

You gentlemen may laugh, but that is true, all right; it sounds ridiculous, I know, but it is a fact. Now, if the problem were put up to any of you men to develop the science of shoveling as it was put up to us, that is, to a group of men who had deliberately set out to develop the science of doing all kinds of laboring work, where do you think you would begin? When you started to study the science of shoveling I make the assertion that you would be within two days—just as we were within two days—well on the way toward development of the science of shoveling. At least you would have outlined in your minds those elements which required careful, scientific study in order to understand the science of shoveling. I do not want to go into all of the details of shoveling, but I will give you some of the elements, one or two of the most important elements of the science of shoveling; that is, the elements that reach further and have more serious consequences than any other. Probably the most important element in the science of shoveling is this: There must be some shovel load at which a first-class shoveler will do his biggest day's work. What is that load? To illustrate: When we went to the Bethlehem Steel Works and observed the shovelers in the yard of that company, we found that each of the good shovelers in that yard owned his own shovel; they preferred to buy their own shovels rather than to have the company furnish them. There was a larger tonnage of ore shoveled in that works than of any other material and rice coal came next in tonnage. We would see a first-class shoveler go from shoveling rice coal with a load of 3½ pounds to the shovel to handling ore from the Massaba Range, with 38 pounds to the shovel. Now, is 3½ pounds the proper shovel load or is 38 pounds the proper shovel load? They cannot both be right. Under scientific management the answer to this question is not a matter of anyone's opinion; it is a question for accurate, careful, scientific investigation.

Under the old system you would call in a first-rate shoveler and say, "See here, Pat, how much ought you to take on at one shovel load?" And if a couple of fellows agreed, you would say that's about the right load and let it go at that. But under scientific management absolutely every element in the work of every man in your establishment, sooner or later becomes the subject of exact, precise, scientific investigation and knowledge to replace the old, "I believe so," and "I guess so." Every motion, every small fact becomes the subject of careful, scientific investigation.

What we did was to call in a number of men to pick from, and from these we selected two first-class shovelers. Gentlemen, the words I used were "first-class shovelers." I want to emphasize that. Not poor shovelers. Not men unsuited to their work, but first-class shovelers. These men were then talked to in about this way, "See here, Pat and Mike, you fellows understand your job all right; both of you fellows are first-class men; you know what we think of you; you are all right now; but we want to pay you fellows double wages. We are going to ask you to do a lot of damn fool things, and when you are doing them there is going to be some one out alongside of you all the time, a young chap with a piece of paper and a stop watch and pencil, and all day long he will tell you to do these fool things, and he will be writing down what you are doing and snapping the watch on you and all that sort of business. Now, we just want to know whether you fellows want to go into that bargain or not? If you want double wages while that is going on all right, we will pay you double; if you don't all right, you needn't take the job unless you want to; we just called you in to see whether you want to work this way or not.

"Let me tell you fellows just one thing: If you go into this bargain, if you go at it, just remember that on your side we want no monkey business of any kind; you fellows will have to play square; you fellows will have to do just what you are supposed to be doing; not a damn bit of soldiering on your part; you must do a fair day's work; we don't want any rushing, only a fair day's work and you know what that is as well as we do. Now, don't take this job unless you agree to these conditions, because if you start to try to fool this same young chap with the pencil and paper he will be onto you in 15 minutes from the time you try to fool him, and just as surely as

he reports you fellows as soldiering you will go out of this works
and you will never get in again. Now, don't take this job unless you
want to accept these conditions; you need not do it unless you
want to; but if you do, play fair."

Well, these fellows agreed to it, and, as I have found almost
universally to be the case, they kept their word absolutely and
faithfully. My experience with workmen has been that their word is
just as good as the word of any other set of men that I know of,
and all you have to do is to have a clear, straight, square understanding with them and you will get just as straight and fair a deal
from them as from any other set of men. In this way the shoveling
experiment was started. My remembrance is that we first started
them on work that was very heavy, work requiring a very heavy
shovel load. What we did was to give them a certain kind of heavy
material ore, I think, to handle with a certain size of shovel. We
sent these two men into different parts of the yard, with two
different men to time and study them, both sets of men being
engaged on the same class of work. We made all the conditions the
same for both pairs of men, so as to be sure that there was no error
in judgment on the part of either of the observers and that they
were normal, first-class men.

The number of shovel loads which each man handled in the
course of the day was counted and written down. At the end of the
day the total tonnage of the material handled by each man was
weighed and this weight was divided by the number of shovel loads
handled, and in that way, my remembrance is, our first experiment
showed that the average shovel load handled was 38 pounds, and
that with this load on the shovel the man handled, say, about 25
tons per day. We then cut the shovel off, making it somewhat
shorter, so that instead of shoveling a load of 38 pounds it held a
load of approximately 34 pounds. The average, then, with the 34
pound load, of each man went up, and instead of handling 25 he had
handled 30 tons per day. These figures are merely relative, used to
illustrate the general principles, and I do not mean that they were
the exact figures. The shovel was again cut off, and the load made
approximately 30 pounds, and again the tonnage ran up, and again
the shovel load was reduced, and the tonnage handled per day
increased, until at about 21 or 22 pounds per shovel we found that
these men were doing their largest day's work. If you cut the shovel
load off still more, say until it averages 18 pounds instead of 21½,

the tonnage handled per day will begin to fall off, and at 16 pounds it will be still lower, and so on right down. Very well; we now have developed the scientific fact that a workman well suited to his job, what we call a first-class shoveler, will do his largest day's work when he has a shovel load of 21½ pounds.

Now, what does that fact amount to? At first it may not look to be a fact of much importance, but let us see what it amounted to right there in the yard of the Bethlehem Steel Co. Under the old system, as I said before, the workmen owned their shovels, and the shovel was the same size whatever the kind of work. Now, as a matter of common sense, we saw at once that it was necessary to furnish each workman each day with a shovel which would hold just 21½ pounds of the particular material which he was called upon to shovel. A small shovel for the heavy material, such as ore, and a large scoop for light material, such as ashes. That meant, also, the building of a large shovel room, where all kinds of laborers' implements were stored. It meant having an ample supply of each type of shovel, so that all the men who might be called upon to use a certain type in any one day could be supplied with a shovel of the size desired that would hold just 21½ pounds. It meant, further, that each day each laborer should be given a particular kind of work to which he was suited, and that he must be provided with a particular shovel suited to that kind of work, whereas in the past all the laborers in the yard of the Bethlehem Steel Co. had been handled in masses, or in great groups of men, by the old-fashioned foreman, who had from 25 to 100 men under him and walked them from one part of the yard to another. You must realize that the yard of the Bethlehem Steel Co. at that time was a very large yard. I should say that it was at least 1½ or 2 miles long and, we will say, a quarter to a half mile wide, so it was a good large yard; and in that yard at all times an immense variety of shoveling was going on.

There was comparatively little standard shoveling which went on uniformly from day to day. Each man was likely to be moved from place to place about the yard several times in the course of the day. All of this involved keeping in the shovel room 10 or 15 kinds of shovels, ranging from a very small flat shovel for handling ore up to immense scoops for handling rice coal, and forks with which to handle coke, which, as you know, is very light. It meant the study and development of the implement best suited to each type of material to be shoveled, and assigning, with the minimum of trouble, the proper shovel to each one of the four to six hundred laborers at work in that yard. Now, that meant mechanism, human mechanism. It meant organizing and planning work at least a day in advance. And, gentlemen, here is an important fact, that the greatest difficulty which we met with in this planning did not come from the workmen. It came from the management's side. Our greatest difficulty was to get the heads of the various departments each day to inform the men in the labor office what kind of work and how much of it was to be done on the following day.

This planning the work one day ahead involved the building of a labor office where before there was no such thing. It also involved the equipping of that office with large maps showing the layout of the yards so that the movements of the men from one part of the yard to another could be laid out in advance, so that we could assign to this little spot in the yard a certain number of men and to another part of the yard another set of men, each group to do a certain kind of work. It was practically like playing a game of chess in which four to six hundred men were moved about so as to be in the right place at the right time. And all this, gentlemen, follows from the one idea of developing the science of shoveling; the idea that you must give each workman each day a job to which he is well suited and provide him with just that implement which will enable him to do his biggest day's work. All this, as I have tried to make clear to you, is the result that followed from the one act of developing the science of shoveling.

In order that our workmen should get their share of the good that came from the development of the science of shoveling and that we should do what we set out to do with our laborers,— namely, pay them 60 per cent higher wages than were paid to any similar workmen around that whole district. Before we could pay them these extra high wages it was necessary for us to be sure that we had first-class men and that each laborer was well suited to his job, because the only way in which you can pay wages 60 per cent higher than other people pay and not overwork your men is by having each man properly suited and well trained to his job. Therefore, it became necessary to carefully select these yard laborers; and in order that the men should join with us heartily and help us in their selection it became necessary for us to make it possible for each man to know each morning as he came in to work that on the previous day he had earned his 60 per cent premium, or that he had failed to do so. So here again comes in a lot of work to be done by the management that had not been done before. The first thing each workman did when he came into the yard in the morning—and I may say that a good many of them could not read and write—was to take two pieces of paper out of his pigeonhole; if they were both white slips of paper, the workman knew he was all right. One of those slips of paper informed the man in charge of the tool room what implement the workman was to use on his first job and also in what part of the yard he was to work. It was in this way that each one of the 600 men in that yard received his orders for the kind of work he was to do and the implement with which he was to do it, and he was also sent right to the part of the yard where he was to work, without any delay whatever. The old-fashioned way was for the workmen to wait until the foreman got good and ready and had found out by asking some of the heads of departments what work he was to do, and then he would lead the gang off to some part of the yard and go to work. Under the new method each man gets his orders almost automatically; he goes right to the tool room, gets the proper implement for the work he is to do, and goes right to the spot where he is to work without any delay.

The second piece of paper, if it was a white piece of paper, showed this man that he had earned his 60 per cent higher wages; if it was a yellow piece of paper the workman knew that he had not earned enough to be a first-class man, and that within two or three days something would happen, and he was absolutely certain what this something would be. Every one of them knew that after he had received three or four yellow slips a teacher would be sent down to him from the labor office. Now, gentlemen, this teacher was no college professor. He was a teacher of shoveling; he understood the science of shoveling; he was a good shoveler himself, and he knew how to teach other men to be good shovelers. This is the sort of man who was sent out of the labor office. I want to emphasize the following point, gentlemen: The workman, instead of hating the teacher who came to him—instead of looking askance at him and saying to himself, "Here comes one of those damn nigger drivers to drive me to work"—looked upon him as one of the best friends he had around there. He knew that he came out there to help him, not to nigger drive him. Now, let me show you what happens. The teacher comes, in every case, not to bulldoze the man, not to drive him to harder work than he can do, but to try in a friendly, brotherly way to help him, so he says, "Now, Pat, something has gone wrong with you. You know no workman who is not a high-priced workman can stay on this gang, and you will have to get off of it if we can't find out what is the matter with you. I believe you have forgotten how to shovel right. I think that's all there is the matter with you. Go ahead and let me watch you awhile. I want to see if you know how to do the damn thing, anyway."

Now, gentlemen, I know you will laugh when I talk again about the science of shoveling. I dare say some of you have done some shoveling. Whether you have or not, I am going to try to show you something about the science of shoveling, and if any of you have done much shoveling, you will understand that there is a good deal of science about it.

There is a good deal of refractory stuff to shovel around a steel works; take ore, or ordinary bituminous coal, for instance. It takes a good deal of effort to force the shovel down into either of these materials from the top of the pile, as you have to when you are unloading a car. There is one right way of forcing the shovel into materials of this sort, and many wrong ways. Now, the way to shovel refractory stuff is to press the forearm hard against the upper part of the right leg just below the thigh, like this (indicating), take the end of the shovel in your right hand and when you push the shovel into the pile, instead of using the muscular effort of your arms, which is tiresome, throw the weight of your body on the shovel like this (indicating); that pushes your shovel in the pile with hardly any exertion and without tiring the arms in the least. Nine out of ten workmen who try to push a shovel in a pile of that sort will use the strength of their arms, which involves more than twice the necessary exertion. Any of you men who don't know this fact just try it. This is one illustration of what I mean when I speak of the science of shoveling, and there are many similiar elements of this science. Now, this teacher would find, time and time again, that the shoveler had simply forgotten how to shovel; that he had drifted back to his old wrong and inefficient way of shoveling, which prevented him from earning his 60 per cent higher wages. So he would say to him, "I see all that is the matter with you is that you have forgotten how to shovel; you have forgotten what I showed you about shoveling some time ago. Now, watch me," he says, "this is the way to do the thing." And the teacher would stay by him two, three, four, or five days, if necessary, until he got the man back again into the habit of shoveling right.

Now, gentlemen, I want you to see clearly that, because that is one of the characteristic features of scientific management; this is not nigger driving; this is kindness; this is teaching; this is doing what I would like mighty well to have done to me if I were a boy trying to learn how to do something. This is not a case of cracking a whip over a man and saying, "Damn you, get there." The old way of treating with workmen, on the other hand, even with a good foreman, would have been something like this: "See here, Pat, I have sent for you to come up here to the office to see me; four or five times now you have not earned your 60 per cent increase in wages; you know that every workman in this place has got to earn 60 per cent more wages than they pay in any other place around here, but you're no good and that's all there is to it; now, get out of this." That's the old way. "You are no good; we have given you a fair chance; get out of this," and the workman is pretty lucky if it isn't "get to hell out of this," instead of "get out of this."

The new way is to teach and help your men as you would a brother; to try to teach him the best way and show him the easiest way to do his work. This is the new mental attitude of the management toward the men, and that is the reason I have taken so much of your time in describing this cheap work of shoveling. It may seem to you a matter of very little consequence, but I want you to see, if I can, that this new mental attitude is the very essence of scientific management; that the mechanism is nothing if you have not got the right sentiment, the right attitude in the minds of the men, both on the management's side and on the workman's side. Because this helps to explain the fact that until this summer there has never been a strike under scientific management.

The men who developed the science of shoveling spent, I should say, four or five months studying the subject and during that time they investigated not only the best and most efficient movements that the men should make when they are shoveling right, but they also studied the proper time for doing each of the elements of the science of shoveling. There are many other elements which go to make up this science, but I will not take up your time describing them.

Now, all of this costs money. To pay the salaries of men who are studying the science of shoveling is an expensive thing. As I remember it there were two college men who studied this science of shoveling and also the science of doing many other kinds of laboring work during a period of about three years; then there were a lot of men in the labor office whose wages had to be paid, men who were planning the work which each laborer was to do at least a day in advance; clerks who worked all night so that each workman might know the next morning when he went to work just what he had accomplished and what he had earned the day before; men who wrote out the proper instructions for the day's work for each workman. All of this costs money; it costs money to measure or weigh up the materials handled by each man each day. Under the old method the work of 50 or 60 men was weighed up together; the work done by a whole gang was measured together. But under scientific management we are dealing with individual man and not with gangs of men. And in order to study and develop each man you must measure accurately each man's work. At first we were told that this would be impossible. The former managers of this work told me "You cannot possibly measure up the work of each individual laborer in this yard; you might be able to do it in a small yard, but our work is of such an intricate nature that it is impossible to do it here."

I want to say that we had almost no trouble in finding some cheap way of measuring up each man's work, not only in that yard but throughout the entire plant.

But all of that costs money, and it is a very proper question to ask whether it pays or whether it doesn't pay, because, let me tell you, gentlemen, at once, and I want to be emphatic about it, scientific management has nothing in it that is philanthropic; I am not objecting to philanthropy, but any scheme of management which has philanthropy as one of its elements ought to fail; philanthropy has no part in any scheme of management. No self-respecting workman wants to be given things, every man wants to earn things, and scientific management is no scheme for giving people something they do not earn. So, if the principles of scientific management do not pay, then this is a miserable system. The final test of any system is, does it pay?

At the end of some three and a half years we had the opportunity of proving whether or not scientific management did pay in its application to yard labor. When we went to the Bethlehem Steel Co. we found from 400 to 600 men at work in that yard, and when we got through 140 men were doing the work of the 400 to 600, and these men handled several million tons of material a year.

We were very fortunate to be able to get accurate statistics as to the cost of handling a ton of materials in that yard under the old system and under the new. Under the old system the cost of handling a ton of materials had been running between 7 and 8 cents, and all you gentlemen familiar with railroad work know that this is a low figure for handling materials. Now, after paying for all the clerical work which was necessary under the new system for the time study and the teachers, for building and running the labor office and the implement room, for constructing a telephone system for moving men about the yard, for a great variety of duties not performed under the old system, after paying for all these things incident to the development of the science of shoveling and managing the men the new way, and including the wages of the workmen, the cost of handling a ton of material was brought down from between 7 and 8 cents to between 3 and 4 cents, and the actual saving, during the last six months of the three and one-half years I was there, was at the rate of $78,000 a year. That is what the company got out of it; while the men who were on the labor gang received an average of sixty per cent more wages than their brothers got or could get anywhere around that part of the country. And none of them were overworked, for it is no part of scientific management ever to overwork any man; certainly overworking these men could not have been done with the knowledge of anyone connected with scientific management, because one of the first requirements of scientific management is that no man shall ever be given a job which he cannot do and thrive under through a long term of years. It is no part of scientific management to drive anyone. At the end of three years we had men talk to and investigate all of these yard laborers and we found that they were almost universally satisfied with their jobs.

V

Labor in the Age of Reform

18. Samuel Gompers,
"Labor and Its Attitude Toward Trusts"

WHILE MANY traditionalists and conservatives joined with reformers in
the fight for government regulation of "the trusts," resistance to legislation of that order came from perhaps an unexpected quarter—most of
organized labor. Among the socialist trade unionists, the trusts represented a necessary final stage of industrial evolution before public expro-
priation. For Gompers, the antisocialist president of the 1.5-million
member American Federation of Labor, the argument took more subtle
directions. First, Gompers observed that government had not usually be-
haved as a friend; thus organized labor could hardly expect to benefit
from any enhancement of the state's power. The antitrust laws in particular hung threateningly over the union's very existence; indeed in 1908,
in the so-called Danbury Hatters' case, the Supreme Court upheld a
claim of treble damages against a union under the Sherman Act (Loewe
v. Lawlor). More might be gained, said Gompers, by emphasizing the
values of voluntarism, in business and in labor organizations. What the
AFL sought was the same kind of freedom for associational activity that
the corporations so evidently enjoyed. Gompers thus joined with corporate leaders such as Elbert Gary of U.S. Steel in pleading the legitimacy
of modern industrial forms.

SOURCE: Address by Samuel Gompers to the Chicago Conference
on Trusts (October 1907), reprinted in the *American Federationist* (November 1907), pp. 880–886.

*Address by Samuel Gompers, President of
the American Federation of Labor, Before
the Chicago Conference on Trusts, October 1907*

There is perhaps no issue before the people today in which
greater general interest is felt than that of trusts, their develop-

ment, their policy, their effect upon civic and individual life. Few issues are more completely befogged to the average mind, and this is not necessarily the fault of the average mind. Many forces are interested in befogging the issue. Then, too, the growth of trusts has been so marvelously rapid and their influence is felt in so many directions that it is only natural that the phenomenom of trust development should be viewed with amazement and a strong sense of protest by those whose chief knowledge of its existence is gained in the pains and penalties of an economic readjustment greater than civilization has ever known before.

To say that there are "good trusts and bad trusts" is to state a certain bromidic truism. But the statement needs a broad foundation and some explanation in order to take its place in the educational vocabulary of the new era.

Instead of discussing the various kinds of trusts, good and bad, let us understand clearly that the trust is the logical development of the present economic era. With the invention of good artificial light, of machinery and power, and their application to industry, came the modern industrial plants. With their advent and development the day of individual workman and individual employer passed, never to return.

The perception of what a trust really is becomes the more confused, because the great aggregations of capital, loosely called by that name, differ much in their characteristics. Some strive to monopolize certain valuable and necessary sources of natural wealth, in order to completely control production, and, in addition, undertake to monopolize every avenue of distribution so completely that the consumer may be delivered to them, bound hand and foot, helpless against their most exhorbitant demands, and all this for the enrichment of the few individuals who have contrived, in the shifting elements of a new era, to gain such control.

Yet this abuse of methods and functions does not at all invalidate the fact that this is absolutely the era of association as contrasted with individual effort, nor does the foregoing characterization apply to all trusts.

Serious problems, indeed, confront us, but they are not hopeless. For this consideration this conference is partly called. *In intelligent and associated use of the powers of the many* will be found the solution. Disorganized and violent denunciation is more harmful than helpful. Constructive and associated effort must check and correct the abuses which have grown so rapidly in this era of concentrated methods of production and distribution. . . .

We can not, if we would, turn back to the primitive conditions of industry which marked the early part of the last century. It is therefore idle chatter to talk of annihilating trusts.

In the association of many persons in order to secure the large sums of money necessary to finance modern industry, lay the germ of the trust. We not only can not prevent the association of these vast organizations of capital in what we call trusts, but in some sense we should not wish to do so. . . .

It lessens the waste in production which is bound to occur under individual initiative. In fact, the trust may be said to have successfully solved the problem of the greatest economy in production. It has, however, other important functions which as a rule it does not yet properly perform and the failure in these respects very justly arouses a wide-spread, and intense feeling of protest among the masses of our people. . . .

Much of the protest against trust methods is justly and legitimately based on the fact that trust promoters, managers, and owners seize and keep for themselves a far greater share of the profits of modern production and distribution than that to which they are entitled.

Many of these gentlemen are merely fortunate accidents in the crystallization of a new era. They too, often, forget that they are bound to give accounting, to do justice to that great force which makes industry possible—the people—in their two capacities, as *producers* and *consumers*.

Speaking for the American Federation of Labor, including as it does more than two millions of wage-workers, it is scarcely presumption when I say that I have the right and in part, at least, the honor to represent the masses in the two capacities of producers and consumers.

It must be borne in mind that the American Federation of Labor speaks for labor—that is, for the masses as a whole, whether organized or unorganized. The trade union is the only successful attempt to give voice to the "voiceless masses." In every trade, in every community where trade unions exist, they are recognized as the spokesmen of the workers and in fact of all except the employing and the idle rich classes. None concede this more promptly than the unorganized themselves, who from ignorance or adverse environment may not yet be able to join the ranks of the organized workers, but they look to that protector of their rights as wage-workers and are glad to be represented by their more advanced fellow-workers.

The public itself does not seriously question that the trade unions speak for all labor and hence for the masses. This is seen even more clearly in places of moderate size than in our largest cities where the constant and great influx of ignorant foreign immigration continually tends to disturb the normal industrial balance.

It must be remembered that the trade union *while not a trust* is just as inevitable and logical a development as the trust itself. The trade union finds its greatest development under the same economic conditions which produce the trust; that, is the introduction of machinery, the subdivision of industry, the adoption of vast and complicated systems of production which obliterate the individuality of the worker and thus force him into an association, but not a trust, with his fellows in order that collectively they may protect their rights as wage-workers and as citizens and also guard the interests of all workers.

Let me reiterate most emphatically here and now that *the trade union is not, and from its very nature can not be, a trust*. It is sometimes derisively called a trust by those who expose their own ignorance of economic first principles in making such a statement.

The trade union is the *voluntary association of the many for the benefit of all* the community. The trust is the voluntary association of the few for their own benefit. The trade union puts no limit upon its membership, except that of skill and character, it welcomes every wage-worker. In fact, its strength and influence rest in its universal adoption by the wage-workers as the permanent and potent method of voicing their needs. Were every wage-worker in the country a member of organized labor, still would there be no labor trust. . . .

The trade union, through association, makes production more effective, but unlike the trust it does not seek a monopoly of the benefits for the few. The trade union ever seeks to distribute the benefits of modern methods of production among the many. It sets an example that trust promoters may well follow. . . .

It is only fair to say that the greatest and most enlightened combinations of capital in industry have not seriously questioned the right and, indeed, the advisability of organization among employes. There is economy of time and power and means of placing responsibility in "collective bargaining" with employes which bring the best results for the benefit of all.

Organized labor has less difficulty in dealing with large firms and corporations today than with many individual employers or small firms.

We have recently seen examples of the bitter antagonism to labor by certain small employers, whose ideas of industry seem to be medieval rather than modern. To some extent they have grasped the idea of organization or association among themselves, but they fail to concede the necessity of organization among wage-workers. In an opera bouffe fashion they emulate the robber barons of the middle ages, whose sole idea of profit was to plunder the individual whom they could find at a disadvantage.

The workers of the country have pretty thoroughly mastered the broad economic truth that organization is the watchword of modern industry. Labor concedes the right of organization among employers. It is perfectly willing to deal with such associations, provided its own rights are not denied or invaded. To put it more strongly, provided its rights are recognized and conceded. . . .

The organized wage-workers are here, as ever, in the vanguard of public opinion, co-operating with their fellow-citizens in an earnest effort to find the equitable remedy for the abuses uncovered.

The courts of our country, too, must come in for their share of attention. The function of the judiciary is a most vital one to the perpetuation of our institutions and to the progress of our nation. It is to the courts that we must look in many instances for protection against assaults upon our rights as citizens.

Yet it must cause us all regret to be compelled to say that the courts in too many instances allow themselves to be bound by precedents which either have no application to present industrial conditions or else such precedents are twisted to apply most injuriously to cases to which they never were intended to apply.

Let me illustrate on one point—the abuse of injunctions. In this respect we find the courts creating new dicta which invariably oppress the wage-worker and encourage the abuse of corporate power.

The injunction has been changed from its original beneficent intent (to protect property rights) and made an instrument of oppression to deprive citizens (when they are wage-earners) of their personal rights and liberties. By its abuse men are restrained from doing perfectly lawful things and then found in contempt and sentenced to imprisonment without trial by jury. It is an alarming state of affairs when a judge may first lay down his ex parte conception (through injunction) of what a citizen may or may not do and then hale the alleged offender before him for judgment and sentence without trial by jury or opportunity for defense. The injunction process as now employed aims to deny liberty of the press and liberty of speech. In a case now pending, Mr. Van Cleave, of St. Louis, endeavors to enjoin the *American Federationist*, the official magazine of the American Federation of Labor, from stating the fact that his employes have found him unfair.

This may be considered far-fetched in one sense and having nothing to do with trusts, but the deterioration or invasion of the courts bears a marked coincidence to the comparative growth of corporate influence in recent years. I do not charge nor intimate that judges are bribed or anything of that sort, but there is no doubt in the mind of any careful observer that vast corporations wielding many sorts of influence do find themselves exempt from interference at the hands of the courts even when they break the laws and that, conversely, the wage-workers find their rights and liberties being curtailed by these same courts who are so complaisant and so dilatory about enforcing sentence even when a trust has been found guilty of violation of law. . . .

The masses—the consumers—are somewhat to blame in that they have so far mostly contented themselves with restless protest instead of constructive effort.

For the consumer to shout "down with the trusts" because he finds his pocket-book affected is no more reasonable than the cry of "smash the machines" which was once heard from wage-workers whose means of livelihood were threatened during the period of adjustment in certain trades while machinery was replacing hand labor. . . .

Let the aggregations of wealth which seek to control our industries remember that in the last analysis they must depend upon the labor and the intelligence and the willingness of the masses. Without workers, who are law abiding and intelligent citizens, to produce their goods, and, in turn, consume them, the trusts might as well be in the desert of Sahara.

Let the trusts remember that they will be required to give an account of their stewardship to the people. An assumption of Divine right and trusteeship is not enough; the accounting must square with the assumption. . . .

Labor aims to co-operate with all influential and powerful forces for the attainment of the greatest good to all our people. . . .

Labor and industry can not be halted or turned back to conform to old conceptions and old conditions. It deals with the present and for the future. There must be the largest liberty of action, the freest possible opportunities for the highest development and greatest expansion of labor, industry, and commerce to make for the common good, for the common progress and for civilization.

19.   *Lochner* v. *New York*

JUSTICE RUFUS W. PECKHAM's *majority opinion in the Lochner case (1905) has long symbolized the obtuseness of the Old Guard in refusing to take note of the changing knowledge of social conditions. Until the end of the century, the Court had generally regarded state legislation— under each state's "police power" to provide for health, safety, and wel- fare—as immune from judicial interference. But for the traditionalists on the Court, the notion of "liberty of contract"—a nonconstitutional prin- ciple that Americans had exalted in the permissive environment of the nineteenth century—took on larger and larger proportions as legislators increasingly heeded the social origins of many modern evils. Funda- mentally opposed to the growing intervention of the states in the alloca- tion of social and economic opportunities among their citizens, a small Court majority—for which Peckham here served as spokesman—insisted that unless the Court intervened, the nation's legislatures would under- mine the traditional concepts of individual liberty as conceived in the Constitution. For more than a decade before the Lochner case, the Court had been edging toward the view that it could, by reference to the Fifth and Fourteenth Amendment clauses which forbade deprivation of "life, liberty, or property without due process of the law," void popular social measures when they seemed unwise according to the Court's own judgment. The argument was essentially tautological: a legislative mea- sure, the Court argued, violated "due process" not merely when it failed to meet formal procedural lawmaking standards but also when it failed to meet the test of what was conventionally reasonable. In the Lochner case, this theory gained its first complete realization. Of course, as Holmes suggests in his famous dissent, it is the very function of statute law to alter the society's conventions along the lines required by the* knowledge of new conditions. Justice Harlan, in a separate dissent joined by two other usually conservative justices, also urged that the Court leave to the legislatures the job of judging what laws were needed to meet new problems (compare "The Rule of Reason" in Document 16 above). The Lochner decision never achieved the status of "good law"; but it was occasionally revived, as in the incredible Adkins v. Children's Hospital case (1923), and it unquestionably stalled for at least a generation much necessary attention to severe injustices in American life.

All three opinions are presented here. Holmes's classic dissent is unabridged.

SOURCE: *Lochner v. New York, 198 U.S. 45 (1905)*.

Mr. Justice Peckham Delivered the Opinion of the Court

The indictment, it will be seen, charges that the plaintiff in error violated the one hundred and tenth section of article 8, chapter 415, of the Laws of 1897, known as the labor law of the State of New York, in that he wrongfully and unlawfully required and permitted an employé working for him to work more than sixty hours in one week. There is nothing in any of the opinions delivered in this case, either in the Supreme Court or the Court of Appeals of the State, which construes the section, in using the word "required," as referring to any physical force being used to obtain the labor of an employé. It is assumed that the word means nothing more than the requirement arising from voluntary contract for such labor in excess of the number of hours specified in the statute. There is no pretense in any of the opinions that the statute was intended to meet a case of involuntary labor in any form. All the opinions assume that there is no real distinction, so far as this question is concerned, between the words "required" and "permitted." The mandate of the statute that "no employé shall be required or permitted to work," is the substantial equivalent of an enactment that "no employé shall contract or agree to work," more than ten hours per day, and as there is no provision for special emergencies the statute is mandatory in all cases. It is not an act merely fixing the number of hours which shall constitute a legal day's work, but an absolute prohibition upon the employer, permitting, under any circumstances, more than ten hours work to be done in his establishment. The employé may desire to earn the extra money, which would arise from his working more than the prescribed time, but this statute forbids the employer from permitting the employé to earn it.

The statute necessarily interferes with the right of contract between the employer and employés, concerning the number of hours in which the latter may labor in the bakery of the employer. The general right to make a contract in relation to his business is part of the liberty of the individual protected by the Fourteenth Amendment of the Federal Constitution. *Allgeyer v. Louisiana*, 165 U.S. 578. Under that provision no State can deprive any person of life, liberty or property without due process of law. The right to purchase or to sell labor is part of the liberty protected by this amendment, unless there are circumstances which exclude the right. There are, however, certain powers, existing in the sovereignty of each State in the Union, somewhat vaguely termed police powers, the exact description and limitation of which have not been attempted by the courts. Those powers, broadly stated and without, at present, any attempt at a more specific limitation, relate to the safety, health, morals and general welfare of the public. Both property and liberty are held on such reasonable conditions as may be imposed by the governing power of the State in the exercise of those powers, and with such conditions the Fourteenth Amendment was not designed to interfere. *Mugler v. Kansas*, 123 U.S. 623; *In re Kemmler*, 136 U.S. 436; *Crowley v. Christensen*, 137 U.S. 86; *In re Converse*, 137 U.S. 624.

The State, therefore, has power to prevent the individual from making certain kinds of contracts, and in regard to them the Federal Constitution offers no protection. If the contract be one which the State, in the legitimate exercise of its police power, has the right to prohibit, it is not prevented from prohibiting it by the Fourteenth Amendment. Contracts in violation of a statute, either of the Federal or state government, or a contract to let one's property for immoral purposes, or to do any other unlawful act, could obtain no protection from the Federal Constitution, as coming under the liberty of person or of free contract. Therefore, when the State, by its legislature, in the assumed exercise of its police powers, has passed an act which seriously limits the right to labor or the right of contract in regard to their means of livelihood between persons who are *sui juris* (both employer and employé), it becomes of great importance to determine which shall prevail—the right of the individual to labor for such time as he may choose, or the right of the State to prevent the individual from laboring or from entering into any contract to labor, beyond a certain time prescribed by the State.

This court has recognized the existence and upheld the exercise of the police powers of the States in many cases which might fairly be considered as border ones, and it has, in the course of its determination of questions regarding the asserted invalidity of such statutes, on the ground of their violation of the rights secured by the Federal Constitution, been guided by rules of a very liberal nature, the application of which has resulted, in numerous instances, in upholding the validity of state statutes thus assailed. Among the later cases where the state law has been upheld by this court is that of *Holden v. Hardy*, 169 U.S. 366. A provision in the act of the legislature of Utah was there under consideration, the act limiting the employment of workmen in all underground mines or workings, to eight hours per day, "except in cases of emergency, where life or property is in imminent danger." It also limited the hours of labor in smelting and other institutions for the reduction or refining of ores or metals to eight hours per day, except in like cases of emergency. The act was held to be a valid exercise of the police powers of the State. A review of many of the cases on the subject, decided by this and other courts, is given in the opinion. It was held that the kind of employment, mining, smelting, etc., and the character of the employés in such kinds of labor, were such as to make it reasonable and proper for the State to interfere to prevent the employés from being constrained by the rules laid down by the proprietors in regard to labor. . . .

It must, of course, be conceded that there is a limit to the valid exercise of the police power by the State. There is no dispute concerning this general proposition. Otherwise the Fourteenth Amendment would have no efficacy and the legislatures of the States would have unbounded power, and it would be enough to say that any piece of legislation was enacted to conserve the morals, the health or the safety of the people; such legislation would be valid, no matter how absolutely without foundation the claim might be. The claim of the police power would be a mere pretext— become another and delusive name for the supreme sovereignty of the State to be exercised free from constitutional restraint. This is not contended for. In every case that comes before this court, therefore, where legislation of this character is concerned and where the protection of the Federal Constitution is sought, the question necessarily arises: Is this a fair, reasonable and appropriate exercise of the police power of the State, or is it an unreasonable, unnecessary and arbitrary interference with the right of the individual to his personal liberty or to enter into those contracts in relation to labor which may seem to him appropriate or necessary for the support of himself and his family? Of course the liberty of contract relating to labor includes both parties to it. The one has as much right to purchase as the other to sell labor.

This is not a question of substituting the judgment of the court for that of the legislature. If the act be within the power of the State it is valid, although the judgment of the court might be totally opposed to the enactment of such a law. But the question would still remain: Is it within the police power of the State? and that question must be answered by the court.

The question whether this act is valid as a labor law, pure and simple, may be dismissed in a few words. There is no reasonable ground for interfering with the liberty of person or the right of free contract, by determining the hours of labor, in the occupation of a baker. There is no contention that bakers as a class are not equal in intelligence and capacity to men in other trades or manual occupations, or that they are not able to assert their rights and care for themselves without the protecting arm of the State, interfering with their independence of judgment and of action. They are in no sense wards of the State. Viewed in the light of a purely labor law, with no reference whatever to the question of health, we think that a law like the one before us involves neither the safety, the morals nor the welfare of the public, and that the interest of the public is not in the slightest degree affected by such an act. The law must be upheld, if at all, as a law pertaining to the health of the individual engaged in the occupation of a baker. It does not affect any other portion of the public than those who are engaged in that occupation. Clean and wholesome bread does not depend upon whether the baker works but ten hours per day or only sixty hours a week. The limitation of the hours of labor does not come within the police power on that ground.

It is a question of which of two powers or rights shall prevail—the power of the State to legislate or the right of the individual to liberty of person and freedom of contract. The mere assertion that the subject relates though but in a remote degree to the public health does not necessarily render the enactment valid. The act must have a more direct relation, as a means to an end, and the end itself must be appropriate and legitimate, before an act can be held to be valid which interferes with the general right of an individual to be free in his person and in his power to contract in relation to his own labor. . . .

Although found in what is called a labor law of the State, the Court of Appeals has upheld the act as one relating to the public health—in other words, as a health law. . . .

We think the limit of the police power has been reached and passed in this case. There is, in our judgment, no reasonable foundation for holding this to be necessary or appropriate as a health law to safeguard the public health or the health of the individuals who are following the trade of a baker. If this statute be valid, and if, therefore, a proper case is made out in which to deny the right of an individual, *sui juris*, as employer or employé, to make contracts for the labor of the latter under the protection of the provisions of the Federal Constitution, there would seem to be no length to which legislation of this nature might not go. . . .

We think that there can be no fair doubt that the trade of a baker, in and of itself, is not an unhealthy one to that degree which would authorize the legislature to interfere with the right to labor, and with the right of free contract on the part of the individual, either as employer or employé. In looking through statistics regarding all trades and occupations, it may be true that the trade of a baker does not appear to be as healthy as some other trades, and is also vastly more healthy than still others. To the common understanding the trade of a baker has never been regarded as an unhealthy one. . . .

The act is not, within any fair meaning of the term, a health law, but is an illegal interference with the rights of individuals, both employers and employés, to make contracts regarding labor upon such terms as they may think best, or which they may agree upon with the other parties to such contracts. Statutes of the nature of that under review, limiting the hours in which grown and intelligent men may labor to earn their living, are mere meddlesome interferences with the rights of the individual, and they are not saved from condemnation by the claim that they are passed in the exercise of the police power and upon the subject of the health of the individual whose rights are interfered with, unless there be some fair ground, reasonable in and of itself, to say that there is material danger to the public health or to the health of the employés, if the hours of labor are not curtailed. . . .

This interference on the part of the legislatures of the several States with the ordinary trader and occupations of the people seems to be on the increase. . . .

It is impossible for us to shut our eyes to the fact that many of the laws of this character, while passed under what is claimed to be the police power for the purpose of protecting the public health or welfare, are, in reality, passed from other motives. We are justified in saying so when, from the character of the law and the subject upon which it legislates, it is apparent that the public health or welfare bears but the most remote relation to the law. The purpose of a statute must be determined from the natural and legal effect of the language employed; and whether it is or is not repugnant to the Constitution of the United States must be determined from the natural effect of such statutes when put into operation, and not from their proclaimed purpose. . . . The court looks beyond the mere letter of the law in such cases. . . .

Reversed.

Mr. Justice Harlan, with Whom Mr. Justice White and Mr. Justice Day Concurred, Dissenting

I do not stop to consider whether any particular view of this economic question presents the sounder theory. What the precise facts are it may be difficult to say. It is enough for the determination of this case, and it is enough for this court to know, that the question is one about which there is room for debate and for an honest difference of opinion. There are many reasons of a weighty, substantial character, based upon the experience of mankind, in support of the theory that, all things considered, more than ten hours' steady work each day, from week to week, in a bakery or confectionery establishment, may endanger the health, and shorten the lives of the workmen, thereby diminishing their physical and mental capacity to serve the State, and to provide for those dependent upon them.

If such reasons exist that ought to be the end of this case, for the State is not amenable to the judiciary, in respect of its legislative enactments, unless such enactments are plainly, palpably, beyond all question, inconsistent with the Constitution of the United States. We are not to presume that the State of New York has acted in bad faith. Nor can we assume that its legislature acted without due deliberation, or that it did not determine this question upon the fullest attainable information, and for the common good. We cannot say that the State has acted without reason nor ought we to proceed upon the theory that its action is a mere sham. Our duty, I submit, is to sustain the statute as not being in conflict with the Federal Constitution, for the reason—and such is an all-sufficient reason—it is not shown to be plainly and palpably inconsistent with that instrument. Let the State alone in the management of its purely domestic affairs, so long as it does not appear beyond all question that it has violated the Federal Constitution. This view necessarily results from the principle that the health and safety of the people of a State are primarily for the State to guard and protect.

I take leave to say that the New York statute, in the particulars here involved, cannot be held to be in conflict with the Fourteenth Amendment, without enlarging the scope of the Amendment far beyond its original purpose and without bringing under the supervision of this court matters which have been supposed to belong exclusively to the legislative departments of the several States when exerting their conceded power to guard the health and safety of their citizens by such regulations as they in their wisdom deem best. Health laws of every description constitute, said Chief Justice Marshall, a part of that mass of legislation which "embraces everything within the territory of a State, not surrendered to the General Government; all which can be most advantageously exercised by the States themselves." *Gibbons v. Ogden*, 9 Wheat. 1, 203. A decision that the New York statute is void under the Fourteenth Amendment will, in my opinion, involve consequences of a far-reaching and mischievous character; for such a decision would seriously cripple the inherent power of the States to care for the lives, health and well-being of their citizens. Those are matters which can be best controlled by the States. The preservation of the just powers of the States is quite as vital as the preservation of the powers of the General Government.

When this court had before it the question of the constitutionality of a statute of Kansas making it a criminal offense for a contractor for public work to permit or require his employés to perform labor upon such work in excess of eight hours each day, it was contended that the statute was in derogation of the liberty both of employés and employer. It was further contended that the Kansas statute was mischievous in its tendencies. This court, while disposing of the question only as it affected public work, held that the Kansas statute was not void under the Fourteenth Amendment. But it took occasion to say what may well be here repeated: "The responsibility therefore rests upon legislators, not upon the courts. No evils arising from such legislation could be more far-reaching than those that might come to our system of government if the judiciary, abandoning the sphere assigned to it by the fundamental law, should enter the domain of legislation, and upon grounds merely of justice or reason or wisdom annul statutes that had received the sanction of the people's representatives. We are reminded by counsel that it is the solemn duty of the courts in cases before them to guard the constitutional rights of the citizen against merely arbitrary power. That is unquestionably true. But it is equally true—indeed, the public interests imperatively demand —that legislative enactments should be recognized and enforced by the courts as embodying the will of the people, unless they are plainly and palpably, beyond all question, in violation of the fundamental law of the Constitution." *Atkin v. Kansas*, 191 U.S. 207, 223.

The judgment in my opinion should be affirmed.

Mr. Justice Holmes Dissenting

I regret sincerely that I am unable to agree with the judgment in this case, and that I think it my duty to express my dissent.

This case is decided upon an economic theory which a large part of the country does not entertain. If it were a question whether I agreed with that theory, I should desire to study it further and long before making up my mind. But I do not conceive that to be my duty, because I strongly believe that my agreement or disagreement has nothing to do with the right of a majority to embody their opinions in law. It is settled by various decisions of this court that state constitutions and state laws may regulate life in many ways which we as legislators might think as injudicious or if you like as tyrannical as this, and which equally with this interfere with the liberty to contract. Sunday laws and usury laws are ancient examples. A more modern one is the prohibition of lotteries. The liberty of the citizen to do as he likes so long as he does not interfere with the liberty of others to do the same, which has been a shibboleth for some well-known writers, is interfered with by school laws, by the Post Office, by every state or municipal institution which takes his money for purposes thought desirable, whether he likes it or not. The Fourteenth Amendment does not enact Mr. Herbert Spencer's Social Statics. The other day we sustained the Massachusetts vaccination law. *Jacobson* v. *Massachusetts*, 197 U.S. 11. United States and state statutes and decisions cutting down the liberty to contract by way of combination are familiar to this court. *Northern Securities Co.* v. *United States*, 193 U.S. 197. Two years ago we upheld the prohibition of sales of stock on margins or for future delivery in the constitution of California. *Otis* v. *Parker*, 187 U.S. 606. The decision sustaining an eight hour law for miners is still recent. *Holden* v. *Hardy*, 169 U.S. 366. Some of these laws embody convictions or prejudices which judges are likely to share. Some may not. But a constitution is not intended to embody a particular economic theory, whether of paternalism and the organic relation of the citizen to the State or of *laissez faire*. It is made for people of fundamentally differing views, and the accident of our finding certain opinions natural and familiar or novel and even shocking ought not to conclude our judgment upon the question whether statutes embodying them conflict with the Constitution of the United States.

General propositions do not decide concrete cases. The decision will depend on a judgment or intuition more subtle than any articulate major premise. But I think that the proposition just stated, if it is accepted, will carry us far toward the end. Every opinion tends to become a law. I think that the word liberty in the Fourteenth Amendment is perverted when it is held to prevent the natural outcome of a dominant opinion, unless it can be said that a rational and fair man necessarily would admit that the statute proposed would infringe fundamental principles as they have been understood by the traditions of our people and our law. It does not need research to show that no such sweeping condemnation can be passed upon the statute before us. A reasonable man might think it a proper measure on the score of health. Men whom I certainly could not pronounce unreasonable would uphold it as a first instalment of a general regulation of the hours of work. Whether in the latter aspect it would be open to the charge of inequality I think it unnecessary to discuss.

20. The Pittsburgh Survey—John A. Fitch, "The Steel Workers"

FEW CONTEMPORARY *documents depict so graphically, and at such close range, the actual conditions of living and working in the wage-earning class as the so-called Pittsburgh Survey. The investigation was made under the sponsorship of the Russell Sage Foundation, which was headed at the time by Robert W. De Forest, co-director of the New York Tenement House Report (Document 12, above). The director of the survey was Paul U. Kellogg, editor of Charities, the country's principal journal of social work. A leader in the young profession of social work, Kellogg recruited an eminent staff for the survey, including John R. Commons of Wisconsin, Robert A. Woods of Boston, and Florence Kelley of Chicago. The results stimulated social research of a similar nature for other communities throughout the country. Together, such efforts expunged the ignorance which had shielded the nation's well-to-do from the condition of their own society; especially, they tore into standard assumptions about the "natural" depravity of the poor and the "stewardship" of the employing classes. The excerpts presented here include a statement of purpose by Kellogg and a lengthy description of the bleak lives of steel operatives living in a company-dominated town.*

SOURCE: John A. Fitch, *The Steel Workers*, Vol. III in Paul U. Kellogg (ed.), *The Pittsburgh Survey Findings* (New York: The Russell Sage Foundation, 1911), pp. v–vii, 3–6, 206–220, 223–226, 227–242.

Editor's Foreword

Bound by a hundred ties to the dramatic story of the Pittsburgh people, this inquiry is, nevertheless, of more than local significance. Steel is a basic industry in America. It has been a beneficiary of the most fiercely contested governmental policies since Civil War times. Its products enter into every tool and structure and means of traffic in civilization. By the side of half a hundred mill sites along the Ohio and its tributaries, at our newest lake ports and above the old mineral beds of the Superior Basin; in the sun-baked Southwest, in the mountain valleys of the New South, and, by anticipation, in the ore regions of Alaska, what men may earn by digging, reducing, rolling, and fabricating this master metal, what leisure and resource they may gain in the process of it all, set the standards of life for hundreds of communities. A constructive statesmanship demands that Americans look well to what those standards tend to become for so numerous and vital an element in the population.

Moreover, the largest employer of steel workers in Pittsburgh is the largest employer of steel workers in the country as a whole; and the largest employer of labor in America today. That employer is in the saddle. So far as the mills and the shifts that man them go, the steel operators possess what many another manager and industrial president has hankered after and has been denied—untrammeled control. What has this exceptional employer done with this exceptional control over the human forces of production? Here our findings state concretely the problems of an industrial democracy in ways which cannot be lightly thrust aside.

Such a social interpretation of steel making could not but bulk large in the scheme of the Pittsburgh Survey. It depicts the industry which gives wealth and business preëminence to the region, which directly determines the well-being of a great company of wage-earners and their families, and which influences all other lines of employment in and about Pittsburgh. Mr. Fitch deals with the work-relationships of the steel men. The family end of their wages problem is the subject of Miss Byington's "Homestead: The Households of a Mill Town." Of the series of six books in which the Pittsburgh Survey is published, these two, therefore, are companion volumes. Mr. Fitch entered upon his commission without any promptings other than the general instincts toward an independent, resourceful citizenship inbred by the spirit of the Northwestern prairies and that quickening sense of economic justice which stirs the University of Wisconsin. To Professor John R. Commons of that University, both for his initial field work and for his consecutive suggestions and advice, author and editor are indebted. For information and insight, acknowledgment is due to steel workers of the greater city and the neighboring mill towns, Braddock, Duquesne, Homestead, McKeesport, to engineers, foremen, superintendents and higher corporation officials, many of whom are facing in their everyday work problems which are beyond the power of isolated men to solve.

Underlying the initial reasons for such a portrayal of labor conditions in the steel industry, is another reason which developed in the course of the inquiry, and which, as with the Mariner's tale, leaves no choice open as to the telling. The issues which Mr. Fitch takes up are of a sort which are not publicly discussed in the mill towns of the Pittsburgh district. Old employes do not dare petition their employers to consider them. Men have been discharged for calling meetings to discuss them. It would mean instant dismissal for large numbers of men should they act together to affect these things in the way that farmers would take up freight rates or the price of apples at a grange hall; and dismissal would mean the entire dislocation of life. An old resident is quoted by Miss Byington as saying, "If you want to talk in Homestead, you must talk to yourself."

It is fully time to bring these issues out into the open, where a man will not risk his livelihood by discussing it. That is the manner of America.

As the author points out, the steel industry could be interpreted from other points of view,—from that of its tremendous administrative burdens, of its fierce commercial competition in the past, of its wonderful technical progress. For these there are many spokesmen. Mr. Fitch makes articulate what the steel industry means to the men who are employed in it—for whom it makes up the matter of life, and who have no voice.

PAUL U. KELLOGG
Director Pittsburgh Survey

Chapter I. Introductory

There is a glamor about the making of steel. The very size of things—the immensity of the tools, the scale of production—grips the mind with an overwhelming sense of power. Blast furnaces, eighty, ninety, one hundred feet tall, gaunt and insatiable, are continually gaping to admit ton after ton of ore, fuel, and stone. Bessemer converters dazzle the eye with their leaping flames. Steel ingots at white heat, weighing thousands of pounds, are carried from place to place and tossed about like toys. Electric cranes pick up steel rails or fifty-foot girders as jauntily as if their tons were ounces. These are the things that cast a spell over the visitor in these workshops of Vulcan. The display of power on every hand, majestic and illimitable, is overwhelming; you must go again and yet again before it is borne in upon you that there is a human problem in steel production.

The purpose of this study is other than to paint word pictures of steel making, or to describe processes for engineer or metallurgist; the purpose is rather to discuss iron and steel, not in terms of ore, and tonnage, and machinery, but in terms of the working life. However ponderous the machinery, somewhere men are controlling its movements. However automatic a process, it is under the guidance of human intelligence. The glare of the fires, the tumult of the converters, the throb of the engines are less wonderful, less difficult of comprehension than the lives of the men who control and guide.

The human problem in the iron and steel industry is more than a labor problem, for it reaches beyond the questions of hours and wages, and beyond the relations of employer with employe, and touches vitally the principles of democracy itself.

It is a problem modified and complicated by many separate and more or less unrelated forces. The nineteenth century was one of constant development in the metal trades. In the later seventies and early eighties came the substitution of steel for iron; in the past fifteen years, the steel industry itself has been practically revolutionized, and so rapid and continuous is this movement that today is in advance of yesterday and tomorrow will see today's record eclipsed. Yet there were forces at work half a century ago that have a bearing upon the present situation; the rise of trade unionism in the iron industry, its rise and fall in the steel industry, the policies of the union, its successes and its failures,—all have contributed their part. Moreover, the cut-throat competition between the leading steel companies and the consolidation of their interests in the greatest employing corporation of the times, contributed directly to making conditions what they are.

The labor problem in the steel industry is not a new one therefore; it is rather a developing one. Each of these three great organic changes, involving in turn the machinery, the men, and the management, has affected it.

Through the revolutionary changes in method, machinery has displaced men to a remarkable extent. The proportion of skilled steel workers needed for the operation of a plant has decreased. At the same time, the large companies have so increased their capacity that they are employing more men than ever before, until today 60 per cent of the men employed in the steel industry are unskilled, and that 60 per cent is greater in numbers than was the total working force twenty years ago. The demand for unskilled labor in the steel industry has made Pittsburgh, during the last dozen years especially, a veritable Mecca to the immigrant. Steel manufacturers have not been at all averse to the rush of foreigners to the mills, for southeastern Europeans are well adapted to the necessities of the industry. For example, of the nearly 7000 men employed at Homestead, more than half are Slavs, and two-thirds are foreign born. Thus a race problem has been added to the labor problem, complicating it.

There were labor troubles in the late forties in the Pittsburgh iron mills. In 1858 a few puddlers of unusual temerity met and formed a labor union which by the end of the sixties had a national organization with some thousands of members, and occupied a position of strength. Later, other trades of iron workers were organized, and in 1876 four separate organizations in Pittsburgh came together to form the Amalgamated Association of Iron and Steel Workers. Prior to 1860 the employers, practically untrammeled by any trade-union restrictions, had been free to bring their best efforts to the adjustment of conditions. That the men were not satisfied with the conditions thus adjusted is evidenced by the steady growth of the unions from that time to 1892, when the Amalgamated Association reported a membership of over 24,000. During this period of thirty years the employes made definite and conscious efforts to control working conditions. In 1892 came the famous Homestead strike, and with the failure of that strike the power of the union was broken. By 1901 the Amalgamated Association had been driven from every important steel mill in the country. Since that time the employers have again been free to work out their own policies.

But unionism and non-unionism are bound up with a third and larger movement. The formation of the United States Steel Corporation has brought more than 50 per cent of the steel workers of the country under one employer, with a resulting promotion of uniformity of conditions of labor. Administrative decisions from a single head affect, without chance of protest, vast masses of men.

These are the facts historically considered. They give us the bearings of work which in America offers a livelihood to a quarter of a million men. This book deals with conditions in 1907 and 1908 in Allegheny County, Pennsylvania, which for forty years has been the producing center of the iron and steel industry in the United States. In the course of stupendous changes in processes and in corporate organization, unionism has been driven out from the mills of this Pittsburgh District. With its elimination has come an increase in hours until the eight-hour day has practically disappeared. A majority of the employes engaged in processes of making steel work twelve hours. Many work seven days in the week, either without a full day of rest or with a free Sunday one week and twenty-four hours of continuous duty the next. Speeding-up methods have augmented production in every department. Even where no new processes or machines have been introduced, the output has increased and in many cases is double what it was fifteen years ago. The stress inevitable under such a system of work is heightened by the heat and dangers of accident which are to be found in handling a great tonnage of molten metal. There are positions commonly spoken of as "hot jobs," where men work close to ladles of fluid iron or steel, or where heat radiates from ingots and from furnaces. Such positions are uncomfortable, to say the least, at any season of the year; but when a July sun is blazing upon the roof they are wellnigh intolerable. These physical conditions, coupled with the prolonged tension, result at many points in the working life of the mills, in human overstrain.

Entering into the relations between the Steel Corporation and its employes are two co-operative factors: a restricted scheme of stock-ownership by employes, and, more recently, the development of a system of preventing accidents in which committees of the men are enlisted. These in no wise affect or limit the underlying labor policy in both Corporation and independent mills. That is a determination to control, in pursuance of which object the employers inflexibly exclude the men from any voice in the conditions of their employment. Consistent with this policy, repressive measures have been introduced designed to enable the companies to retain the advantages which they gained for themselves when they eliminated the unions. These measures are doubtless intended to preserve industrial efficiency, but they have resulted in a thoroughgoing and far-reaching censorship that curtails free speech and the free activity of citizens. The effect of these measures is seen in every department of community life wherever, in Allegheny County, steel is made.

There is one issue the strands of which run unbroken through all the complicated forces mentioned, indistinct at first because uncertainly defined, but standing out finally clear and unmistakable,— responsibility. However divided this responsibility may have been at different periods in the history of the industry, control is today in the hands of the employers. They can change or continue conditions at their will. And beside this issue is another and mightier one,—that of democracy. Through all the following pages of this book it is hoped that these issues will not for one moment be forgotten. With them in mind, the facts presented become a question and a challenge.

But it was not alone because the steel companies wished to rid themselves of these improper restrictions that they crushed out unionism; they wished also to be free from the proper and legitimate activities of the union.

This latter becomes evident when we consider what has been done by the employers when free from union control. They have not stopped with introducing a necessary and proper discipline in their plants, but have taken advantage of their unlimited control to introduce the negative and destructive policies summarized above. Like the union, which in the days of its strength sometimes demanded all of the benefit of an increase in tonnage due to a new invention, and would not accept a reduction in the rate of pay, the steel companies are now demanding all of the benefit of increased tonnage, whether due to inventions or to physical effort, and will not permit any proportionate advance in workmen's earnings. More than this, they are taking advantage of the situation to exact far more of the worker than was expected of him years ago, and it is my belief far more than is expected now in other industries.

The causes that developed the present labor policy were, as stated above, economic in their nature. But a proper economic policy from the standpoint of the individual may be absolutely uneconomic from the standpoint of society. Such men as have plundered our forests and wasted our coal deposits have followed out an economic policy individually sound, but that policy is today denounced as at enmity with the public good. If the man who wastes and destroys *natural* resources is a public enemy, what of the corporations that exploit *human* resources?

If the employes could be charged formerly with a share of the responsibility for conditions in the steel industry, that time has gone by. The employers accepted the full burden of that responsibility by driving out unionism; they have increased their accountability by their stern measures designed to retain for themselves the control now exercised.

A repressive régime that makes it impossible for men to protest against conditions that are inimical to their welfare serves now, and has served since the destruction of unionism, to keep the employers in the saddle.

Chapter XVI. Repression

It now becomes necessary to discuss the reasons for the apparent acquiescence of the steel workers in existing conditions. The obvious deterrent to collective action on their part is the fact that they are non-union. But that merely suggests the question: Why don't they organize? To understand the absence of united action and resistance to the policies of the companies one must understand the obstacles that stand in the way.

In the first place, there is the so-called profit-sharing system of the United States Steel Corporation. This plan was announced by the Corporation to take effect in 1903. There were at that time about 168,000 employes of the Corporation, and these were divided, according to annual earnings, into six classes. It was provided that 25,000 shares of preferred stock should be set aside, and during January, 1903, the employes should have opportunity to subscribe, each one for as many shares as he wished, within the limits of a sum represented by a certain percentage of his annual salary.

Every year since 1903 there has been an additional stock issue, and the employes have usually over-subscribed the amount of stock allotted. . . .

The terms of purchase are very advantageous. Stock is to be paid for in monthly instalments, to be deducted from wages in such amounts as the subscriber may designate, not to exceed 25 per cent of the monthly wages or salary. Three years are allowed for full payment and 5 per cent interest is charged on deferred payments.

In the allotments of stock, preference has been given the employes whose incomes fall in the lower classes, although at least one full share of stock has been allotted each subscriber. No employe has ever been refused. Of the six classes designated, 25.69 per cent of the stock has been subscribed by the sixth class (workmen with an income under $800 per year, or, roughly, under $15 per week, in which, as we have seen, fall 71 per cent of the labor force). Skilled men, foremen and minor superintendents would fall in the fifth class, which has subscribed most heavily—56.38 per cent. Officials earning over $2,500 have subscribed the remaining 17.93 per cent. Of these, those earning over $5,000 have subscribed 6.91 per cent.

A plan by which the great working force of 200,000 employes can share in the year's profits of the United States Steel Corporation commends itself for its fair intent. It is possible that a plan by which, as here, employes can share through a system of stock ownership, open to all, has advantages over a percentage based on wages or output. Such a plan, as is often urged, may tend in entirely natural ways to a community of interest between men and management.

But other factors have been injected into the stock ownership plan of the United States Steel Corporation which remove it from the class of straight profit-sharing. On these factors it must be judged. The full text of the original offer appears in the appendix. In order to show the superimposed features which differentiate this plan from straight profit-sharing, I will quote from it briefly:

> As soon as the stock shall have been fully paid for, it will be issued in the name of the original subscriber and the certificate will be given to him, and he can then sell it any time he chooses. But as an inducement for him to keep it and to remain continuously in the employ of the Corporation or of one or another of the subsidiary companies, and to have the same interest in the business that a stockholder or working partner would have, the following offer is made, viz.:
>
> If he will not sell or part with the stock, but will keep it and in January of each year, for five years, commencing with January, 1904, will exhibit the certificate to the treasurer of his company, together with a letter from a proper official, to the effect that he has been continuously in the employ of the Corporation or of one or another of its subsidiary companies during the preceding year, and has shown a proper interest in its welfare and progress, he will during each of such five years receive checks at the rate of five dollars a share per year. . . .

If he shall remain continuously in the service of the Corporation or of one or another of its subsidiary companies for five years, at the end of the fifth year the Corporation intends that he shall receive a still further dividend, which cannot now be ascertained or stated, but which will be derived from the following source, viz.:

All who subscribe for stock in January, 1903, and commence to pay for it, but who discontinue at any time during the five years, of course will not receive the $5.00 per share for such of the five years as remain after they discontinue. The Corporation will, however, pay into a special fund each year the $5.00 payments that would have been made to such subscribers had they continued. This fund shall be credited with 5 per cent annual interest, and at the end of the five years' period the total amount thus accumulated will be divided into as many parts as shall be equal to the number of shares then remaining in the hands of men who shall have continued in such employ for the whole five years, and the Corporation will then by its own final determination award to each man whom it shall find deserving thereof as many parts of such accumulated fund as shall be equal to the number of shares then held by him under this plan. . . .

There can be no doubt of the value to the employes of the stock issue plan as a business proposition. An average net return on an investment of 17 to 25 per cent per year, for the first five years, and after that 7 per cent, is not bad. In spite of this there is not unanimity of feeling regarding the plan among the employes of the Steel Corporation. Some who hold stock criticise the policy very severely, while they admit that it is a good investment. This criticism is not all of it logical, perhaps. Some of it is aroused by the mere fact that the plan was worked out by capitalists, whose every move is regarded by certain classes of men in a sinister light. Others are logical in their reasoning provided they are correct in their premises, and when they see the United States Steel Corporation giving with one hand and taking away with the other they connect the two in their minds, and they do not view the dividends with pleasure. Many of the men with whom I talked spoke bitterly of the stock issues. One of the Homestead men said to me: "Many of the workingmen have been fooled by the preferred stock plan, and they really believe that the company has meant to do great things for them, in giving them the bonus besides the regular dividend. But I want to tell you that the first stock issue in 1903 was followed by a cut in wages in 1904 that made up to the company several times over all the extra bonuses they will pay in five years. The plan is to keep the men quiet, and it does it too. No stockholder wants to try to organize a union when the terms of the agreement state that only those who show a proper interest in the affairs of the company will receive a bonus."

There are employes who jump to the conclusion that the stock issues and the savings department of the Carnegie Steel Company, and all such plans, are for the purpose of finding out how much a workingman can save, and thus just how much of a wage reduction he can stand. A steel worker in one of the mill towns held that the reduction of 1904 in his mill took from each class of workmen almost exactly what the representatives of each class had been paying each month on their stock. A letter published in a labor paper from a Homestead steel worker just after the reduction in wages went into effect in February, 1908, is a good example of the sentiment entertained by many of the skilled workmen in the employ of the Corporation. A part of it reads as follows:

> With a blare of trumpets the United States Steel Corporation has announced a large distribution of profits to its preferred stock-holders, especially to its employes, but nothing has been said about the big reduction in wages at its Homestead plant which took effect February 1, 1908. This is the second heavy cut in wages at this plant since the preferred stock scheme was devised by the big corporation, and will amply reimburse the United States Steel Corporation for its generosity to its workmen. The present reduction averages about 20 per cent.[1] How does this strike you after their last year profit, amounting to $160,000,000 net earning to 1907?

Another steel worker, in discussing this same reduction in a letter to the same paper remarked, "The United States Steel Corporation is making a grand-stand play in giving away cash bonuses on preferred stock. Any man with two spoonfuls of horse sense knows that when they give away one dollar they know where they are going to get another in its place."

Whether or not there has been a connection between extra dividends and wage reductions, I have no light to help the reader to judge, but the workman who pointed out the effectiveness of the deferred dividend policy in promoting a passive acceptance of conditions was not far wrong.

Profit-sharing in principle is good. A scheme that recognizes that

1. The writer was incorrect in supposing that this reduction was general throughout the plant. It affected the plate mills chiefly.

the employe is a vital and necessary part of the successful prosecution of the business, and therefore admits him to a share in the profits of an industry, is to be commended. Such a profit-sharing is only a fair recognition of the part played by the employe in making profits possible. But the stock-issue plan of the Steel Corporation is not that kind of profit-sharing.

In the first place, there is no suggestion that the special dividends and bonuses that the employe receives are, at best, other than kindly meant gifts distributed by a benevolent overlord. The whole tenor of the apparently inspired newspaper and magazine articles dealing with the subject is suggestive less of the spirit of wages than of almsgiving; and as such is a form of injustice. If the amounts distributed are a deserved and just remuneration for value received, then the Corporation is humiliating and misusing these men in pretending to *give* money instead of paying it.

A larger reason for condemning this stock-issue system is that it brings those employes who invest in stock more surely under the domination of the Corporation. The bonus paid each year for five years is to go to those who have shown "*a proper interest in the welfare and progress*" of the Corporation, and the extra dividends at the end of the five-year period are awarded to those whom the Corporation finds "*deserving thereof.*" There is nothing to prevent an employe of the Corporation purchasing stock on the same basis as the outsider, but in that case he will receive only ordinary dividends. The extraordinary return received by the holder of employes' stock is based on his acquiescence as an employe. So long as his large profits are potentially dependent upon submission to every policy and project of the Corporation, so long will the principle underlying these special bonuses be vicious. . . . Would a stock-holding employe be showing a "proper interest in the welfare and progress" of the Corporation if he should protest and encourage his fellow workmen to protest against Sunday work? I do not know, for I have never met a stock-holding employe who had tried it. Nor have I met one who had tried to bring his fellow employes together into an association for purposes of collective bargaining; but I have no illusions in regard to such an employe being considered "deserving" of extra stock bonuses.

Efforts to encourage loyalty in a working force have much to commend them, from the standpoint of administrative efficiency. They may make for the smooth running of a plant, for increased productivity, and better returns for stockholders and men. But a plan which penalizes independent thinking and democratic action does not make for healthy progress. That the profit-sharing plan has been subordinated to this ulterior purpose is further affirmed by the practical repetition of its worst features in the bonus system. There only officials are concerned, many of them the minor operating heads upon whose independence and fraternalism, in the absence of trade union activity, the men must depend for the working out of common justice in the plants. A share of the year's bonus is held back in the form of stock. It remains with the company for five years and if a man leaves his position, or is discharged in this time, he forfeits it. Similarly he forfeits the special bonus distributed at the end of each five-year period.

But the positive influence of these systems of rewards, binding the working force to the company, is supplemented by the negative influence, far more sinister, of a system of espionage.

I doubt whether you could find a more suspicious body of men than the employes of the United States Steel Corporation. They are suspicious of one another, of their neighbors, and of their friends. I was repeatedly suspected of being an agent of the Corporation, sent out to sound the men with regard to their attitude toward the Corporation and toward unionism. The fact is, the steel workers do not dare openly express their convictions. They do not dare assemble and talk over affairs pertaining to their welfare as mill men. . . .

When I met the men in their homes, too, there was suspicion to be broken down. Sometimes I could not get an opportunity to see the man whom I was seeking. Business engagements would suddenly be remembered which prevented an interview. Several men refused to talk about mill work. A highly paid employe of the Corporation refused even to see me. I had been at his house, and finding that he was out, I left word that I would return at a specified hour. Returning at the time named, my ring brought the housewife to the door, who told me that her husband was at home, but that he would not see me or talk to me because the company had forbidden its employes to talk with strangers about mill work. . . .

These skilled steel workers are very much like other Americans. They are neither less nor more intelligent, courageous, and self-reliant than the average citizen. Their extreme caution, the constant state of apprehension in which they live, can have but one cause. It is the burnt child that dreads the fire. It would hardly be expected that the loss of one strike, disastrous though it was, should have so disheartened the workers that they would never attempt to revive collective bargaining. It has been through a series of such attempts that the men have learned to respect the vigilance and power of their employers, and they have learned the cost of defiance.

In 1895 it was reported in the Amalgamated Association Convention that the Homestead steel workers had received "another reduction, ranging from 48 per cent to 60 per cent." A meeting with a thousand men in attendance had been held January 16 to protest, and officers of the Amalgamated Association had addressed the meeting. The next day the Carnegie Steel Company "discharged men by fives and tens for daring to attend a public meeting." Secret meetings were then held, and 25 men employed in the 119-inch mill were organized into a lodge of the Amalgamated Association. It was not long before the officers of this lodge were discharged, and the president of the lodge was told that it was for organizing. . . .

The officials of the steel companies make no secret of their hostility to unionism, and I have been told by two leading employers that they would not tolerate it. Any movement toward organization, they assured me, would mean discharge. That this was no idle boast is evident from the record of all attempts at organization since 1892.

All of the steel companies have effective methods of learning what is going on among the workmen. The Jones and Laughlin Company has some organization that keeps it sufficiently informed as to the likelihood of sedition breaking out, and the United States Steel Corporation has regular secret service departments. Its agents are thought by the men to be scattered through all of the mills of the Corporation, working shoulder to shoulder at the rolls or furnaces with honest workmen, ready to record any "disloyal" utterances or to enter into any movement among their fellows. The workmen feel this espionage. They believe it exists, but they do not know who the traitors are. It may be that the friend of long standing who works at the next furnace is one of them, or, possibly, the next-door neighbor at home; they do not know. Is it any wonder, therefore, that they suspect each other and guard their tongues?

This book is not intended to be condemnatory except as the facts speak for themselves. There may be considerable defense, from the standpoint of shop management, for much that has been pointed out to be socially bad. But no justification of any sort presents itself for this "spy system."

Let us look at it clearly and understandingly. It is detective work of a different stripe from that which would weed out grafting among foremen, or would protect tools and metals from theft. The steel companies have large properties which they must protect. But I assume that neither the officials of the Jones and Laughlin Company nor the directors of the United States Steel Corporation would bribe a bookkeeper in a competing company to give them its trade secrets. If a representative of organized labor during a recess in a conference with an employer were left alone, on his honor, in the employer's private office, and he took advantage of the opportunity to examine the correspondence lying on the desk, I have no doubt that these same steel company officials would agree with me that such action was despicable. They would be right. That is the other side. What do they think of buying information about their workmen, not intended for them; of sending paid spies into the workmen's committees? Such things are justified in war. Does war exist in western Pennsylvania?

Chapter XVII. Citizenship in the Mill Towns

The question next arises—and the answer must determine our judgment of the employers' policies—what does it all mean to the men and the families of the men who work in the mills? What is the effect upon standards and ideals, down deep in the heart of the community life?

Steel making is carried on in a score of mill towns in the Allegheny and Monongahela valleys. In these towns, more clearly than in the greater city of Pittsburgh, the influence both of the labor conditions and of the policies of suppression are to be seen. With the men deprived of collective action through work-organizations, do the older social institutions of church and town afford channels through which democratic action and ideals may find expression and conditions be improved, or are they too benumbed by the influence of the administrative policies we have outlined?

In the industrial district surrounding Pittsburgh a wonderful opportunity exists for organized Christian service. But the churches do not see this opportunity because their point of view is individual, not social. There are in the churches of Allegheny County ministers who are doing heroic service, but there are too many, preaching every Sunday to steel workers' families, who never have stepped inside a steel mill and who do not know a Bessemer converter from a puddling furnace. It is because of this lack of knowledge of some of the real problems of life that the ministers sometimes deliver their heaviest blows against secondary evils while the prime wrongs, the ones that dry up the roots of the community life, may escape their wrath. To make my point clearer, I will refer to one of the biggest problems in the steel mills today—that of Sunday work. There is no doubt of the evil of the practice that makes men toil seven days in the week. Its results are bad physically, intellectually and morally. The ministers have combatted Sunday work, but they have directed their energies more frequently against drug stores, confectionery and fruit stores and amusements, than they have against the United States Steel Corporation with its thousands of employes working the "long turn." They have, it is true, requested the superintendents of the steel mills to eliminate Sunday work as much as possible, but there has been no determined effort to enforce the Sunday closing law against the steel works, as there has been in the other quarters named. This is partly due to the fact that the ministers have not informed themselves properly as to the extent of Sunday work. Some of them are in possession of the essential facts, but many others seem to be in almost complete ignorance.[1] Another reason is the fact that the steel companies are considered too powerful for successful attack. If this be true, we are in a bad way. If the forces of righteousness in a community dare not attack corporate wrongdoing, but must devote their energies only to the small offender, the time will not be long deferred when the hands of those who would see justice done will be effectually tied.

I speak of this attitude of mind of the leaders of the churches because of the effect of it upon the workers. I would not criticise the churches because they do not prevent Sunday work in the mills. It is quite true that they cannot do that—not in a day. The fact,

1. This can scarcely be urged in extenuation since the publication of the findings of the Pittsburgh Survey in *Charities and The Commons* in January–March, 1909, and in the Pittsburgh newspapers.

however, that the ministers do not generally understand the workingman's problem, and do not seek to understand, well enough to sympathize fully with the hardships of their lives, has tended to make the workers lose interest in the church. Even deeper has been the estrangement which has arisen because of the hesitancy of the clergy to speak as boldly against the large offender as against the small.

There is an instinctive feeling among the steel workers that the church is "on the other side." The thought that the church people "do not understand" has led to bitterness. A steel worker during the slack times in the winter of 1908, spoke to me of the practice of starting the mills on Sunday evening when it was known that they would be idle again before the end of the week. "And still the good church people," he remarked, "wonder why we don't go to church." Another man told me that the minister of the church of which his wife was a member had urged him to attend more frequently. He replied that he was too tired from his week's work to go to church Sunday morning, and Sunday evening he was back at work again in the mill before church services began. He asked the minister why he didn't "do something to get him a chance to go to church." I must quote the statement of a skilled steel worker who gave utterance to what was expressed to me numbers of times, though not always with the same amount of feeling:

> There are a good many churches in this borough, supported generally by women. The preachers don't have any influence in securing better conditions for the men and they don't try to have. They never visit the mills, and they don't know anything about the conditions the men have to face. They think the men ought to go to church after working twelve hours Saturday night. They could accomplish a lot if they would try to use their influence in the right direction. Let them quit temperance reform until they get better conditions for the men. It is no time to preach to a man when he is hungry. Feed him first, then preach to him: so with the workingman. Get a decent working day with decent conditions for a man, then ask him to stop drinking. Let the preacher find out how the men work; go and see them in the heat and smoke and heavy toil; let them notice the crushed hands, broken arms and amputated limbs and find out what the workingman is up against, and then try to better his condition.

Of course, the hostile attitude toward the church of some of the workingmen is not entirely reasonable, although it is a feeling characteristic of the majority. They are defiant, and they make demands beyond the churches' strength. There are, on the other hand, a good many steel workers who are loyal members of churches, and the church would, I think, have the confidence of all if it would boldly withstand industrial oppression and corporate wrongdoing in the spirit of the Man who violently drove the money changers out of the temple and who denounced to their faces those who laid heavy burdens upon the poor. Then the church could also serve to keep the best spirit alive in the homes in spite of the long working days, and it might help to provide for the social life of the mill men who are now almost entirely barred from the better forms of social observance.

Thus it was that my residence in the mill towns brought it home to me that three institutions organized to promote enjoyment and progress are not, in these communities, exerting their proper influence. As was shown in an earlier chapter, the schedule of hours does not permit the home and the library to fulfill their natural functions. We have now seen how lethargy within and pressure without are tending to nullify or misdirect the influence of the church.

But this does not mean that the workingmen in the mill towns have no opportunity whatever for pleasure or society. It is only the moral and intellectual forces that are insulated. Young men who work in the mills cannot have their spirits utterly dampened by a long working day, and they often take trouble to dress for an evening's entertainment or to meet their friends socially. This does not last long, for youth itself is not long-lived in the steel mills; but whether young or old, men cannot thus easily be deprived of the social instinct. It is essential that they should meet together somehow and somewhere in fellowship and in relaxation from their work. The saloon and the lodge remain as the social centers for the steel workers.

There are other reasons, to be sure, than the desire to mingle with one's fellows, for the popularity of the saloon; drinking is traditional among iron and steel workers. But there is no doubt that the craving for companionship is one of the strongest reasons for its hold upon a community of workingmen. The nature of mill work is such as to make the saloon habit one of the most natural ones in the world. Practically every man is affected by the heat even if he does not have a "hot job." The whole atmosphere is such as to induce perspiration and enhance thirst. All the workers drink water in great quantities as long as they are in the mill. Sometimes a man drinks too much, so that he leaves at the end of a day's work feeling half nauseated. Such a man steps into a saloon for a glass of something to set his stomach right. Or if a man does not overdrink during the day, he is still chronically thirsty, and it is to satisfy a real longing for drink that he stops for his beer. The dust of the mills, too, that the men have been breathing for twelve hours, sends another quota to their beer or whiskey to clear out their throats. Then comes the largest contingent of all, the men wearied with the heat and the work, some almost overcome and dragging their feet. These feel the necessity of a stimulant, and they get it day after day, regardless of the waste of physical and nervous energy involved in keeping themselves keyed up to their work by an artificial aid. I do not think I am far wrong when I say that a large majority of steel workers sincerely believe that the regular use of alcoholic drinks is essential to keep them from breaking down. It is seldom a pleasure-seeking crowd that fills the saloons after the whistle has blown at the end of a turn. The men line up at the bar, each one taking one drink and paying for it himself. The first line of men put down their glasses and leave, and the bar is filled again with a second group. There are very few who take more than one drink on coming from the mill.

There is more conviviality on Saturday nights and after pay days than on an ordinary midweek night. Then is the time the men relax; then the treating is done. The saloon becomes a social center and the men find the fellowship that they crave. It is a following of the line of least resistance that makes the saloon supplant all better forms of social life. A man does not need to change his clothing and get a shave before he is made welcome here. He may come covered with the grime of the mill and not feel out of place. In slack times, when the mills are not running, the saloon becomes a regular meeting place, and men go there primarily for companionship, the drinking becoming secondary. Ordinarily one does not see very much drunkenness. The men want to be fit for work the next day. On the eve of a holiday some will go too far, but these are most likely to be the unskilled workmen. The only men whom I found in a state of intoxication when I looked for them at their homes were blast furnace men—men who had been working for months without a holiday or a Sunday. The men I refer to had had a brief holiday and they spent it in the only way they knew. The better class of steel workers, who view their fellows with a sympathetic eye, explain the holiday intoxication of a certain element in the industry as a logical result of steady work and the long day. After weeks and months of work, twelve hours a day, and no holidays, a man gets far behind in his accumulation of the pleasure that he feels to be his due. When a holiday comes it is all too short to collect the overdue bill; pleasure of a concentrated sort must be sought in order to make up for lost time.

As a result of all these cumulative promptings, the saloons take more of the steel worker's money than do many of the legitimate business interests of the mill towns. During 1907 there were 30 saloons in Duquesne, a mill town of 10,000 or 12,000 population. I was told in 1908, by one who was in a position to know, that the leading saloonkeeper in this borough drew from the bank, regularly, every two weeks, just before pay day, between $200 and $300 to be used as change in anticipation of the bills of large denomination that would be handed over the bar. Braddock, where the Edgar Thomson steel works are located, had in 1907, 65 saloons. Braddock and North Braddock together had a population of about 25,000. I was told that a considerably larger sum was required for change on pay days here than in Duquesne, the average to each saloon being $500, making over $30,000 in all. I cannot vouch for the truth of this statement it was a report which reached me indirectly and may be only an expression of some one's opinion and not based on facts. But information in regard to the situation in McKeesport in 1906 came to me through such channels that there can be little doubt as to its accuracy. McKeesport had about 40,000 people in 1906, and 69 saloons. On the Thursdays preceding the semi-monthly pay days, which fall on Fridays and Saturdays, the three leading saloonkeepers of the city were accustomed to draw from their bank accounts from $1200 to $1500 each in dollar bills and small denominations, to be used as change. Other saloonkeepers drew varying amounts, and the totals thus drawn each fortnight footed up to $60,000. On the Mondays after pay days the saloonkeepers usually deposited double the amount drawn. These periodic leaps in deposits never failed to coincide with pay days, and, the inevitable conclusion is that about $60,000 of the steel workers' wages were regularly expended in the saloons within the two days. If this seems overdrawn, let me cite the case of George

Holloway, who was blacklisted in 1901 after leading a strike in the Wood plant of the American Sheet and Tin Plate Company in McKeesport. With what was generally understood to be borrowed funds—for Holloway was left almost penniless by the strike—he started a saloon in McKeesport. I saw and talked with him in the fall of 1907, and he told me that in 1905, four years from the time of entering business, he had sold out. He has established a son in a saloon in the west, and with the rest of his family he is now living in McKeesport on the income of his investments, a retired capitalist.

The liquor situation in an American town bears a very direct relation to the political life. This is true in these boroughs. In earlier chapters we have seen how the steel companies deny the employes the right to organize in unions. In spite of this, the situation is not hopeless so long as the workingman is secure in his possession of the ballot. It is commonly understood that the United States Steel Corporation is the dominant force in politics in the mill towns, except in McKeesport, where authority seems to be divided with the brewing interests.[1]

Repeatedly I was told that workmen have been discharged at Duquesne for refusing to vote the way the company wished. I was told by one employe that he had been called into the office of his superintendent and remonstrated with for working against the company ticket, and an indirect threat was made of discharge. I was told by men of unimpeachable standing in Braddock, who were not steel works employes, that in the spring of 1908, preceding the May primaries, men were induced to vote for the candidates favored by the Corporation by promises of a resumption in industry if the right men were nominated. But the most damaging testimony that I received regarding the interference of the Steel Corporation in politics came from a source clearly authoritative.

For obvious reasons I cannot give my informant's name. "A short time before the primaries of May, 1908," he said, "orders came from the New York office of the United States Steel Corporation, to the general superintendent of the Edgar Thomson plant

1. In McKeesport, during the strike of 1901, when the threat was made that the Dewees Wood plant would be dismantled on account of the alleged hostility of the people of the town, the mayor issued a statement in which he charged that the property of the Steel Corporation in this city was assessed at 40 per cent of its market value, while the houses of the citizens were assessed at 70 per cent. (*Outlook*, August 17, 1901, p. 889.)

at Braddock, directing him to order the department superintendents to line up their employes for the Penrose candidates for the legislature. The general superintendent called a meeting of the department superintendents and delivered the orders. This created considerable dismay, for local option was an issue in the primaries and the Penrose candidates were opposed to local option. Some of the superintendents were already prominently identified with the local option party and had been assisting in organizing the campaign. How they could with honor or self-respect abandon the issue at this point was not clear to the officials. But the answer to the objections was clear and to the point. They were told that their first duties were to the Corporation. They must, accordingly, break any or all promises and work for Penrose, because the United States Steel Corporation needed him in the Senate."

After this information had come to me, I received other corroborative testimony. I had a talk with a man who had been prominent in the local option campaign previous to the primaries of 1908 at Braddock. I wrote down what he said, and after he had read my manuscript he indorsed every word. His statement was as follows:

> The most damnable feature of the whole campaign was the attitude of the United States Steel Corporation. There is not such a perfect political organization in the country as the steel trust. They aim to control the politics of every borough and town where their works are located, and usually they do control. They plan their campaigns far in advance; they are laying their wires now to control the borough council three years ahead. You ought to see the way they line up their men at the polls and vote them by thousands. What does a secret ballot amount to? In every ward in this borough the steel works employes are in the majority. There are two or three foremen in nearly every ward, and it is up to them to round up the vote. If there are not enough foremen in a ward, they send them over from the next ward to help out. Naturalized foreigners can be handled easily, but so can men of three and four generations of American blood. These men have been so long dominated by the Corporation that they dare not disobey. They have a sort of superstitious feeling that somehow the boss will know if they vote wrong. And the workingmen are not the only ones that can be managed. Before the May primaries we perfected an organization in this borough to fight for local option. Several of the foremen and assistant superintendents in the mills were among our most active workers. Some of them helped in the speaking campaign. One day an order came that the thing must stop. The United States Steel Corporation needs to have Boies Penrose in the Senate, and the

political life of Penrose is bound up with the liquor interests of the state. So a blow to liquor is a blow to Penrose, and the steel trust cannot have that. So the superintendents and foremen were ordered to line up their men for Penrose and the saloon. One young man who had been speaking in the campaign refused to stop, and he was called into the office and plainly told that he must either quit local option or quit the mills. That was not unusual though. The bread and butter argument is always used. As a result, the local optionists were badly broken up. The speaking campaign practically stopped and men whom we had counted on and who had been with us, actually turned around and made a show at least of opposing local option. Then the company gave it out that if the Penrose candidates to the legislature were nominated, the mill would be likely to resume operations, and the men who had been idle half or two-thirds of the time since October, clutched at that half promise like drowning men.

It is probably unnecessary to add that Penrose carried Allegheny County.

In the chapter on repression I showed how through policies of seducing and spying, the Steel Corporation kept a strong hand on the men to prevent any collective or outspoken action with respect to the terms of their employment. A negative policy—that of enforcing silence. It is a policy of sitting on the safety-valve. A policy which runs parallel to it is here described. If the first was repression, this other is coercion.

Chapter XVIII. The Spirit of the Workers

Under common conditions workingmen are apt to develop common feelings with respect to some of the deeper and more fundamental questions of their lives. This is especially true in a crisis or a peculiarly aggravated state of affairs, when minor differences are forgotten and feeling is keen. This was so at Homestead in 1892 when H. C. Frick sent the armed Pinkerton guards to drive the striking workmen off the company premises; it was so in Homestead again in February, 1908, when with the panic at its height and the mills operating on barely one-fourth time, the Carnegie Steel Company cut wages 10 to 30 per cent of men who were not, during those months, earning enough to live on. It has been so at different times in the Monongahela valley in the last decade when men have been discharged and then blacklisted for meeting in a public hall to form an organization.

Since 1892 a common feeling has been slowly making headway. The lengthening of the working day, the choking of democratic institutions, and the coercive sway of the employers have worked out more than a well organized industrial machine. The years from 1892 down are illuminated here and there with flashes of indignation. These have died away and the public has forgotten, but each time the embers have glowed a little redder, a little more surely. Among the many fine workingmen that I grew to know in Pittsburgh was one whose gentleness of breeding and native courtesy would have marked him in any company. I asked him once how far socialism had progressed in the mill towns. His eye suddenly flashed as he answered, "Ninety-nine per cent of the men are socialists, if by that you mean one who hates a capitalist."

The steel worker sees on every side evidences of an irresistible power, baffling and intangible. It fixes the conditions of his employment; it tells him what wages he may expect to receive and where and when he must work. If he protests, he is either ignored or rebuked. If he talks it over with his fellow workmen, he is likely to be discharged. As a steel worker said to me, the same one quoted above, "The galling thing about it all is the necessity of accepting in silence any treatment that the Corporation may see fit to give. We have no right to independent action, and when we are wronged there is no redress." . . .

No great problem, whether social or other, can be worked out with success without enthusiasm and hope. The difficulty of reaching a solution of the labor problem in the steel industry is augmented by a certain element among the workers with whom hope is dead and enthusiasm forgotten. There are a large number of whom this is true. They are the older men, generally, who have hoped, years back, and waited, for a revival of something like democracy in western Pennsylvania. But "Hope deferred maketh the heart sick." The years have done their work, and these men, with spirit dead, face a future in which they expect nothing and ask for nothing. They look dull-eyed on a world from which the brightness is gone. Writers have always loved to make use of striking epithets in describing the power wielded by forceful men who are counted the successful ones of their times. Latterly we have heard much of "merchant princes" and "captains of industry." Kindred to these is the term "iron-master." It is a name to roll over one's tongue, and suggests might and power. But it has a grim significance to those who know the men upon whose toil these strutting "iron-masters" have raised themselves. To them the name does not suggest heroics. . . .

There is a deep unrest among the voters in the mill towns with regard to things political, and in this uneasiness or dissatisfaction there is a marked tendency in the direction of theories commonly called socialistic. This situation has grown not so much from a study of socialist literature, and an intellectual acceptance of the principles involved, as it is a turning away from an adherence to a political organization that has invited the support of the workingmen, yet failed to interest itself in any important legislation for their benefit. . . . Most of the Pittsburgh steel workers vote the republican ticket, because they see no immediate hope of success through a workingmen's party; but they are ready to accept any political theory that promises something worth while to labor. If the workmen in the mills were once convinced that in an approaching election there existed a possibility of the election of the socialist candidates, there would follow what could not adequately be termed a landslide; it would be an avalanche. . . .

It is not necessary for me to attempt to interpret the minds of the immigrant workmen. That has been done by others in the Pittsburgh Survey far better qualified to speak. It is necessary to refer to them, however, that we may keep freshly in mind the leading aspects of the labor problem in the steel mills. The so-called English-speaking workmen number less than half of the total employed. Fully 60 per cent of the workmen are immigrants, the Slavic races largely preponderating. Most of these are unskilled laborers; few of them are citizens; a majority are unable to speak the English language. The way in which this mass of illiterate, unassimilated foreigners complicates the labor problem in the steel mills has been pointed out in an earlier chapter.

In a sense the immigrants are an unknown factor in the problem. It would seem, as has been pointed out before, that their presence in such large numbers would have a tendency to make more stable the existing conditions in the industry. But a good case also might be made for an opposite thesis. A skilled American-born workman pointed out to me that the foreigners occupy a strategic position, and that a new union movement might naturally start from among them that would be irresistible. The foreigners already have organizations through which they could work, in the fraternal orders that are everywhere to be found among them as auxiliaries to their churches; and so compact are their organizations and so loyal are they to their churches, that a priest might easily give the word that in a short time would tie up the whole industry. While this view fails to take into account the lines of cleavage between Protestant and Catholic, and between the Roman church and the Greek, it is worthy of consideration. The strength of the organizations under the banner of any one of these creeds is enough to be formidable.

In the summer of 1909 there was a demonstration of the spirit of immigrant workmen that opened the eyes of the public to qualities heretofore unknown. For many weeks at McKees Rocks they persisted in their strike against the Pressed Steel Car Company. It had been thought that the Slavs were too sluggish to resist their employers, and unable to organize along industrial lines. It was proved in this conflict that neither theory was correct; and, stranger still, it was demonstrated that American-born and immigrant workmen can and will work side by side for common ends. It is encouraging to note the awakening of social consciousness among the Slav workmen; it is quickening to catch the spirit of their leaders; but it must be remembered, too, that they are as a body ignorant and illiterate. When they become fully awake to their power, they may be an element of strength added to the cause of social justice, or they may be a menace to life and property in their indiscriminate fury.

I have told in these chapters the facts as I found them in the Pittsburgh District. And yet in the face of them all, I know that there are some who will deny the existence of any labor problem, or of any injustice in the institutions of society, that may not be remedied by individual effort. I have heard a minister, a man of rare talents and usefulness, say from his pulpit that there need be no suffering nor discontent among the working people, because in a single Western state, he alleged, there is enough unused land to provide sustenance for them all if they would leave the cities and occupy it. I have been assured by employers that it is impossible for any great injustice to exist in an industry because the workmen can always quit their jobs and find others. If these statements were true, they would represent a poor makeshift for a social program. The best they offer is a way of escape from unwholesome conditions, while the real evil is not attacked. But the statements are misleading at best, and they suggest a theory with reference to the labor problem that is utterly unsound. They fail to note that the labor problem is social, not individual. They assume a mobility on the part of labor that does not and cannot exist; they are ill considered and unfair.

It is not to be assumed that the minister would desire the wheels of industry to be stopped. When, therefore, he advises dissatisfied city workmen to go to the farms, he is instead of offering a suggestion designed to relieve society of a burden, recommending a transfer of the burden from the shoulders of one group to those of another. The movement would be impossible without greatly increased immigration, in order to fill the places of those who have gone to the farms; and if the overhanging industrial evils were not attacked, the new contingent would have to escape to the land after a time. The logical following out of this theory would eventually involve the appropriation of the last vacant farm; what would be the remedy when this enforced stationary condition arrived, it remains for the supporters of the theory to explain.

The suggestion that the right to quit offers anything in the way of refuge from unjust conditions reveals ignorance of the true facts. Young, unmarried men may shift about quite freely without incurring great danger, and many of them do. But married men cannot jeopardize the interests of their families by leaving the known for the unknown. Even skilled men cannot be sure of finding readily other positions in their own trades, and to begin again, as apprentices, to master other trades is of course out of the question. Beginners' wages are not sufficient to support families. Many employers prefer married men because they are more stable, and this is merely another way of saying that married men dare not quit, and so do not make trouble.

To be effective, the right-to-quit theory would have to be accompanied by absolute mobility on the part of labor. For many reasons this cannot exist, and any theory that requires such mobility for its justification is blind. The minister, the banker, the man of affairs, when they take the attitude mentioned, are unconsciously measuring all workmen, from the poorest, most illiterate laborer up, by their own standards, and out of their own experiences. It is nothing to the business man to travel from Boston to St. Louis, and to know the demands of trade over thousands of miles of country; it is easy for the student or the professional man to acquaint himself with localities where opportunity is relatively good. Such men, with their wide outlook on life, their unusual opportunity to know industrial conditions, and their exceptional equipment, find that America is rich in opportunity. They blame the factory or mill hand, bound to twelve daily hours of toil, and without any of the means for discovering the most advantageous industry, because he does not know all that they know. It would be as reasonable for an engineer to scorn a professor of Greek for not knowing how to build a bridge.

This attitude is unfair because it subjects workingmen to tests that their more favored critics are not willing to meet. Home means much to the educated man and to the man of affairs. He will not lightly tear himself loose from the city or the locality where all his closet friends reside and go so far away that they perhaps may never follow, and he may never return. Is it a small thing that the working people also love their homes and the associations of years? The home community often means more to a workman of slender means than it does to those more fortunate, for he knows just who are the trusted friends there who can be counted on in disaster. It cannot be made to sound very impressive to a New York or Pennsylvania workman, that there are good chances on the farms of Iowa or the Dakotas.

Those who defend existing conditions in the steel mills and in other similar industries have another favorite argument. It is the "high wage" theory. A certain foreman in one of the Pittsburgh mills had this theory, and he undertook to become my guide on a tour of the mill, in order that he might demonstrate its truth to me. He showed me a Hungarian laborer sitting on a box with nothing for the moment demanding his attention. This man was idle half the time, I was told, and drew $2.00 a day. We passed an engineer, dozing in the cab of his dinkey engine, and it appeared that he received $3.50 a day for doing that. We came to where a heat of steel was being poured, and men were pointed out to me by my guide, working in the glare of the metal, who were getting $5.00, $6.00 and even $7.00 a day, and some of them were known to be dissatisfied. To my guide it was an evidence of depravity. . . .

It was shown in the chapter on Wages and the Cost of Living that steel workers are not highly paid. But even if their earnings were very high, it would be folly to claim that they are compensated for their lack of opportunity to live the lives of normal men who work a normal day and rest at night, or for their lost privileges of free speech, or for their stolen political rights. These are things for which you cannot pay a man.

But here, as in every other phase of the labor problem, the social aspect overshadows the individual. Were a man to consider himself recompensed by high wages for long hours and lack of touch with the world or for extreme danger, society is not thereby recompensed. Men stunted, whether physically or mentally, are a burden to the communities in which they live; and the man or the industry that has placed a barrier before a man's growth is to that extent a social enemy. For the rearing of children, strong in body and mind, with aspirations toward mental and moral growth and with ideals that shall make for honest citizenship, there is need of strong fathers and mothers, healthy in body and mind. There must be time in the home for the development of a sentiment not wholly concerned with bread-winning. That person, or corporation, or set of ideas that stands in the way is a public enemy, and there is none greater.

21.   The Industrial Workers of the World

HAMPERED by the courts, as well as by their own shortsightedness, the country's lawmakers failed to accommodate the growing, restive wage-earning classes. As a result, for many, American society in its current form appeared to offer no substantial rewards. This was especially true for migrant labor and for the relatively unskilled workers recruited for western mining and lumber operations. Ignored or rejected by the traditional craft workers organized in the AFL, the Railroad Brotherhoods, and the United Mine Workers of the eastern coal regions; usually separated by great distances from their home communities and even their immediate families; and often treated as criminals by police, sheriffs, and militia even in the absence of legal charges, such workers appreciated no tangible stake in the society that hosted them. Their reaction, rather understandably, was virtually to declare war on the entire political and economic structure, including the wage system, the elections system, representative government, and even the concept of national political identification. As one Wobbly explained: "If you were a bum without a blanket; if you had left your wife and kids when you went west for a job, and had never located them since; if your job never kept you long enough in a place to qualify you to vote; if you slept in a lousy, sour bunk-house, and ate food just as rotten as they could give you and get by with it . . . if every

*person who represented law and order and the nation beat you up, rail-
roaded you to jail, and the good Christian people cheered and told them
to go to it, how the hell do you expect a man to be patriotic?" The Industrial Workers of the World, a quasi-Marxist, syndicalist association
founded in the United States in 1905, gave organizational expression to
these sentiments.*

SOURCE: Document A: Preamble to the Constitution of the Industrial Workers of the World as Adopted at the First Convention in 1905 and Amended in 1908.

A. Preamble of the I.W.W. Constitution (1908)

The working class and the employing class have nothing in
common. There can be no peace so long as hunger and want are
found among millions of working people and the few, who make
up the employing class, have all the good things of life.

Between these two classes a struggle must go on until the
workers of the world organize as a class, take possession of the earth
and the machinery of production, and abolish the wage system.

We find that the centering of management of the industries into
fewer and fewer hands makes the trade unions unable to cope with
the ever growing power of the employing class. The trade unions
foster a state of affairs which allows one set of workers to be pitted
against another set of workers in the same industry, thereby helping defeat one another in wage wars. Moreover, the trade unions
aid the employing class to mislead the workers into the belief that
the working class have interests in common with their employers.

These conditions can be changed and the interest of the working
class upheld only by an organization formed in such a way that all
its members in any one industry, or in all industries if necessary,
cease work whenever a strike or lockout is on in any department
thereof, thus making an injury to one an injury to all.

Instead of the conservative motto, "A fair day's wage for a fair
day's work," we must inscribe on our banner the revolutionary
watchword, "Abolition of the wage system."

It is the historic mission of the working class to do away with
capitalism. The army of production must be organized, not only for
the everyday struggle with capitalists, but also to carry on production when capitalism shall have been overthrown. By organizing

industrially we are forming the structure of the new society within the shell of the old.

B. Arturo M. Giovannitti, "The Cage" (1913)

ALTHOUGH the I.W.W. mainly attracted western miners, farm laborers, and lumberjacks, it sought a broader base among eastern factory workers. The AFL's neglect of unskilled workers, especially immigrant workers from southern and eastern Europe, gave the I.W.W. its opportunity. In January 1912, several thousand textile workers in Lawrence, Massachusetts—chiefly Italian operatives—struck their mills after the mill owners cut wages across the board. The Textile Workers Union (AFL) and the city Central Labor Union refused to sanction or support the strike. Consequently, the I.W.W. sent its own organizers into the town. The Lawrence strike produced considerable violence, largely provoked and perpetrated by company-hired thugs, the police, and the militia. At one point, the strikers stormed a factory building and smashed windows and some machinery. On a different occasion, the militia fired into a crowd, wounding several and killing a young woman worker. Although there was no question about who fired the fatal shots, the local authorities arrested on murder charges three of the Wobbly leaders—Joseph Caruso, Joe Ettor, and Arturo Giovannitti.

Arturo Giovannitti (1883–1962) was born in Abruzzi, Italy, the son of a physician and chemist who gave him the opportunity for a liberal education in the public schools. He emigrated to the United States in 1901 and shortly afterward entered Union Theological Seminary in New York to study for the Presbyterian ministry. Although he never graduated, he practiced his "trade" in several cities before contact with the conditions of the poor drove him into socialism. Giovannitti, Ettor, and Caruso were imprisoned for seven months before their case came to trial. The trial lasted two more months, culminating in their exoneration. Giovannitti wrote "The Cage" in a single night, inspired by a huge demonstration in Lawrence protesting his imprisonment.

The editorial comments of the Atlantic Monthly, which printed "The Cage" in March 1913, are also worth quoting at least in part. "We are not prepared to debate the question whether Syndicalism has a soul," the editors wrote, "but if it has, 'The Cage' gives a picture of it. The philosophy of the poem sounds harshly materialistic, yet we must not forget that to the very poor, bread, bed, and sunshine may suggest something very different from materialism. They are helps—almost essential helps—to spiritual freedom. . . . But even if the poem offers no suggestion of some evolution toward an idealism still to come, if sunshine and a chance to feel its warmth are really all these revolutionists desire, then to be shut away from it is to them at least an utter calamity." Having made this condescending bow toward objectivity and sympathy, (reminiscent in style of Bishop Lawrence's "Relationship of Wealth to Morals" in Document 2) the Atlantic editors concluded with a rejection of Giovannitti's view of law and justice: "It was the law which freed Giovannitti. This law, read by 'dead men' out of 'dead books,' had in it the spark of the eternal life of justice. The logic of facts is against the poet's repudiation of the past. So thinks the conservative, and rightly." (June 1913, pp. 853–854). The reader is left to wonder if "the logic of facts" would read the same to the editors if it were they who were freed by a law which had also imprisoned them for nine months on such extraordinary charges.

SOURCE: Document B: Arturo M. Giovannitti, "The Cage," The Atlantic Monthly (March 1913). Reprinted by permission of The Atlantic Monthly.

Salem Jail, Sunday, October 20, 1912

I

In the middle of the great greenish room stood the green iron cage.

All was old and cold and mournful, ancient with the double antiquity of heart and brain in the great greenish room.

Old and hoary was the man who sat upon the faldstool, upon the fireless and godless altar.

Old were the tomes that mouldered behind him on the dusty shelves.

Old was the painting of an old man that hung above him.

Old the man upon his left, who awoke with his cracked voice the dead echoes of dead centuries; old the man upon his right who wielded a wand; and old all those who spoke to him and listened to him before and around the green iron cage.

Old were the words they spoke, and their faces were drawn and white and lifeless, without expression or solemnity; like the ikons of old cathedrals.

For of naught they knew, but of what was written in the old yellow books. And all the joys and pains and loves and hatreds and furies and labors and strifes of man, all the fierce and divine passions that battle and rage in the heart of man, never entered into the great greenish room but to sit in the green iron cage.

Senility, dullness and dissolution were all around the green iron
cage, and nothing was new and young and alive in the great
room, except the three men who were in the cage.

II

Throbbed and thundered and clamored and roared outside of the
great greenish room the terrible whirl of life, and most pleasant was the hymn of its mighty polyphony to the listening ears
of the gods.

Whirred the wheels of the puissant machines, rattled and clanked
the chains of the giant cranes, crashed the falling rocks; the
riveters crepitated; and glad and sonorous was the rhythm of
the bouncing hammers upon the loud-throated anvils.

Like the chests of wrathfully toiling Titans, heaved and sniffed and
panted the sweaty boilers, like the hissing of dragons sibilated
the white jets of steam, and the sirens of the workshops
shrieked like angry hawks, flapping above the crags of a dark
and fathomless chasm.

The files screeched and the trains thundered, the wires hummed,
the dynamos buzzed, the fires crackled; and like a thunderclap
from the Cyclopean forge roared the blasts of the mines.

Wonderful and fierce was the mighty symphony of the world, as
the terrible voices of metal and fire and water cried out into
the listening ears of the gods the furious song of human toil.

Out of the chaos of sound, welded in the unison of one will to sing,
rose clear and nimble the divine accord of the hymn:—

> Out of the cañons of the mountains,
>   Out of the whirlpools of the lakes,
> Out of the entrails of the earth,
>   Out of the yawning gorges of hell,
> From the land and the sea and the sky,
>   From wherever comes bread and wealth and joy,

And from the peaceful abodes of men, rose majestic and fierce,
louder than the roar of the volcano and the bellow of the
typhoon, the anthem of human labor to the fatherly justice of
the Sun.

But in the great greenish room there was nothing but the silence of
dead centuries and of ears that listen no more; and none heard

the mighty call of life that roared outside, save the three men who were in the cage.

III

All the good smells, the wholesome smells, the healthy smells of life and labor were outside the great room.

The smell of rain upon the grass and of the flowers consumed by their love for the stars.

The heavy smell of smoke that coiled out of myriads of chimneys of ships and factories and homes.

The dry smell of sawdust and the salty smell of the iron filings.

The odor of magazines and granaries and warehouses, the kingly smell of argosies and the rich scent of market-places, so dear to the women of the race.

The smell of new cloth and new linen, the smell of soap and water and the smell of newly printed paper.

The smell of grains and hay and the smell of stables, the warm smell of cattle and sheep that Virgil loved.

The smell of milk and wine and plants and metals,

And all the good odors of the earth and of the sea and of the sky, and the fragrance of fresh bread, sweetest aroma of the world, and the smell of human sweat, most holy incense to the divine nostrils of the gods, and all the olympian perfumes of the heart and the brain and the passions of men, were outside of the great greenish room.

But within the old room there was nothing but the smell of old books and the dust of things decayed, and the suffocated exhalation of old graves, and the ashen odor of dissolution and death.

Yet all the sweetness of all the wholesome odors of the world outside were redolent in the breath of the three men in the cage.

IV

Like crippled eagles fallen were the three men in the cage, and like little children who look into a well to behold the sky were the men that looked down upon them.

No more would they rise to their lofty eyries, no more would they soar above the snow-capped mountains—yet, tho' their pinions were broken, nothing could dim the fierce glow of their eyes, which knew all the altitudes of heaven.

Strange it was to behold the men in the cage while life clamored outside, and strange it seemed to them that they should be there because of what dead men had written in old books.

So of naught did they think but of the old books and the green cage.

Thought they: All things are born, grow, decay, and die and are forgotten.

Surely all that is in this great room will pass away. But what will endure the longer, the folly that was written into the old books or the madness that was beaten into the bands of this cage?

Which of these two powers has enthralled us, the thought of dead men who wrote the old books, or the labor of living men who have wrought this cage?

Long and intently they thought, but they found no answer.

v

But one of the three men in the cage, whose soul was tormented by the fiercest fire of hell, which is the yearning after the Supreme Truth, spoke and said unto his comrades:—

'Aye, brothers, all things die and pass away, yet nothing is truly and forever dead until each one of the living has thrown a regretless handful of soil into its grave.

'Many a book has been written since these old books were written, and many a proverb of the sage has become the jest of the fool, yet this cage still stands as it stood for numberless ages.

'What is it then that made it of metal more enduring than the printed word?

'Which is its power to hold us here?

'Brothers, it is the things we love that enslave us.

'Brothers, it is the things we yearn for that subdue us.

'Brothers, it is not hatred for the things that are, but love for the things that are to be, that makes us slaves.

'And what man is more apt to become a thrall, brothers, and to be locked in a green iron cage, than he who yearns the most for the Supreme of the things that are to be—he who most craves for Freedom?

'And what subtle and malignant power save this love of loves could be in the metal of this cage that it is so mad to imprison us?'

So spoke one of the men to the other two, and then out of the silence of the æons spoke into his tormented soul the metallic soul of the cage.

VI

'Iron, the twin brother of fire, the first born out of the matrix of the earth, the witness everlasting to the glory of thy labor, am I, O Man!

'Not for this was I meant, O Man! Not to imprison thee, but to set thee free and sustain thee in thy strife and in thy toil.

'I was to lift the pillars of thy Temple higher than the mountains;

'I was to lower the foundations of thy house deeper than the abysmal sea;

'I was to break down and bore through all the barriers of the world to open the way to thy triumphal chariot.

'All the treasures and all the bounties of the earth was I to give as an offering into thy hands, and all its forces and powers to bring chained like crouching dogs at thy feet.

'Hadst thou not sinned against the nobility of my nature and my destiny, hadst thou not humiliated me, an almighty warrior, to become the lackey of gold, I would never have risen against thee and enthralled thee, O Man!

'While I was hoe and ploughshare and sword and axe and scythe and hammer, I was the first artificer of thy happiness; but the day I was beaten into the first lock and the first key, I became fetters and chains to thy hands and thy feet, O Man!

'My curse is thy curse, O Man! and even if thou shouldst pass out of the wicket of this cage, never shalt thou be free until thou returnest me to the joy of labor.

'O Man! bring me back into the old smithy, purify me again with the holy fire of the forge, lay me again on the mother breast of the anvil, beat me again with the old honest hammer—O Man! remould me with thy wonderful hands into an instrument of thy toil,

'Remake of me the sword of thy justice,
Remake of me the tripod of thy worship,

Remake of me the sickle for thy grain,
   Remake of me the oven for thy bread,
And the andirons for thy peaceful hearth, O Man!
   And the trestles for the bed of thy love, O Man!
And the frame of thy joyous lyre, O Man!'

VII

Thus spake to one of the three men, out of the silence of centuries,
the metallic soul of the cage.

And he listened unto its voice, and while it was still ringing in his
soul,—which was tormented with the fiercest fire of hell,
which is the yearning after the Supreme Truth (Is it Death? Is
it Love?),—there arose one man in the silent assembly of old
men that were around the iron cage.

And that man was the most hoary of all, and most bent and worn
and crushed was he under the heavy weight of the great
burden he bore without pride and without joy.

He arose, and addressing himself—I know not whether to the old
man that sat on the black throne, or to the old books that
were mouldering behind him, or to the picture that hung
above him—he said (and dreary as a wind that moans through
the crosses of an old graveyard was his voice):—

'I will prove to you that these three men in the cage are criminals
and murderers and that they ought to be put to death.'

Love, it was then that I heard for the first time the creak of the
moth that was eating the old painting and the old books, and
the worm that was gnawing the old bench, and it was then
that I saw that all the old men around the great greenish room
were dead.

They were dead like the old man in the old painting, save that they
still read the old books he could read no more, and still spoke
and heard the old words he could speak and hear no more, and
still passed the judgment of the dead, which he no more could
pass, upon the mighty life of the world outside that throbbed
and thundered and clamored and roared the wonderful
anthem of Labor to the fatherly justice of the Sun.

VI

The Race Question
and the Immigrant Problem

22. Plessy v. Ferguson

Plessy v. Ferguson (1896) is the landmark Supreme Court decision that established in American law the "separate but equal" doctrine as the principle on which American society might justify differential treatment of its citizens according to race. The decision came in the midst of a decade in which white Americans dramatically overhauled official policy on the American Negro's place in the society. With the willing acquiescence of most northern whites of all classes, the southern states completed the reversal of post-Civil War Reconstruction by disfranchising their black citizens and driving them from whatever vantage points they might have gained by that time in the competition for social and economic opportunities. Thirteen years earlier, the Court had already given impetus to such a development when it voided the Federal Civil Rights Act of 1875, which had forbidden racial discrimination in the operation of inns, conveyances, amusements, and other public conveniences. In that case, as in the Plessy case, Justice Harlan vigorously dissented: "I cannot resist the view," he wrote in 1883, "that the substance and spirit of the recent amendments of the Court have been sacrificed by a subtle and ingenious verbal criticism. . . . It was perfectly well known that the great danger to the equal enjoyment by citizens of their rights, as citizens, was to be apprehended not altogether from unfriendly state legislation, but from the hostile action of corporations and individuals in the States. And it is presumed that it was intended by that section [of the Constitution] to clothe Congress with the power and authority to meet that danger."

The Court in 1883 was far from accepting the degree of legislative control over private corporations that Harlan's opinion suggested (whatever the Constitution might say about it, one might add). But in the Plessy case, the Court decided that, although it had ruled that the public could not force corporations to serve certain of the state's citizens of nonwhite racial backgrounds, the public could forbid those corporations to serve those citizens except in redundant accommodations at the corporation's own expense. Similarly, it was the very same Court for which Justice Brown spoke that in the 1890's was in the process of revolutionizing the constitutional concept of "due process" so as to sanctify the principle of "liberty of contract" against state corporation, railroad, and labor regulations. Yet, in the Plessy case, Brown found it possible to allude to antimiscegenation laws as examples of a perfectly "reasonable" exercise of the police power, even though, Brown conceded, such laws "may be said in a technical sense to interfere with the freedom of contract." Compare Harlan's comments in this case and in the "Rule of Reason" case of 1911 (Document 16 above) on "the tendency these days to enlarge the functions of the courts by means of judicial interference with the will of the people as expressed by the legislature."

The illogic of Justice Brown's opinion is manifest on many levels. It is perhaps best illustrated by his remarkable observation at the outset that "a statute which implies merely a legal distinction between the white and colored races . . . has no tendency to destroy the legal equality of the two races." There is a certain legalistic cogency to the point, but it defies practical application. In a few words, then, the Court's decision is demonstrably founded in its own assumptions about the inferiority of Negroes (a fact which, incidentally, points to the low cynicism in Brown's rejection of "the plaintiff's argument . . . that the enforced separation of the two races stamps the colored race with a badge of inferiority"). Yet, it is still more important to note that the decision was also founded on the manifest racial assumptions of most contemporary white Americans, North and South. The Court had no difficulty finding precedents in pre- and post-Civil War court decisions; indeed, the strongest precedent came from Massachusetts, the supposed center of abolitionism, in which case Brown could cite Chief Justice Shaw's argument in defense of segregated schools! Although much of Brown's logic is truly tortured and many precedents are squeezed from remote case analogues, what emerges plainly is that the Court was simply unwilling to flout the clearest popular sentiments of the day. For that reason, it refused to set in motion a broad re-examination of the principles on which innumerable existing discriminatory state and congressional statutes were based. It was to take another sixty years before the Court enjoyed a social mood that permitted such a re-examination.

SOURCE: Plessy v. Ferguson, 163 U.S. 537 (1896), reprinted from Charles Aiken (ed.), Leading Decisions of the Supreme Court (San Francisco, Calif.: Chandler Publishing Company, n.d.).

This was a petition for writs of prohibition and certiorari, originally filed in the Supreme Court of the State by Plessy, the plaintiff in error, against the Hon. John H. Ferguson, judge of the criminal District Court for the parish of Orleans, and setting forth in substance the following facts:

That petitioner was a citizen of the United States and a resident of the State of Louisiana, of mixed descent, in the proportion of seven eighths Caucasian and one eighth African blood; that the mixture of colored blood was not discernible in him, and that he was entitled to every recognition, right, privilege and immunity secured to the citizens of the United States of the white race by its Constitution and laws; that on June 7, 1892, he engaged and paid for a first class passage on the East Louisiana Railway from New Orleans to Covington, in the same State, and thereupon entered a passenger train, and took possession of a vacant seat in a coach where passengers of the white race were accommodated; that such railroad company was incorporated by the laws of Louisiana as a common carrier, and was not authorized to distinguish between citizens according to their race. But, notwithstanding this, petitioner was required by the conductor, under penalty of ejection from said train and imprisonment, to vacate said coach and occupy another seat in a coach assigned by said company for persons not of the white race, and for no other reason than that petitioner was of the colored race; that upon petitioner's refusal to comply with such order, he was, with the aid of a police officer, forcibly ejected from said coach and hurried off to and imprisoned in the parish jail of New Orleans, and there held to answer a charge made by such officer to the effect that he was guilty of having criminally violated an act of the General Assembly of the State, approved July 10, 1890, in such case made and provided. . . .

Mr. Justice Brown, After Stating the Case, Delivered the Opinion of the Court

This case turns upon the constitutionality of an act of the General Assembly of the State of Louisiana, passed in 1890, providing for separate railway carriages for the white and colored races. Acts 1890, No. 111, p. 152.

The first section of the statute enacts "that all railway companies carrying passengers in their coaches in this State, shall provide equal but separate accommodations for the white, and colored races, by providing two or more passenger coaches for each passenger train, or by dividing the passenger coaches by a partition so as to secure separate accommodations: *Provided,* That this section shall not be construed to apply to street railroads. No person or persons, shall be admitted to occupy seats in coaches, other than, the ones, assigned, to them on account of the race they belong to."

By the second section it was enacted "that the officers of such passenger trains shall have power and are hereby required to assign each passenger to the coach or compartment used for the race to which such passenger belongs; any passenger insisting on going into a coach or compartment to which by race he does not belong, shall be liable to a fine of twenty-five dollars, or in lieu thereof to imprisonment for a period of not more than twenty days in the parish prison, and any officer of any railroad insisting on assigning a passenger to a coach or compartment other than the one set aside for the race to which said passenger belongs, shall be liable to a fine of twenty-five dollars, or in lieu thereof to imprisonment for a period of not more than twenty days in the parish prison; and should any passenger refuse to occupy the coach or compartment to which he or she is assigned by the officer of such railway, said officer shall have power to refuse to carry such passenger on his train, and for such refusal neither he nor the railway company which he represents shall be liable for damages in any of the courts of this State."

The third section provides penalties for the refusal or neglect of the officers, directors, conductors and employés of railway companies to comply with the act, with a proviso that "nothing in this act shall be construed as applying to nurses attending children of the other race." The fourth section is immaterial. . . .

The constitutionality of this act is attacked upon the ground that it conflicts both with the Thirteenth Amendment of the Constitution, abolishing slavery, and the Fourteenth Amendment, which prohibits certain restrictive legislation on the part of the States.

1. That it does not conflict with the Thirteenth Amendment, which abolished slavery and involuntary servitude, except as a punishment for crime, is too clear for argument. Slavery implies involuntary servitude—a state of bondage; the ownership of mankind as a chattel, or at least the control of the labor and services of one man for the benefit of another, and the absence of a legal right to the disposal of his own person, property and services. This

amendment was said in the *Slaughter-house cases*, 16 Wall. 36, to have been intended primarily to abolish slavery, as it had been previously known in this country, and that it equally forbade Mexican peonage or the Chinese coolie trade, when they amounted to slavery or involuntary servitude, and that the use of the word "servitude" was intended to prohibit the use of all forms of involuntary slavery, of whatever class or name. . . .

So, too, in the *Civil Rights cases*, 109 U.S. 3, 24, it was said that the act of a mere individual, the owner of an inn, a public conveyance or place of amusement, refusing accommodations to colored people, cannot be justly regarded as imposing any badge of slavery or servitude upon the applicant, but only as involving an ordinary civil injury, properly cognizable by the laws of the State, and presumably subject to redress by those laws until the contrary appears. "It would be running the slavery argument into the ground," said Mr. Justice Bradley, "to make it apply to every act of discrimination which a person may see fit to make as to the guests he will entertain, or as to the people he will take into his coach or cab or car, or admit to his concert or theatre, or deal with in other matters of intercourse or business."

A statute which implies merely a legal distinction between the white and colored races—a distinction which is founded in the color of the two races, and which must always exist so long as white men are distinguished from the other race by color—has no tendency to destroy the legal equality of the two races, or reëstablish a state or involuntary servitude. Indeed, we do not understand that the Thirteenth Amendment is strenuously relied upon by the plaintiff in error in this connection.

2. By the Fourteenth Amendment, all persons born or naturalized in the United States, and subject to the jurisdiction thereof, are made citizens of the United States and of the State wherein they reside; and the States are forbidden from making or enforcing any law which shall abridge the privileges or immunities of citizens of the United States, or shall deprive any person of life, liberty or property without due process of law, or deny to any person within their jurisdiction the equal protection of the laws.

The proper construction of this amendment was first called to the attention of this court in the *Slaughter-house cases*, 16 Wall. 36, which involved, however, not a question of race, but one of exclusive privileges. The case did not call for any expression of opinion as to the exact rights it was intended to secure to the colored race, but it was said generally that its main purpose was to establish the citizenship of the negro; to give definitions of citizenship of the United States and of the States, and to protect from the hostile legislation of the States the privileges and immunities of citizens of the United States, as distinguished from those of citizens of the States.

The object of the amendment was undoubtedly to enforce the absolute equality of the two races before the law, but in the nature of things it could not have been intended to abolish distinctions based upon color, or to enforce social, as distinguished from political equality, or a commingling of the two races upon terms unsatisfactory to either. Laws permitting, and even requiring, their separation in places where they are liable to be brought into contact do not necessarily imply the inferiority of either race to the other, and have been generally, if not universally, recognized as within the competency of the state legislatures in the exercise of their police power. The most common instance of this is connected with the establishment of separate schools for white and colored children, which has been held to be a valid exercise of the legislative power even by courts of States where the political rights of the colored race have been longest and most earnestly enforced.

One of the earliest of these cases is that of *Roberts* v. *City of Boston*, 5 Cush. 198, in which the Supreme Judicial Court of Massachusetts held that the general school committee of Boston had power to make provision for the instruction of colored children in separate schools established exclusively for them, and to prohibit their attendance upon the other schools. "The great principle," said Chief Justice Shaw, p. 206, "advanced by the learned and eloquent advocate for the plaintiff," (Mr. Charles Sumner,) "is, that by the constitution and laws of Massachusetts, all persons without distinction of age or sex, birth or color, origin or condition, are equal before the law. . . . But, when this great principle comes to be applied to the actual and various conditions of persons in society, it will not warrant the assertion, that men and women are legally clothed with the same civil and political powers, and that children and adults are legally to have the same functions and be subject to the same treatment; but only that the rights of all, as they are settled and regulated by law, are equally entitled to the paternal consideration and protection of the law for their maintenance and security." It was held that the powers of the committee extended to the establishment of separate schools for children of different ages, sexes and colors, and that they might also establish special schools for poor and neglected children, who have become too old to attend the primary school, and yet have not acquired the rudiments of learning, to enable them to enter the ordinary schools. Similar laws have been enacted by Congress under its general power of legislation over the District of Columbia, Rev. Stat. D.C. §§ 281, 282, 283, 310, 319, as well as by the legislatures of many of the States, and have been generally, if not uniformly, sustained by the courts. *State* v. *McCann*, 21 Ohio St. 198; *Lehew* v. *Brummell*, 15 S.W. Rep. 765; *Ward* v. *Flood*, 48 California, 36; *Bertonneau* v. *School Directors*, 3 Woods, 177; *People* v. *Gallagher*, 93 N.Y. 438; *Cory* v. *Carter*, 48 Indiana, 327; *Dawson* v. *Lee*, 83 Kentucky, 49.

Laws forbidding the intermarriage of the two races may be said in a technical sense to interfere with the freedom of contract, and yet have been universally recognized as within the police power of the State. *State* v. *Gibson*, 36 Indiana, 389.

The distinction between laws interfering with the political equality of the negro and those requiring the separation of the two races in schools, threatres and railway carriages has been frequently drawn by this court. Thus in *Strauder* v. *West Virginia*, 100 U.S. 303, it was held that a law of West Virginia limiting to white male persons, 21 years of age and citizens of the State, the right to sit upon juries, was a discrimination which implied a legal inferiority in civil society, which lessened the security of the right of the colored race, and was a step toward reducing them to a condition of servility. Indeed, the right of a colored man that, in the selection of jurors to pass upon his life, liberty and property, there shall be no exclusion of his race, and no discrimination against them because of color, has been asserted in a number of cases. *Virginia* v. *Rives*, 100 U.S. 313; *Neal* v. *Delaware*, 103 U.S. 370; *Bush* v. *Kentucky*, 107 U.S. 110; *Gibson* v. *Mississippi*, 162 U.S. 565. So, where the laws of a particular locality or the charter of a particular railway corporation has provided that no person shall be excluded from the cars on account of color, we have held that this meant that persons of color should travel in the same car as white ones, and that the enactment was not satisfied by the company's providing cars assigned exclusively to people of color, though they were as good as those which they assigned exclusively to white persons. *Railroad Company v. Brown*, 17 Wall. 445.

Upon the other hand, where a statute of Louisiana required those engaged in the transportation of passengers among the States to give to all persons travelling within that State, upon vessels employed in that business, equal rights and privileges in all parts of the vessel, without distinction on account of race or color, and subjected to an action for damages the owner of such a vessel, who excluded colored passengers on account of their color from the cabin set aside by him for the use of whites, it was held to be so far as it applied to interstate commerce, unconstitutional and void. *Hall* v. *De Cuir*, 95 U.S. 485. The court in this case, however, expressly disclaimed that it had anything whatever to do with the statute as a regulation of internal commerce, or affecting anything else than commerce among the States.

In the *Civil Rights case*, 109 U.S. 3, it was held that an act of Congress, entitling all persons within the jurisdiction of the United States to the full and equal enjoyment of the accommodations, advantages, facilities and privileges of inns, public conveyances, on land or water, theatres and other places of public amusement, and made applicable to citizens of every race and color, regardless of any previous condition of servitude, was unconstitutional and void, upon the ground that the Fourteenth Amendment was prohibitory upon the States only, and the legislation authorized to be adopted by Congress for enforcing it was not direct legislation on matters respecting which the States were prohibited from making or enforcing certain laws, or doing certain acts, but was corrective legislation, such as might be necessary or proper for counteracting and redressing the effect of such laws or acts. In delivering the opinion of the court Mr. Justice Bradley observed that the Fourteenth Amendment "does not invest Congress with power to legislate upon subjects that are within the domain of state legislation; but to provide modes of relief against state legislation, or state action, of the kind referred to. It does not authorize Congress to create a code of municipal law for the regulation of private rights; but to provide modes of redress against the operation of state laws, and the action of state officers, executive or judicial, when these are subversive of the fundamental rights specified in the amendment. Positive rights and privileges are undoubtedly secured by the Fourteenth Amendment; but they are secured by way of prohibition against state laws and state proceedings affecting those rights and privileges, and by power given to Congress to legislate for the purpose of carrying such prohibition into effect; and such legislation must necessarily be predicated upon such supposed state laws or state proceedings, and be directed to the correction of their operation and effect." . . . In the present case no question of interference with interstate commerce can possibly arise, since the East Louisiana Railway appears to have been purely a local line, with both its termini within the State of Louisiana. Similar statutes for the separation of the two races upon public conveyances were held to be constitutional in *West Chester &c. Railroad v. Miles*, 55 Penn. St. 209; *Day v. Owen*, 5 Michigan, 520; *Chicago &c. Railway v. Williams*, 55 Illinois, 185; *Chesapeake &c. Railroad v. Wells*, 85 Tennessee, 613; *Memphis &c. Railroad v. Benson*, 85 Tennessee, 627; *The Sue*, 22 Fed. Rep. 843; *Logwood v. Memphis &c. Railroad*, 23 Fed. Rep. 318; *McGuinn v. Forbes*, 37 Fed. Rep. 639; *People v. King*, 18 N.E. Rep. 245; *Houck v. South Pac. Railway*, 38 Fed. Rep. 226; *Heard v. Georgia Railroad Co.*, 3 Int. Com. Com'n, 111; *S.C.*, 1 Ibid. 428.

It is claimed by the plaintiff in error that, in any mixed community, the reputation of belonging to the dominant race, in this instance the white race, is *property*, in the same sense that a right of action, or of inheritance, is property. Conceding this to be so, for the purposes of this case, we are unable to see how this statute deprives him of, or in any way affects his right to, such property. If he be a white man and assigned to a color coach, he may have his action for damages against the company for being deprived of his so called property. Upon the other hand, if he be a colored man and be so assigned, he has been deprived of no property, since he is not lawfully entitled to the reputation of being a white man.

In this connection, it is also suggested by the learned counsel for the plaintiff in error that the same argument that will justify the state legislature in requiring railways to provide separate accommodations for the two races will also authorize them to require separate cars to be provided for people whose hair is of a certain color, or who are aliens, or who belong to certain nationalities, or to enact laws requiring colored people to walk upon one side of the street, and white people upon the other, or requiring white men's houses to be painted white, and colored men's black, or their vehicles or business signs to be of different colors, upon the theory that one side of the street is as good as the other, or that a house or vehicle of one color is as good as one of another color. The reply to all this is that every exercise of the police power must be reasonable, and extend only to such laws as are enacted in good faith for the promotion for the public good, and not for the annoyance or oppression of a particular class. . . .

So far, then, as a conflict with the Fourteenth Amendment is concerned, the case reduces itself to the question whether the statute of Louisiana is a reasonable regulation, and with respect to this there must necessarily be a large discretion on the part of the legislature. In determining the question of reasonableness it is at liberty to act with reference to the established usages, customs and traditions of the people, and with a view to the promotion of their comfort, and the preservation of the public peace and good order. Gauged by this standard, we cannot say that a law which authorizes or even requires the separation of the two races in public conveyances is unreasonable, or more obnoxious to the Fourteenth Amendment than the acts of Congress requiring separate schools for colored children in the District of Columbia, the constitutionality of which does not seem to have been questioned, or the corresponding acts of state legislatures.

We consider the underlying fallacy of the plaintiff's argument to consist in the assumption that the enforced separation of the two races stamps the colored race with a badge of inferiority. If this be so, it is not by reason of anything found in the act, but solely because the colored race chooses to put that construction upon it. The argument necessarily assumes that if, as has been more than once the case, and is not unlikely to be so again, the colored race should become the dominant power in the state legislature, and should enact a law in precisely similar terms, it would thereby relegate the white race to an inferior position. We imagine that the white race, at least, would not acquiesce in this assumption. The argument also assumes that social prejudices may be overcome by legislation, and that equal rights cannot be secured to the negro except by an enforced commingling of the two races. We cannot accept this proposition. If the two races are to meet upon terms of social equality, it must be the result of natural affinities, a mutual appreciation of each other's merits and a voluntary consent of individuals. As was said by the Court of Appeals of New York in *People* v. *Gallagher*, 93 N.Y. 438, 448, "this end can neither be accomplished nor promoted by laws which conflict with the general sentiment of the community upon whom they are designed to operate. When the government, therefore, has secured to each of its citizens equal rights before the law and equal opportunities for improvement and progress, it has accomplished the end for which it was organized and performed all of the functions respecting social advantages with which it is endowed." Legislation is powerless to eradicate racial instincts or to abolish distinctions based upon physical differences, and the attempt to do so can only result in accentuating the difficulties of the present situation. If the civil and political rights of both races be equal one cannot be inferior to the other civilly or politically. If one race be inferior to the other socially, the Constitution of the United States cannot put them upon the same plane.

It is true that the question of the proportion of colored blood necessary to constitute a colored person, as distinguished from a white person, is one upon which there is a difference of opinion in the different States, some holding that any visible admixture of black blood stamps the person as belonging to the colored race, (State v. Chavers, 5 Jones, [N.C.] 1, p. 11); others that it depends upon the preponderance of blood, (Gray v. State, 4 Ohio, 354; Monroe v. Collins, 17 Ohio St. 665); and still others that the predominance of white blood must only be in the proportion of three fourths. (People v. Dean, 14 Michigan, 406; Jones v. Commonwealth, 80 Virginia, 538.) But these are questions to be determined under the laws of each State and are not properly put in issue in this case. Under the allegations of his petition it may undoubtedly become a question of importance whether, under the laws of Louisiana, the petitioner belongs to the white or colored race.

The judgment of the court below is, therefore,   *Affirmed.*

Mr. Justice Harlan Dissenting

While there may be in Louisiana persons of different races who are not citizens of the United States, the words in the act, "white and colored races," necessarily include all citizens of the United States of both races residing in that State. So that we have before us a state enactment that compels, under penalties, the separation of the two races in railroad passenger coaches, and makes it a crime for a citizen of either race to enter a coach that has been assigned to citizens of the other race.

Thus the State regulates the use of a public highway by citizens of the United States solely upon the basis of race.

However apparent the injustice of such legislation may be, we have only to consider whether it is consistent with the Constitution of the United States.

That a railroad is a public highway, and that the corporation which owns or operates it is in the exercise of public functions, is not, at this day, to be disputed. . . .

In respect of civil rights, common to all citizens, the Constitution of the United States does not, I think, permit any public authority to know the race of those entitled to be protected in the enjoyment of such rights. Every true man has pride of race, and under appropriate circumstances when the rights of others, his equals before the law, are not to be affected, it is his privilege to express such pride and to take such action based upon it as to him seems proper. But I deny that any legislative body or judicial tribunal may have regard to the race of citizens when the civil rights of those citizens are involved. Indeed, such legislation, as that here in question, is inconsistent not only with that equality of rights which pertains to citizenship, National and State, but with the personal liberty enjoyed by every one within the United States.

The Thirteenth Amendment does not permit the withholding or the deprivation of any right necessarily inhering in freedom. It not only struck down the institution of slavery as previously existing in the United States, but it prevents the imposition of any burdens or disabilities that constitute badges of slavery or servitude. It decreed universal civil freedom in this country. This court has so adjudged. But that amendment having been found inadequate to the protection of the rights of those who had been in slavery, it was followed by the Fourteenth Amendment, which added greatly to the dignity and glory of American citizenship, and to the security of personal liberty, by declaring that "all persons born or naturalized in the United States, and subject to the jurisdiction thereof, are citizens of the United States and of the State wherein they reside," and that "no State shall make or enforce any law which shall abridge the privileges or immunities of citizens of the United States; nor shall any State deprive any person of life, liberty or property without due process of law, nor deny to any person within its jurisdiction the equal protection of the laws." These two amendments, if enforced according to their true intent and meaning, will protect all the civil rights that pertain to freedom and citizenship. Finally, and to the end that no citizen should be denied, on account of his race, the privilege of participating in the political control of his country, it was declared by the Fifteenth Amendment that "the right of citizens of the United States to vote shall not be denied or abridged by the United States or by any State on account of race, color or previous conditions of servitude."

These notable additions to the fundamental law were welcomed by the friends of liberty throughout the world. They removed the race line from our governmental systems. They had, as this court has said, a common purpose, namely, to secure "to a race recently emancipated, a race that through many generations have been held in slavery, all the civil rights that the superior race enjoy." They declared, in legal effect, this court has further said, "that the law in the States shall be the same for the black as for the white; that all persons, whether colored or white, shall stand equal before the laws of the States, and, in regard to the colored race, for whose protection the amendment was primarily designed, that no discrimination shall be made against them by law because of their color." We also said: "The words of the amendment, it is true, are prohibitory, but they contain a necessary implication of a positive immunity, or right, most valuable to the colored race—the right to exemption from unfriendly legislation against them distinctively as colored— exemption from legal discriminations, implying inferiority in civil society, lessening the security of their enjoyment of the rights which others enjoy, and discriminations which are steps towards reducing them to the condition of a subject race." It was, consequently, adjudged that a state law that excluded citizens of the colored race from juries, because of their race and however well qualified in other respects to discharge the duties of jurymen, was repugnant to the Fourteenth Amendment. *Strauder v. West Virginia*, 100 U.S. 303, 306, 307; *Virginia v. Rives*, 100 U.S. 313; *Ex parte Virginia*, 100 U.S. 339; *Neal v. Delaware*, 103 U.S. 370, 386; *Bush v. Kentucky*, 107 U.S. 110, 116. At the present term, referring to the previous adjudications, this court declared that "underlying all of those decisions is the principle that the Constitution of the United States, in its present form, forbids, so far as civil and political rights are concerned, discrimination by the General Government or the States against any citizen because of his race. All citizens are equal before the law." *Gibson v. Mississippi*, 162 U.S. 565.

The decisions referred to show the scope of the recent amendments of the Constitution. They also show that it is not within the power of a State to prohibit colored citizens, because of their race, from participating as jurors in the administration of justice.

It was said in argument that the statute of Louisiana does not discriminate against either race, but prescribes a rule applicable alike to white and colored citizens. But this argument does not meet the difficulty. Every one knows that the statute in question had its origin in the purpose, not so much to exclude white persons from railroad cars occupied by blacks, as to exclude colored people from coaches occupied by or assigned to white persons. Railroad corporations of Louisiana did not make discrimination among whites in the matter of accommodation for travellers. The thing to accomplish was, under the guise of giving equal accommodation for whites and blacks, to compel the latter to keep to themselves while travelling in railroad passenger coaches. No one would be so wanting in candor as to assert the contrary. The fundamental objection, therefore, to the statute is that it interferes with the personal freedom of citizens. "Personal liberty," it has been well said, "consists in the power of locomotion, of changing situation, or removing one's person to whatsoever places one's own inclination may direct, without imprisonment or restraint, unless by due course of law." 1 Bl. Com. *134. If a white man and a black man choose to occupy the same public conveyance on a public highway, it is their right to do so, and no government, proceeding alone on grounds of race, can prevent it without infringing the personal liberty of each.

It is one thing for railroad carriers to furnish, or to be required by law to furnish, equal accommodations for all whom they are under a legal duty to carry. It is quite another thing for government to forbid citizens of the white and black races from travelling in the same public conveyance, and to punish officers of railroad companies for permitting persons of the two races to occupy the same passenger coach. If a State can prescribe, as a rule of civil conduct, that whites and blacks shall not travel as passengers in the same railroad coach, why may it not so regulate the use of the streets of its cities and towns as to compel white citizens to keep on one side of a street and black citizens to keep on the other? Why may it not, upon like grounds, punish whites and blacks who ride together in street cars or in open vehicles on a public road or street? Why may it not require sheriffs to assign whites to one side of a court-room and blacks to the other? And why may it not also prohibit the commingling of the two races in the galleries of legislative halls or in public assemblages convened for the consideration of the political questions of the day? Further, if this statute of Louisiana is consistent with the personal liberty of citizens, why may not the State require the separation in railroad coaches of native and naturalized citizens of the United States, or of Protestants and Roman Catholics?

The answer given at the argument to these questions was that regulations of the kind they suggest would be unreasonable, and could not, therefore, stand before the law. Is it meant that the determination of questions of legislative power depends upon the inquiry whether the statute whose validity is questioned is, in the judgment of the courts, a reasonable one, taking all the circumstances into consideration? A statute may be unreasonable merely because a sound public policy forbade its enactment. But I do not understand that the courts have anything to do with the policy or expediency of legislation. A statute may be valid, and yet, upon grounds of public policy, may well be characterized as unreasonable. Mr. Sedgwick correctly states the rule when he says that the legislative intention being clearly ascertained, "the courts have no other duty to perform than to execute the legislative will, without any regard to their views as to the wisdom or justice of the particular enactment." Stat. & Const. Constr. 324. There is a dangerous tendency in these latter days to enlarge the functions of the courts, by means of judicial interference with the will of the people as expressed by the legislature. Our institutions have the distinguishing characteristic that the three departments of government are coördinate and separate. Each must keep within the limits defined by the Constitution. And the courts best discharge their duty by executing the will of the law-making power, constitutionally expressed, leaving the results of legislation to be dealt with by the people through their representatives. Statutes must always have a reasonable construction. Sometimes they are to be construed strictly; sometimes, liberally, in order to carry out the legislative will. But however construed, the intent of the legislature is to be respected, if the particular statute in question is valid, although the courts, looking at the public interests, may conceive the statute to be both unreasonable and impolitic. If the power exists to enact a statute, that ends the matter so far as the courts are concerned. The adjudged cases in which statutes have been held to be void, because unreasonable, are those in which the means employed by the legislature were not at all germane to the end to which the legislature was competent.

The white race deems itself to be the dominant race in this country. And so it is, in prestige, in achievements, in education, in wealth and in power. So, I doubt not, it will continue to be for all time, if it remains true to its great heritage and holds fast to the principles of constitutional liberty. But in view of the Constitution, in the eye of the law, there is in this country no superior, dominant, ruling class of citizens. There is no caste here. Our Constitution is color-blind, and neither knows nor tolerates classes among citizens. In respect of civil rights, all citizens are equal before the law. The humblest is the peer of the most powerful. The law regards man as man, and takes no account of his surroundings or of his color when his civil rights as guaranteed by the supreme law of the land are involved. It is, therefore, to be regretted that this high tribunal, the final expositor of the fundamental law of the land, has reached the conclusion that it is competent for a State to regulate the enjoyment by citizens of their civil rights solely upon the basis of race. . . . The recent amendments of the Constitution, it was supposed, had eradicated these principles from our institutions. But it seems that we have yet, in some of the States, a dominant race—a superior class of citizens, which assumes to regulate the enjoyment of civil rights, common to all citizens, upon the basis of race. The present decision, it may well be apprehended, will not only stimulate aggressions, more or less brutal and irritating, upon the admitted rights of colored citizens, but will encourage the belief that it is possible, by means of state enactments, to defeat the beneficent purposes which the people of the United States had in view when they adopted the recent amendments of the Constitution, by one of which the blacks of this country were made citizens of the United States and of the States in which they respectively reside, and whose privileges and immunities, as citizens, the States are forbidden to abridge. Sixty millions of whites are in no danger from the presence here of eight millions of blacks. The destinies of the two races, in this country, are indissolubly linked together, and the interests of both require that the common government of all shall not permit the seeds of race hate to be planted under the sanction of law. What can more certainly arouse race hate, what more certainly create and perpetuate a feeling of distrust between these races, than state enactments, which, in fact, proceed on the ground that colored citizens are so inferior and degraded that they cannot be allowed to sit in public coaches occupied by white citizens? That, as all will admit, is the real meaning of such legislation as was enacted in Louisiana. . . . This question is not met by the suggestion that social equality cannot exist between the white and black races in this country. That argument, if it can be properly regarded as one, is scarcely worthy of consideration; for social equality no more exists between two races when travelling in a passenger coach or a public highway than when members of the same races sit by each other in a street car or in the jury box, or stand or sit with each other in a political assembly, or when they use in common the streets of a city or town, or when they are in the same room for the purpose of having their names placed on the registry of voters, or when they approach the ballot-box in order to exercise the high privilege of voting.

There is a race so different from our own that we do not permit those belonging to it to become citizens of the United States. Persons belonging to it are, with few exceptions, absolutely excluded from our country. I allude to the Chinese race. But by the statute in question, a Chinaman can ride in the same passenger coach with white citizens of the United States, while citizens of the black race in Louisiana, many of whom, perhaps, risked their lives for the preservation of the Union, who are entitled, by law, to participate in the political control of the State and nation, who are not excluded, by law or by reason of their race, from public stations of any kind, and who have all the legal rights that belong to white citizens, are yet declared to be criminals, liable to imprisonment, if they ride in a public coach occupied by citizens of the white race. . . .

The arbitrary separation of citizens, on the basis of race, while they are on a public highway, is a badge of servitude wholly inconsistent with the civil freedom and the equality before the law established by the Constitution. It cannot be justified upon any legal grounds.

If evils will result from the commingling of the two races upon public highways established for the benefit of all, they will be infinitely less than those that will surely come from state legislation regulating the enjoyment of civil rights upon the basis of race. We boast of the freedom enjoyed by our people above all other peoples. But it is difficult to reconcile that boast with a state of the law which, practically, puts the brand of servitude and degradation upon a large class of our fellow-citizens, our equals before the law. The thin disguise of "equal" accommodations for passengers in railroad coaches will not mislead any one, nor atone for the wrong this day done. . . .

May it not now be reasonably expected that astute men of the dominant race, who affect to be disturbed at the possibility that the integrity of the white race may be corrupted, or that its supremacy will be imperilled, by contact on public highways with black people, will endeavor to procure statutes requiring white and black jurors to be separated in the jury box by a "partition," and that, upon retiring from the court room to consult as to their verdict, such partition, if it be a moveable one, shall be taken to their consultation room, and set up in such way as to prevent black jurors from coming too close to their brother jurors of the white race. If the "partition" used in the court room happens to be stationary, provision could be made for screens with openings through which jurors of the two races could confer as to their verdict without coming into personal contact with each other. I cannot see but that, according to the principles this day announced, such state legislation, although conceived in hostility to, and enacted for the purpose of humiliating citizens of the United States of a particular race, would be held to be consistent with the Constitution.

I do not deem it necessary to review the decisions of state courts to which reference was made in argument. Some, and the most important, of them are wholly inapplicable, because rendered prior to the adoption of the last amendments of the Constitution, when colored people had very few rights which the dominant race felt obliged to respect. Others were made at a time when public opinion, in many localities, was dominated by the institution of slavery; when it would not have been safe to do justice to the black man; and when, so far as the rights of blacks were concerned, race prejudice was, practically, the supreme law of the land. Those decisions cannot be guides in the era introduced by the recent amendments of the supreme law, which established universal civil freedom, gave citizenship to all born or naturalized in the United States and residing here, obliterated the race line from our systems of governments, National and State, and placed our free institutions upon the broad and sure foundation of the equality of all men before the law.

23.   Booker T. Washington,
The Atlanta Exposition Address

BOOKER TALIAFERRO WASHINGTON (1856–1915) was born on an Alabama plantation, the son of a house slave and an unknown white man. For almost six years after emancipation, he worked with his brother and stepfather in the nearby coal and salt mines. He detested every minute of the dirt and drudgery, but most of all he hated the absence of any means of getting an education to lift himself out of his predicament. When he was fifteen, he welcomed the chance to leave the mines to work as a houseboy for the Yankee-born mine owner, General Lewis Ruffner. Mrs. Ruffner was a difficult employer, but there is little doubt that it was her compulsive New England ways that imbued Washington with his lifelong affinity for hard work and self-discipline. With Mrs. Ruffner's help, too, Washington made it to Hampton Institute in 1872, where he realized his dream of an education. In 1881, he became the first principal of Tuskegee Institute.

Until 1895, Washington's renown, such as it was, remained confined to his achievements at Tuskegee. It was the Atlanta address that thrust him into the position of leadership and controversy he was to know for the final twenty years of his life. The address's popularity, especially among white Americans, made Washington the "spokesman for his race." Plessy v. Ferguson was still a year away, but the wave of racial animosity which culminated in the complete repression of American black people had already taken on terrifying dimensions. There were few white men in the country, moreover, who had not grown to doubt the wisdom of granting the freedmen any political power at all. The speech highlighted the central tenets of the American gospel of self-help. It was bluntly accommodationist to prevailing white racial as well as economic views. Yet it also expressed Washington's deepest personal convictions about the way to individual success.

*Understandably, Negroes received Washington's speech with consider-
able skepticism and some hostility. For the burden of what he said
focused on black men's shortcomings—in particular their unrealistic
quest for classical education and "culture," their neglect of manual
trades, their emphasis on political matters, and their eagerness to blame
the white man for their low fortunes while they shunned the trades and
enterprise that might overcome their disadvantages. On the other hand,
the speech also won general approval among many black intellectuals
(conspicuously, one might note, W. E. B. Du Bois). In its context, it
bespoke a not unrealistic answer to the problems faced by up to 10 million black men deprived of education, of many essential social amenities,
and most recently of any political leverage.*

*Having established the position and having been rewarded with some
of the fruits of power from the country's political leaders, Washington
remained the defender—and became the symbol—of black accommodation and of self-help. Within a decade, however, the weaknesses of some
of Washington's premises—especially his view that American Negroes
could gain acceptance among whites through assiduous self-discipline
and economic achievement—became too plain to ignore. To more militant Negroes of his own and later generations, "Bookerite" came to
signify an "Uncle Tom."*

SOURCE: Woodson Carter Goodwin (ed.), *Negro Orators and Their
Orations* (Washington, D.C.: Associated Publishers, 1925), pp.
580–583.

An Address Delivered at the Opening of the Cotton States' Exposition in Atlanta, Georgia, September, 1895

Mr. President and Gentlemen of the Board of Directors and
Citizens: One-third of the population of the South is of the Negro
race. No enterprise seeking the material, civil, or moral welfare of
this section can disregard this element of our population and reach
the highest success. I but convey to you, Mr. President and Directors, the sentiment of the masses of my race when I say that in
no way have the value and manhood of the American Negro been
more fittingly and generously recognized than by the managers of
this magnificent Exposition at every stage of its progress. It is a
recognition that will do more to cement the friendship of the two
races than any occurrence since the dawn of freedom.

Not only this, but the opportunity here afforded will awake
among us a new era of industrial progress. Ignorant and inexperienced, it is not strange that in the first years of our new life we

began at the top instead of at the bottom; that a seat in Congress or the State Legislature was more sought than real estate or industrial skill; that the political convention or stump speaking had more attractions than starting a dairy farm or truck garden.

A ship lost at sea for many days suddenly sighted a friendly vessel. From the mast of the unfortunate vessel was seen a signal. "Water, water; we die of thirst!" The answer from the friendly vessel at once came back: "Cast down your bucket where you are." A second time the signal, "Water, water; send us water!" ran up from the distressed vessel, and was answered: "Cast down your bucket where you are." The captain of the distressed vessel, at last heeding the injunction, cast down his bucket, and it came up full of fresh, sparkling water from the mouth of the Amazon River. To those of my race who depend upon bettering their condition in a foreign land, or who underestimate the importance of cultivating friendly relations with the Southern white man, who is his next door neighbor, I would say: "Cast down your bucket where you are"—cast it down in making friends in every manly way of the people of all races by whom we are surrounded.

Cast it down in agriculture, mechanics, in commerce, in domestic service, and in the professions. And in this connection it is well to bear in mind that whatever other sins the South may be called to bear, when it comes to business, pure and simple, it is in the South that the Negro is given a man's chance in the commercial world, and in nothing is this Exposition more eloquent than in emphasizing this chance. Our greatest danger is, that in the great leap from slavery to freedom we may overlook the fact that the masses of us are to live by the productions of our hands, and fail to keep in mind that we shall prosper in proportions as we learn to dignify and glorify common labor, and put brains and skill into the common occupations of life; shall prosper in proportion as we learn to draw the line between the superficial and the substantial, the ornamental gewgaws of life and the useful. No race can prosper till it learns that there is as much dignity in tilling a field as in writing a poem. It is at the bottom of life we must begin, and not at the top. Nor should we permit our grievances to overshadow our opportunities.

To those of the white race who look to the incoming of those of foreign birth and strange tongue and habits for the prosperity of the South, were I permitted I would repeat what I say to my own race, "Cast down your bucket where you are." Cast it down among the 8,000,000 Negroes whose habits you know, whose fidelity and love you have tested in days when to have proved treacherous meant the ruin of your firesides. Cast down your bucket among these people who have, without strikes and labor wars, tilled your fields, cleared your forests, builded your railroads and cities, and brought forth treasures from the bowels of the earth, and helped make possible this magnificent representation of the progress of the South. Casting down your bucket among my people, helping and encouraging them as you are doing on these grounds, and, with education of head, hand and heart, you will find that they will buy your surplus land, make blossom the waste places in your fields, and run your factories. While doing this, you can be sure in the future, as in the past, that you and your families will be surrounded by the most patient, faithful, law-abiding, and unresentful people that the world has seen. As we have proved our loyalty to you in the past, in nursing your children, watching by the sick bed of your mothers and fathers, and often following them with tear-dimmed eyes to their graves, so in the future, in our humble way, we shall stand by you with a devotion that no foreigner can approach, ready to lay down our lives, if need be, in defense of yours, interlacing our industrial, commercial, civil, and religious life with yours in a way that shall make the interests of both races one. In all things that are purely social we can be as separate as the fingers, yet one as the hand in all things essential to mutual progress.

There is no defense or security for any of us except in the higher intelligence and development of all. If anywhere there are efforts tending to curtail the fullest growth of the Negro, let these efforts be turned into stimulating, encouraging, and making him the most useful and intelligent citizen. Effort or means so invested will pay a thousand per cent interest. These efforts will be twice blessed— blessing him that gives and him that takes.

There is no escape through law of man or God from the in- evitable:

> The laws of changeless justice bind
> Oppressor with oppressed;
> And close as sin and suffering joined
> We march to fate abreast.

Nearly sixteen millions of hands will aid you in pulling the load upwards, or they will pull against you the load downwards. We shall constitute one third and more of the ignorance and crime of the South, or one-third its intelligence and progress; we shall contribute one-third to the business and industrial prosperity of the South, or we shall prove a veritable body of death, stagnating, depressing, retarding every effort to advance the body politic.

Gentlemen of the Exposition, as we present to you our humble effort at an exhibition of our progress, you must not expect overmuch. Starting thirty years ago with ownership here and there in a few quilts and pumpkins and chickens (gathered from miscellaneous sources), remember the path that has led from these to the invention and production of agricultural implements, buggies, steam engines, newspapers, books, statuary, carving, paintings, the management of drug stores and banks has not been trodden without contact with thorns and thistles. While we take pride in what we exhibit as a result of our independent efforts, we do not for a moment forget that our part in this exhibition would fall far short of your expectations but for the constant help that has come to our educational life, not only from the Southern States, but especially from Northern philanthropists, who have made their gifts a constant stream of blessing and encouragement.

The wisest among my race understand that the agitation of questions of social equality is the extremest folly, and that progress in the enjoyment of all the privileges that will come to us must be the result of severe and constant struggle rather than of artificial forcing. No race that has anything to contribute to the markets of the world is long in any degree ostracized. It is important and right that all privileges of the law be ours, but it is vastly more important that we be prepared for the exercise of those privileges. The opportunity to earn a dollar in a factory just now is worth infinitely more than the opportunity to spend a dollar in an opera house.

In conclusion, may I repeat that nothing in thirty years has given us more hope and encouragement, and drawn us so near to you of the white race, as this opportunity offered by the Exposition; and here bending, as it were, over the altar that represents the results of the struggles of your race and mine, both starting practically empty-handed three decades ago, I pledge that, in your effort to work out the great and intricate problem which God has laid at the doors of the South, you shall have at all times the patient, sympathetic help of my race; only let this be constantly in mind that, while from representations in these buildings of the products of field, of forest, of mine, of factory, letters, and art, much good will come, yet far above and beyond material benefits will be the higher good, that let us pray God will come, in a blotting out of sectional differences and racial animosities and suspicions, in a determination to administer absolute justice, in a willing obedience among all classes to the mandates of law. This, coupled with our material prosperity, will bring into our beloved South a new heaven and a new earth.

24.   W. E. B. Du Bois,
The Souls of Black Folk

WILLIAM EDWARD BURGHARDT DU BOIS has symbolized American black militancy quite as much as Washington has represented accommodation. Their personal backgrounds were equally divergent. Both were, in a sense, self-made men. Yet by comparison, life greeted Du Bois with sunny cordiality. He was born free, of free-born parents, in the still hopeful year of 1868 in the tranquil Berkshire town of Great Barrington, Massachusetts. His mother had descended from a manumitted slave whose freedom was granted for service in the Continental Army; it was he who began the family properties in Great Barrington. Du Bois's father had been born in Santo Domingo, descended from a line of seafarers; he settled early in New England, and though never remarkably prosperous he maintained his household according to smalltown middle-class standards.

Whereas Washington was born in the condition of oppression, Du Bois experienced the pain of discovering the oppressiveness of living "within the Veil." Education came easily to him, but it served as much to sensitize him to the injustices of racism as Washington's hard-won education had served to open opportunities for success. Washington had viewed Hampton Institute as the end of the rainbow; at Fisk, Du Bois tasted the bitter reminder of his difference from other people. Ultimately he earned a Ph.D. from Harvard, where President Eliot defended the presence of Negroes as "largely a question of the number of colored [students] to white." ("Absolutely lost in the mass of 5000 whites," Eliot observed. ". . . they have no influence of any sort for evil.")

These facts alone might sufficiently explain the two men's conflicting views: Washington had enjoyed a progress upward from slavery; to Du Bois life revealed only greater indignities. Yet, in 1895, Du Bois's principal reservation about Washington's Atlanta address concerned Washington's failure to explain how American black people could gain leadership if they neglected higher education as the Tuskegee educator had proposed. Until Du Bois's direct attack on Washington in the passage printed below, the two had been cordial. By that time, however, racial violence had done much to undermine Washington's optimistic arguments. The time was ripe for an alternative view of how to solve black men's difficulties in America. The Niagara Movement and the NAACP were both derived from Du Bois's proposals for organization and protest.

"Of the Passing of the First-Born" follows Du Bois's reply to Washington; it depicts briefly and sharply the bitterness already growing in Du Bois, although coupled with the still-vital hope of eventual assimilation. This hope ultimately flickered out. Du Bois died in Ghana in 1963.

SOURCE: W. E. B. Du Bois, *The Souls of Black Folk* (Chicago: 1903), pp. 42–54; 152–157.

Of Mr. Booker T. Washington
and Others

From birth till death enslaved; in word, in deed, unmanned!

. . . .

Hereditary bondsmen! Know ye not
Who would be free themselves must strike the blow?

BYRON

Easily the most striking thing in the history of the American Negro since 1876 is the ascendancy of Mr. Booker T. Washington. It began at the time when war memories and ideals were rapidly passing; a day of astonishing commercial development was dawning; a sense of doubt and hesitation overtook the freedmen's sons,—then it was that his leading began. Mr. Washington came, with a single definite programme, at the psychological moment when the nation was a little ashamed of having bestowed so much sentiment on Negroes, and was concentrating its energies on Dollars. His programme of industrial education, conciliation of the South, and submission and silence as to civil and political rights, was not wholly original; the Free Negroes from 1830 up to wartime had striven to build industrial schools, and the American Missionary Association had from the first taught various trades; and Price and others had sought a way of honorable alliance with the best of the Southerners. But Mr. Washington first indissolubly linked these things; he put enthusiasm, unlimited energy, and perfect faith into this programme, and changed it from a by-path into a veritable Way of Life. And the tale of the methods by which he did this is a fascinating study of human life.

It startled the nation to hear a Negro advocating such a programme after many decades of bitter complaint; it startled and won the applause of the South, it interested and won the admiration of the North; and after a confused murmur of protest, it silenced if it did not convert the Negroes themselves.

To gain the sympathy and coöperation of the various elements comprising the white South was Mr. Washington's first task; and this, at the time Tuskegee was founded, seemed, for a black man, well-nigh impossible. And yet ten years later it was done in the word spoken at Atlanta: "In all things purely social we can be as separate as the five fingers, and yet one as the hand in all things essential to mutual progress." This "Atlanta Compromise" is by all odds the most notable thing in Mr. Washington's career. The South interpreted it in different ways: the radicals received it as a complete surrender of the demand for civil and political equality; the conservatives, as a generously conceived working basis for mutual understanding. So both approved it, and to-day its author is certainly the most distinguished Southerner since Jefferson Davis, and the one with the largest personal following.

Next to this achievement comes Mr. Washington's work in gaining place and consideration in the North. Others less shrewd and tactful had formerly essayed to sit on these two stools and had fallen between them; but as Mr. Washington knew the heart of the South from birth and training, so by singular insight he intuitively grasped the spirit of the age which was dominating the North. And so thoroughly did he learn the speech and thought of triumphant commercialism, and the ideals of material prosperity, that the picture of a lone black boy poring over a French grammar amid the weeds and dirt of a neglected home soon seemed to him the acme of absurdities. One wonders what Socrates and St. Francis of Assisi would say to this.

And yet this very singleness of vision and thorough oneness with his age is a mark of the successful man. It is as though Nature must needs make men narrow in order to give them force. So Mr. Washington's cult has gained unquestioning followers, his work has wonderfully prospered, his friends are legion, and his enemies are confounded. To-day he stands as the one recognized spokesman of his ten million fellows, and one of the most notable figures in a nation of seventy millions. One hesitates, therefore, to criticise a life which, beginning with so little, has done so much. And yet the time is come when one may speak in all sincerity and utter courtesy of the mistakes and shortcomings of Mr. Washington's career, as well as of his triumphs, without being thought captious or envious, and without forgetting that it is easier to do ill than well in the world.

The criticism that has hitherto met Mr. Washington has not always been of this broad character. In the South especially has he had to walk warily to avoid the harshest judgments,—and naturally so, for he is dealing with the one subject of deepest sensitiveness to that section. Twice—once when at the Chicago celebration of the Spanish-American War he alluded to the color-prejudice that is "eating away the vitals of the South," and once when he dined with President Roosevelt—has the resulting Southern criticism been violent enough to threaten seriously his popularity. In the North the feeling has several times forced itself into words, that Mr. Washington's counsels of submission overlooked certain elements of true manhood, and that his educational programme was unnecessarily narrow. Usually, however, such criticism has not found open expression, although, too, the spiritual sons of the Abolitionists have not been prepared to acknowledge that the schools founded before Tuskegee, by men of broad ideals and self-sacrificing spirit, were wholly failures or worthy of ridicule. While, then, criticism has not failed to follow Mr. Washington, yet the prevailing public opinion of the land has been but too willing to deliver the solution of a wearisome problem into his hands, and say, "If that is all you and your race ask, take it."

Among his own people, however, Mr. Washington has encountered the strongest and most lasting opposition, amounting at times to bitterness, and even to-day continuing strong and insistent even though largely silenced in outward expression by the public opinion of the nation. Some of this opposition is, of course, mere envy; the disappointment of displaced demagogues and the spite of narrow minds. But aside from this, there is among educated and thoughtful colored men in all parts of the land a feeling of deep regret, sorrow, and apprehension at the wide currency and ascendancy which some of Mr. Washington's theories have gained. These same men admire his sincerity of purpose, and are willing to forgive much to honest endeavor which is doing something worth the doing. They coöperate with Mr. Washington as far as they conscientiously can; and, indeed, it is no ordinary tribute to this man's tact and power that, steering as he must between so many diverse interests and opinions, he so largely retains the respect of all.

But the hushing of the criticism of honest opponents is a dangerous thing. It leads some of the best of the critics to unfortunate silence and paralysis of effort, and others to burst into speech so passionately and intemperately as to lose listeners. Honest and earnest criticism from those whose interests are most nearly touched,—criticism of writers by readers, of government by those governed, of leaders by those led,—this is the soul of democracy and the safeguard of modern society. If the best of the American Negroes receive by outer pressure a leader whom they had not recognized before, manifestly there is here a certain palpable gain. Yet there is also irreparable loss,—a loss of that peculiarly valuable education which a group receives when by search and criticism it finds and commissions its own leaders. The way in which this is done is at once the most elementary and the nicest problem of social growth. History is but the record of such group-leadership; and yet how infinitely changeful is its type and character! And of all types and kinds, what can be more instructive than the leadership of a group within a group?—that curious double movement where real progress may be negative and actual advance be relative retrogression. All this is the social student's inspiration and despair.

Now in the past the American Negro has had instructive experience in the choosing of group leaders, founding thus a peculiar dynasty which in the light of present conditions is worth while studying. When sticks and stones and beasts form the sole environment of a people, their attitude is largely one of determined opposition to and conquest of natural forces. But when to earth and brute is added an environment of men and ideas, then the attitude of the imprisoned group may take three main forms,—a feeling of revolt and revenge; an attempt to adjust all thought and action to the will of the greater group; or, finally, a determined effort at self-realization and self-development despite environing opinion. The influence of all of these attitudes at various times can be traced in the history of the American Negro, and in the evolution of his successive leaders.

Before 1750, while the fire of African freedom still burned in the veins of the slaves, there was in all leadership or attempted leadership but the one motive of revolt and revenge,—typified in the terrible Maroons, the Danish blacks, and Cato of Stono, and veiling all the Americas in fear of insurrection. The liberalizing tendencies of the latter half of the eighteenth century brought, along with kindlier relations between black and white, thoughts of ultimate adjustment and assimilation. Such aspiration was especially voiced in the earnest songs of Phyllis, in the martyrdom of Attucks, the fighting of Salem and Poor, the intellectual accomplishments of Banneker and Derham, and the political demands of the Cuffes.

Stern financial and social stress after the war cooled much of the previous humanitarian ardor. The disappointment and impatience of the Negroes at the persistence of slavery and serfdom voiced itself in two movements. The slaves in the South, aroused undoubtedly by vague rumors of the Haytian revolt, made three fierce attempts at insurrection,—in 1800 under Gabriel in Virginia, in 1822 under Vesey in Carolina, and in 1831 again in Virginia under the terrible Nat Turner. In the Free States, on the other hand, a new and curious attempt at self-development was made. In Philadelphia and New York color-prescription led to a withdrawal of Negro communicants from white churches and the formation of a peculiar socio-religious institution among the Negroes known as the African Church,—an organization still living and controlling in its various branches over a million of men.

Walker's wild appeal against the trend of the times showed how the world was changing after the coming of the cotton-gin. By 1830 slavery seemed hopelessly fastened on the South, and the slaves thoroughly cowed into submission. The free Negroes of the North, inspired by the mulatto immigrants from the West Indies, began to change the basis of their demands; they recognized the slavery of slaves, but insisted that they themselves were freemen, and sought assimilation and amalgamation with the nation on the same terms with other men. Thus, Forten and Purvis of Philadelphia, Shad of Wilmington, Du Bois of New Haven, Barbadoes of Boston, and others, strove singly and together as men, they said, not as slaves; as "people of color," not as "Negroes." The trend of the times, however, refused them recognition save in individual and exceptional cases, considered them as one with all the despised blacks, and they soon found themselves striving to keep even the rights they formerly had of voting and working and moving as freemen. Schemes of migration and colonization arose among them; but these they refused to entertain, and they eventually turned to the Abolition movement as a final refuge.

Here, led by Remond, Nell, Wells-Brown, and Douglass, a new period of self-assertion and self-development dawned. To be sure, ultimate freedom and assimilation was the ideal before the leaders, but the assertion of the manhood rights of the Negro by himself was the main reliance, and John Brown's raid was the extreme of its logic. After the war and emancipation, the great form of Frederick Douglass, the greatest of American Negro leaders, still led the host. Self-assertion, especially in political lines, was the main programme, and behind Douglass came Elliot, Bruce, and Langston, and the Reconstruction politicians, and, less conspicuous but of greater social significance Alexander Crummell and Bishop Daniel Payne.

Then came the Revolution of 1876, the suppression of the Negro votes, the changing and shifting of ideals, and the seeking of new lights in the great night. Douglass, in his old age, still bravely stood for the ideals of his early manhood,—ultimate assimilation *through* self-assertion, and on no other terms. For a time Price arose as a new leader, destined, it seemed, not to give up, but to restate the old ideals in a form less repugnant to the white South. But he passed away in his prime. Then came the new leader. Nearly all the former ones had become leaders by the silent suffrage of their fellows, had sought to lead their own people alone, and were usually, save Douglass, little known outside their race. But Booker T. Washington arose as essentially the leader not of one race but of two,—a compromiser between the South, the North, and the Negro. Naturally the Negroes resented, at first bitterly, signs of compromise which surrendered their civil and political rights, even though this was to be exchanged for larger chances of economic development. The rich and dominating North, however, was not only weary of the race problem, but was investing largely in Southern enterprises, and welcomed any method of peaceful coöperation. Thus, by national opinion, the Negroes began to recognize Mr. Washington's leadership; and the voice of criticism was hushed.

Mr. Washington represents in Negro thought the old attitude of adjustment and submission; but adjustment at such a peculiar time

as to make his programme unique. This is an age of unusual
economic development, and Mr. Washington's programme naturally takes an economic cast, becoming a gospel of Work and
Money to such an extent as apparently almost completely to
overshadow the higher aims of life. Moreover, this is an age when
the more advanced races are coming in closer contact with the less
developed races, and the race-feeling is therefore intensified; and
Mr. Washington's programme practically accepts the alleged inferiority of the Negro races. Again, in our own land, the reaction
from the sentiment of war time has given impetus to race-prejudice
against Negroes, and Mr. Washington withdraws many of the high
demands of Negroes as men and American citizens. In other
periods of intensified prejudice all the Negro's tendency to self-
assertion has been called forth; at this period a policy of submission
is advocated. In the history of nearly all other races and peoples the
doctrine preached at such crises has been that manly self-respect is
worth more than lands and houses, and that a people who voluntarily surrender such respect, or cease striving for it, are not worth
civilizing.

In answer to this, it has been claimed that the Negro can survive
only through submission. Mr. Washington distinctly asks that
black people give up, at least for the present, three things,—

First, political power,

Second, insistence on civil rights,

Third, higher education of Negro youth,—

and concentrate all their energies on industrial education, the accumulation of wealth, and the conciliation of the South. This policy
has been courageously and insistently advocated for over fifteen
years, and has been triumphant for perhaps ten years. As a result of
this tender of the palm-branch, what has been the return? In these
years there have occurred:

1. The disfranchisement of the Negro.

2. The legal creation of a distinct status of civil inferiority for
the Negro.

3. The steady withdrawal of aid from institutions for the higher
training of the Negro.

These movements are not, to be sure, direct results of Mr.
Washington's teachings; but his propaganda has, without a shadow
of doubt, helped their speedier accomplishment. The question

then comes: Is it possible, and probable, that nine millions of men can make effective progress in economic lines if they are deprived of political rights, made a servile caste, and allowed only the most meagre chance for developing their exceptional men? If history and reason give any distinct answer to these questions, it is an emphatic No. And Mr. Washington thus faces the triple paradox of his career:

1. He is striving nobly to make Negro artisans business men and property-owners; but it is utterly impossible, under modern competitive methods, for workingmen and property-owners to defend their rights and exist without the right of suffrage.

2. He insists on thrift and self-respect, but at the same time counsels a silent submission to civic inferiority such as is bound to sap the manhood of any race in the long run.

3. He advocates common-school and industrial training, and depreciates institutions of higher learning; but neither the Negro common-schools, nor Tuskegee itself, could remain open a day were it not for teachers trained in Negro colleges, or trained by their graduates.

This triple paradox in Mr. Washington's position is the object of criticism by two classes of colored Americans. One class is spiritually descended from Toussaint the Savior, through Gabriel, Vesey, and Turner, and they represent the attitude of revolt and revenge; they hate the white South blindly and distrust the white race generally, and so far as they agree on definite action, think that the Negro's only hope lies in emigration beyond the borders of the United States. And yet, by the irony of fate, nothing has more effectually made this programme seem hopeless than the recent course of the United States toward weaker and darker peoples in the West Indies, Hawaii, and the Philippines,—for where in the world may we go and be safe from lying and brute force?

The other class of Negroes who cannot agree with Mr. Washington has hitherto said little aloud. They deprecate the sight of scattered counsels, of internal disagreement; and especially they dislike making their just criticism of a useful and earnest man an excuse for a general discharge of venom from small-minded opponents. Nevertheless, the questions involved are so fundamental and serious that it is difficult to see how men like the Grimkes, Kelly Miller, J. W. E. Bowen, and other representatives of this group, can much longer be silent. Such men feel in conscience bound to ask of this nation three things:

1. The right to vote.
2. Civic equality.
3. The education of youth according to ability.

They acknowledge Mr. Washington's invaluable service in counselling patience and courtesy in such demands; they do not ask that ignorant black men vote when ignorant whites are debarred, or that any reasonable restrictions in the suffrage should not be applied; they know that the low social level of the mass of the race is responsible for much discrimination against it, but they also know, and the nation knows, that relentless color-prejudice is more often a cause than a result of the Negro's degradation; they seek the abatement of this relic of barbarism, and not its systematic encouragement and pampering by all agencies of social power from the Associated Press to the Church of Christ. They advocate, with Mr. Washington, a broad system of Negro common schools supplemented by thorough industrial training; but they are surprised that a man of Mr. Washington's insight cannot see that no such educational system ever has rested or can rest on any other basis than that of the well-equipped college and university, and they insist that there is a demand for a few such institutions throughout the South to train the best of the Negro youth as teachers, professional men, and leaders.

This group of men honor Mr. Washington for his attitude of conciliation toward the white South; they accept the "Atlanta Compromise" in its broadest interpretation; they recognize, with him, many signs of promise, many men of high purpose and fair judgment, in this section; they know that no easy task has been laid upon a region already tottering under heavy burdens. But, nevertheless, they insist that the way to truth and right lies in straightforward honesty, not in indiscriminate flattery; in praising those of the South who do well and criticising uncompromisingly those who do ill; in taking advantage of the opportunities at hand and urging their fellows to do the same, but at the same time in remembering that only a firm adherence to their higher ideals and aspirations will ever keep those ideals within the realm of possibility. They do not expect that the free right to vote, to enjoy civic rights, and to be educated, will come in a moment; they do not expect to see the bias and prejudices of years disappear at the blast of a trumpet; but they are absolutely certain that the way for a people to gain their reasonable rights is not by voluntarily throwing them away and insisting that they do not want them; that the way for a people to gain respect is not by continually belittling and ridiculing themselves; that, on the contrary, Negroes must insist continually, in season and out of season, that voting is necessary to modern manhood, that color discrimination is barbarism, and that black boys need education as well as white boys.

In failing thus to state plainly and unequivocally the legitimate demands of their people, even at the cost of opposing an honored leader, the thinking classes of American Negroes would shirk a heavy responsibility,—a responsibility to themselves, a responsibility to the struggling masses, a responsibility to the darker races of men whose future depends so largely on this American experiment, but especially a responsibility to this nation,—this common Fatherland. It is wrong to encourage a man or a people in evildoing; it is wrong to aid and abet a national crime simply because it is unpopular not to do so. The growing spirit of kindliness and reconciliation between the North and South after the frightful difference of a generation ago ought to be a source of deep congratulation to all, and especially to those whose mistreatment caused the war; but if that reconciliation is to be marked by the industrial slavery and civic death of those same black men, with permanent legislation into a position of inferiority, then those black men, if they are really men, are called upon by every consideration of patriotism and loyalty to oppose such a course by all civilized methods, even though such opposition involves disagreement with Mr. Booker T. Washington. We have no right to sit silently by while the inevitable seeds are sown for a harvest of disaster to our children, black and white.

First, it is the duty of black men to judge the South discriminatingly. The present generation of Southerners are not responsible for the past, and they should not be blindly hated or blamed for it. Furthermore, to no class is the indiscriminate endorsement of the recent course of the South toward Negroes more nauseating than to the best thought of the South. The South is not "solid"; it is a land in the ferment of social change, wherein forces of all kinds are fighting for supremacy; and to praise the ill the South is to-day perpetrating is just as wrong as to condemn the good. Discriminating and broad-minded criticism is what the South needs,—needs it for the sake of her own white sons and daughters, and for the insurance of robust, healthy mental and moral development.

To-day even the attitude of the Southern whites toward the blacks is not, as so many assume, in all cases the same; the ignorant Southerner hates the Negro, the workingmen fear his competition, the money-makers wish to use him as a laborer, some of the educated see a menace in his upward development, while others—usually the sons of the masters—wish to help him to rise. National opinion has enabled this last class to maintain the Negro common schools, and to protect the Negro partially in property, life, and limb. Through the pressure of the money-makers, the Negro is in danger of being reduced to semi-slavery, especially in the country districts; the workingmen, and those of the educated who fear the Negro, have united to disfranchise him, and some have urged his deportation; while the passions of the ignorant are easily aroused to lynch and abuse any black man. To praise this intricate whirl of thought and prejudice is nonsense; to inveigh indiscriminately against "the South" is unjust; but to use the same breath in praising Governor Aycock, exposing Senator Morgan, arguing with Mr. Thomas Nelson Page, and denouncing Senator Ben Tillman, is not only sane, but the imperative duty of thinking black men.

It would be unjust to Mr. Washington not to acknowledge that in several instances he has opposed movements in the South which were unjust to the Negro; he sent memorials to the Louisiana and Alabama constitutional conventions, he has spoken against lynching, and in other ways has openly or silently set his influence against sinister schemes and unfortunate happenings. Notwithstanding this, it is equally true to assert that on the whole the distinct impression left by Mr. Washington's propaganda is, first, that the South is justified in its present attitude toward the Negro because of the Negro's degradation; secondly, that the prime cause of the Negro's failure to rise more quickly is his wrong education in the past; and, thirdly, that his future rise depends primarily on his own efforts. Each of these propositions is a dangerous half-truth. The supplementary truths must never be lost sight of: first, slavery and race-prejudice are potent if not sufficient causes of the Negro's position; second, industrial and common-school training were necessarily slow in planting because they had to await the black teachers trained by higher institutions,—it being extremely doubtful if any essentially different development was possible, and certainly a Tuskegee was unthinkable before 1880; and, third, while it is a great truth to say that the Negro must strive and strive mightily to help himself, it is equally true that unless his striving be not simply seconded, but rather aroused and encouraged, by the initiative of the richer and wiser environing group, he cannot hope for great success.

In his failure to realize and impress this last point, Mr. Washington is especially to be criticised. His doctrine has tended to make the whites, North and South, shift the burden of the Negro problem to the Negro's shoulders and stand aside as critical and rather pessimistic spectators; when in fact the burden belongs to the nation, and the hands of none of us are clean if we bend not our energies to righting these great wrongs.

The South ought to be led, by candid and honest criticism, to assert her better self and do her full duty to the race she has cruelly wronged and is still wronging. The North—her co-partner in guilt —cannot salve her conscience by plastering it with gold. We cannot settle this problem by diplomacy and suaveness, by "policy" alone. If worse come to worst, can the moral fibre of this country survive the slow throttling and murder of nine millions of men?

The black men of America have a duty to perform, a duty stern and delicate,—a forward movement to oppose a part of the work of their greatest leader. So far as Mr. Washington preaches Thrift, Patience, and Industrial Training for the masses, we must hold up his hands and strive with him, rejoicing in his honors and glorying in the strength of this Joshua called of God and of man to lead the headless host. But so far as Mr. Washington apologizes for injustice, North or South, does not rightly value the privilege and duty of voting, belittles the emasculating effects of caste distinctions, and opposes the higher training and ambition of our brighter minds,—so far as he, the South, or the Nation, does this,—we must unceasingly and firmly oppose them. By every civilized and peaceful method we must strive for the rights which the world accords to men, clinging unwaveringly to those great words which the sons of the Fathers would fain forget: "We hold these truths to be self-evident: That all men are created equal; that they are endowed by their Creator with certain unalienable rights; that among these are life, liberty, and the pursuit of happiness."

Of the Passing of the First-Born

O sister, sister, thy first-begotten,
The hands that cling and the feet that follow,
The voice of the child's blood crying yet,
Who hath remembered me? who hath forgotten?
Thou hast forgotten, O summer swallow,
But the world shall end when I forget.

SWINBURNE

"Unto you a child is born," sang the bit of yellow paper that fluttered into my room one brown October morning. Then the fear of fatherhood mingled wildly with the joy of creation; I wondered how it looked and how it felt,—what were its eyes, and how its hair curled and crumpled itself. And I thought in awe of her,—she who had slept with Death to tear a man-child from underneath her heart, while I was unconsciously wandering. I fled to my wife and child, repeating the while to myself half wonderingly, "Wife and child? Wife and child?"—fled fast and faster than boat and steam-car, and yet must ever impatiently await them; away from the hard-voiced city, away from the flickering sea into my own Berkshire Hills that sit all sadly guarding the gates of Massachusetts.

Up the stairs I ran to the wan mother and whimpering babe, to the sanctuary on whose altar a life at my bidding had offered itself to win a life, and won. What is this tiny formless thing, this newborn wail from an unknown world,—all head and voice? I handle it curiously, and watch perplexed its winking, breathing, and sneezing. I did not love it then; it seemed a ludicrous thing to love; but her I loved, my girl-mother, she whom now I saw unfolding like the glory of the morning—the transfigured woman. Through her I came to love the wee thing, as it grew strong; as its little soul unfolded itself in twitter and cry and half-formed word, and as its eyes caught the gleam and flash of life. How beautiful he was, with his olive-tinted flesh and dark gold ringlets, his eyes of mingled blue and brown, his perfect little limbs, and the soft voluptuous roll which the blood of Africa had moulded into his features! I held him in my arms, after we had sped far away to our Southern home,—held him, and glanced at the hot red soil of Georgia and the breathless city of a hundred hills, and felt a vague unrest. Why was his hair tinted with gold? An evil omen was golden hair in my life. Why had not the brown of his eyes crushed out and killed the blue?—for brown were his father's eyes, and his father's father's. And thus in the Land of the Color-line I saw, as it fell across my baby, the shadow of the Veil.

Within the Veil was he born, said I; and there within shall he live,—a Negro and a Negro's son. Holding in that little head—ah, bitterly!—the unbowed pride of a hunted race, clinging with that tiny dimpled hand—ah, wearily!—to a hope not hopeless but unhopeful, and seeing with those bright wondering eyes that peer into my soul a land whose freedom is to us a mockery and whose liberty a lie. I saw the shadow of the Veil as it passed over my baby, I saw the cold city towering above the blood-red land. I held my face beside his little cheek, showed him the star-children and the twinkling lights as they began to flash, and stilled with an even-song the unvoiced terror of my life.

So sturdy and masterful he grew, so filled with bubbling life, so tremulous with the unspoken wisdom of a life but eighteen months distant from the All-life,—we were not far from worshipping this revelation of the divine, my wife and I. Her own life builded and moulded itself upon the child; he tinged her every dream and idealized her every effort. No hands but hers must touch and garnish those little limbs; no dress or frill must touch them that had not wearied her fingers; no voice but hers could coax him off to Dreamland, and she and he together spoke some soft and unknown tongue and in it held communion. I too mused above his little white bed; saw the strength of my own arm stretched onward through the ages through the newer strength of his; saw the dream of my black fathers stagger a step onward in the wild phantasm of the world; heard in his baby voice the voice of the Prophet that was to rise within the Veil.

And so we dreamed and loved and planned by fall and winter, and the full flush of the long Southern spring, till the hot winds rolled from the fetid Gulf, till the roses shivered and the still stern sun quivered its awful light over the hills of Atlanta. And then one night the little feet pattered wearily to the wee white bed, and the tiny hands trembled; and a warm flushed face tossed on the pillow, and we knew baby was sick. Ten days he lay there,—a swift week and three endless days, wasting, wasting away. Cheerily the mother nursed him the first days, and laughed into the little eyes that smiled again. Tenderly then she hovered round him, till the smile fled away and Fear crouched beside the little bed.

Then the day ended not, and night was a dreamless terror, and joy and sleep slipped away. I hear now that Voice at midnight calling me from dull and dreamless trance,—crying, "The Shadow of Death! The Shadow of Death!" Out into the starlight I crept, to rouse the gray physician,—the Shadow of Death, the Shadow of Death. The hours trembled on; the night listened; the ghastly dawn glided like a tired thing across the lamplight. Then we two alone looked upon the child as he turned toward us with great eyes, and stretched his string-like hands,—the Shadow of Death! And we spoke no word, and turned away.

He died at eventide, when the sun lay like a brooding sorrow above the western hills, veiling its face; when the winds spoke not, and the trees, the great green trees he loved, stood motionless. I saw his breath beat quicker and quicker, pause, and then his little soul leapt like a star that travels in the night and left a world of darkness in its train. The day changed not; the same tall trees peeped in at the windows, the same green grass glinted in the setting sun. Only in the chamber of death writhed the world's most piteous thing—a childless mother.

I shirk not. I long for work. I pant for a life full of striving. I am no coward, to shrink before the rugged rush of the storm, nor even quail before the awful shadow of the Veil. But hearken, O Death! Is not this my life hard enough,—is not that dull land that stretches its sneering web about me cold enough,—is not all the world beyond these four little walls pitiless enough, but that thou must needs enter here,—thou, O Death? About my head the thundering storm beat like a heartless voice, and the crazy forest pulsed with the curses of the weak; but what cared I, within my home beside my wife and baby boy? Wast thou so jealous of one little coign of happiness that thou must needs enter there,—thou, O Death?

A perfect life was his, all joy and love, with tears to make it brighter,—sweet as a summer's day beside the Housatonic. The world loved him; the women kissed his curls, the men looked gravely into his wonderful eyes, and the children hovered and fluttered about him. I can see him now, changing like the sky from sparkling laughter to darkening frowns, and then to wondering thoughtfulness as he watched the world. He knew no color-line, poor dear,—and the Veil, though it shadowed him, had not yet darkened half his sun. He loved the white matron, he loved his black nurse; and in his little world walked souls alone, uncolored and unclothed. I—yea, all men—are larger and purer by the infinite breadth of that one little life. She who in simple clearness of vision sees beyond the stars said when he had flown, "He will be happy There; he ever loved beautiful things." And I, far more ignorant, and blind by the web of mine own weaving, sit alone winding words and muttering, "If still he be, and he be There, and there be a There, let him be happy, O Fate!"

Blithe was the morning of his burial, with bird and song and sweet-smelling flowers. The trees whispered to the grass, but the children sat with hushed faces. And yet it seemed a ghostly unreal day,—the wraith of Life. We seemed to rumble down an unknown street behind a little white bundle of posies, with the shadow of a song in our ears. The busy city dinned about us; they did not say much, those pale-faced hurrying men and women; they did not say much,—they only glanced and said, "Niggers!"

We could not lay him in the ground there in Georgia, for the earth there is strangly red; so we bore him away to the northward, with his flowers and his little folded hands. In vain, in vain!—for where, O God! beneath thy broad blue sky shall my dark baby rest in peace,—where Reverence dwells, and Goodness, and a Freedom that is free?

All that day and all that night there sat an awful gladness in my heart,—nay, blame me not if I see the world thus darkly through the Veil,—and my soul whispers ever to me, saying, "Not dead, not dead, but escaped; not bond, but free." No bitter meanness now shall sicken his baby heart till it dies a living death, no taunt shall madden his happy boyhood. Fool that I was to think or wish that this little soul should grow choked and deformed within the Veil! I might have known that yonder deep unworldly look that ever and anon floated past his eyes was peering far beyond this narrow Now. In the poise of his little curl-crowned head did there not sit all that wild pride of being which his father had hardly crushed in his own heart? For what, forsooth, shall a Negro want with pride amid the studied humiliations of fifty million fellows? Well sped, my boy, before the world had dubbed your ambition insolence, had held your ideals unattainable, and taught you to cringe and bow. Better far this nameless void that stops my life than a sea of sorrow for you.

Idle words; he might have borne his burden more bravely than we,—aye, and found it lighter too, some day; for surely, surely this is not the end. Surely there shall yet dawn some mighty morning to lift the Veil and set the prisoned free. Not for me,—I shall die in my bonds,—but for fresh young souls who have not known the night and waken to the morning; a morning when men ask of the workman, not "Is he white?" but "Can he work?" When men ask artists, not "Are they black?" but "Do they know?" Some morning this may be, long, long years to come. But now there wails, on that dark shore within the Veil, the same deep voice, *Thou shalt forego!* And all have I foregone at that command, and with small complaint,—all save that fair young form that lies so coldly wed with death in the nest I had builded.

If one must have gone, why not I? Why may I not rest me from this restlessness and sleep from this wide waking? Was not the world's alembic, Time, in his young hands, and is not my time waning? Are there so many workers in the vineyard that the fair promise of this little body could lightly be tossed away? The wretched of my race that line the alleys of the nation sit fatherless and unmothered; but Love sat beside his cradle, and in his ear Wisdom waited to speak. Perhaps now he knows the All-love, and needs not to be wise. Sleep, then, child,—sleep till I sleep and waken to a baby voice and the ceaseless patter of little feet—above the Veil.

25. Robert A. Woods and Albert J. Kennedy, "The Negroes of Cambridgeport"

ROBERT WOODS *and Albert Kennedy were the leading social-work professionals in Massachusetts during the Progressive Era—Boston's counterparts to Chicago's Jane Addams and Florence Kelley and New York's Coit Stanton and Lillian Wald. Their research into slum and labor conditions, their operation of settlement houses for the poor (particularly South End House), and their lobbying at the State House contributed remarkably to enlightened legislation and civic improvement. They embodied the best of progressive humanitarianism. Their patronizing though genuinely sympathetic attitude toward Negroes is therefore especially instructive on the assumptions about Negro inferiority prevalent "even" among the most humane individuals of the era. Compare* The Tenement House Problem *and the* Pittsburgh Survey *above (Documents 12, 20).*

SOURCE: R. A. Woods and A. T. Kennedy, *The Zone of Emergence*, edited by Sam B. Warner, Jr. (Cambridge, Mass.: Harvard University Press, 1962), pp. 66–69. Copyright 1962 by the Joint

Center for Urban Studies of the Massachusetts Institute of Technology and Harvard University. Reprinted by permission of Harvard University Press.

Next to the native stock the Negroes are longest resident in the Port. . . . There are two Negro centers: one immediately about Burleigh Street and the other on Howard Street. The Burleigh Street colony, one time situated on the swamp, is very old, and the houses are small, two-story shacks. The Howard Street colony began to grow about 1890, and is much more desirable in housing and surroundings. There are 2,500 persons living in the Burleigh Street district and its surrounding colonies, and 1,000 in the Howard Street quarter.

The population is organized on state lines. Of 1,649 born south, 554 came from North Carolina and 528 from Virginia. The female population from North Carolina and Virginia is from 10 to 30 per cent higher than the male, which shows a settled family life that permits of sending south for relatives and friends. The two colonies also run on state lines, the Burleigh Street region being predominantly North Carolinian, and the Howard Street center Virginian. Churches, lodges, etc., are affected by state divisions.

There is also a growing group of Negroes from Nova Scotia and the West Indies. The former are from the same stock as the Southern Negro, and such immigrants mix easily with the native stock. The West Indian Negro has been coming to Cambridge since 1903, working his passage on boats plying between the Islands and Canada, and coming through the Providences; but some come directly. This immigration has been stimulated by the American invasion of the West Indies and the stories circulated concerning high wages and the superior conditions of living in the States. West Indians are often well educated, and have a directness of manner and felicity of speech which is most attractive. They are skilled workmen and have been printers, cabinet makers, wood workers, carpenters, etc. They remain British and take little part in American life; living in hope of an ultimate return. A few attend the Episcopal and the Catholic churches. They do not intermarry with the Southern stock, preferring to send back for wives. Their social life centers in Boston, but there are several cricket clubs and a good literary club in Cambridgeport.

The majority of Negroes of the Port work in Boston as waiters,

porters, hotel and personal servants. In the Port a few are team-
sters, porters, and a very few work in the factories. There are no
places open to them in the industries; the sentiment among the
operatives being overwhelmingly against them as fellow workmen.
The colony has a few professional and business men, and one
newspaper. There are no distinctly colored stores, largely because
the Negro lacks initiative, and partly because of the impossibility of
organizing racial buying sentiment. A number of them own their
own homes, and a few are well off. The majority live close to the
margin, partly through lack of industry and foresight, and partly
because of industrial conditions. There is much friendly and neigh-
borly aid and they do not call on organized charity more than other
peoples.

Their social life is very luxuriant. They have a childish delight in
multiplicity of organization, and every Negro at some time forms
an organization or association. Even the humblest seem pressed to
fulfill their social obligations. Boston sets the standard for Cambridgeport life. The ranking families, churches, business, professional, trade and social organizations are over the river. Many
Cambridgeport Negroes belong to Boston organizations, especially
lodges; and to Company L of the Sixth Regiment. In the Port the
chief social force is the church, which numbers about 1,000 communicants, and raises in the vicinity of $7,000 a year. The course of
church life is not smooth, as money comes with difficulty and there
are many calls for denominational aid. The clergy are ill-paid, and
the work beset with personal difficulties. The charity of the church
goes to its own members or South.

In addition to the lodges there are a number of philanthropic
and social clubs, and a dozen or more cultural clubs. The 'Forum'
is notable with 200 members, and it has secured capable speakers;
both white and black, for its Sunday afternoon meeting. There are
various Alumni Associations of High Schools and Institutes, danc-
ing classes and small group clubs.

The Negro has to bear up in his relations to whites under the
double handicap of racial incapacity (measured by white standards) and racial discrimination. The latter difficulty causes the
race constant irritation and soreness. This comes out most plainly
in the Negro attitude to the public school. The punishment of a
colored child or a failure in promotion is felt to be discrimination
of race. Yet the colored child is not the equal of the white child in

comprehension, execution and order. He gravitates toward the end of the class, and is suspicious, quarrelsome, and hard to handle. There are a few Negro children who are excellent scholars, and two cases may be instanced where Negroes outdistanced white children of good families. They attend the evening grammar schools in limited numbers, but do not use manual training courses of the Rindge School [sic]. A few attend the High School. On the whole there is a deepseated feeling that it is useless to attend school because of the impossibility of using commercially such education as one may secure.

26.   The Immigration Commission Report

BETWEEN 1880 and 1910, 12.5 million immigrants settled in the United States, accounting for about one-third of the total population increase in the country during those years. An additional 3 million foreigners had immigrated, but returned to their home countries sometime during the same period. Fairly constantly between 1890 and 1920, slightly less than 15 per cent of the American population was foreign born; another 25 per cent were children of at least one foreign-born parent. Immigration reached a remarkable climax in the 1905–1914 period, when the figures exceeded a million a year six times, peaking in 1907 at 1,285,349 and coming almost that high again in 1913 and 1914 just before the war ended the European exodus. Not only did the newcomers arrive in spectacularly larger numbers than ever before; about 80 per cent of them were from Italy, Austria-Hungary, and Russia, rather than from Britain, Ireland, and Germany, the three countries which until the 1890's had accounted for about 85 per cent of all American immigrants. A strikingly large number, moreover—2 million between 1900–1910, for example—could neither read nor write their native languages; while even those who might be classified as "skilled" would find few opportunities to use the skills they possessed in the more highly mechanized industry of the United States.

Understandably, the Immigration Problem loomed large among national issues and Congress established the inevitable commission to investigate. The conclusions of the commission's report—sometimes called the Dillingham Report after Senator William P. Dillingham (Republican of Vermont), the commission's chairman—were entirely predictable. Although several renowned scholars were recruited to do most of the spadework, they tended to seek statistics which lent support to commonly held assumptions. For example, having documented that the new immigration derived from different sources than the old, the commission simply asserted (without offering relevant criteria) that "the new immigration as a class is far less intelligent than the old"; the evidence it did offer spoke to the new immigrant's illiteracy (which the commission admitted was a function of poverty rather than of intelligence), to his "race," to his temperament, and to his motivations. The subtitles of the commission's report say much about what troubled the investigators most and which they identified with the Immigration Problem—for example, Immigration and Criminals, Immigration of the Mentally Defective, Immigration and Crime, Immigration and the Public Health, and so on.

SOURCE: Presented by Senator William P. Dillingham, Senate Document Number 747, 61st Cong., 3rd Sess. (December 5, 1910); reprinted from Abstracts of Reports of the Immigration Commission (Washington, D.C.: Government Printing Office, 1911).

Brief Statement of the Investigations

PLAN AND SCOPE OF THE INQUIRY

Briefly stated, the plan of work adopted by the Commission included a study of the sources of recent immigration in Europe, the general character of incoming immigrants, the methods employed here and abroad to prevent the immigration of persons classed as undesirable in the United States immigration law, and finally a thorough investigation into the general status of the more recent immigrants as residents of the United States, and the effect of such immigration upon the institutions, industries, and people of this country. As above suggested, the chief basis of the Commission's work was the changed character of the immigration movement to the United States during the past twenty-five years.

During the fiscal year 1907, in which the Commission was created, a total of 1,285,349 immigrants were admitted to the United States. Of this number 1,207,619 were from Europe, including Turkey in Asia, and of these 979,661, or 81 per cent, came from the southern and eastern countries, comprising Austria-Hungary, Bulgaria, Greece, Italy, Montenegro, Poland, Portugal, Roumania, Russia, Servia, Spain, Turkey in Europe, and Turkey in Asia.

Twenty-five years earlier, in the fiscal year 1882, 648,186 European immigrants came to the United States, and of these only

84,973, or 13.1 per cent, came from the countries above enumerated, while 563,213, or 86.9 per cent, were from Belgium, Great Britain and Ireland, France, Germany, the Netherlands, Scandinavia, and Switzerland, which countries furnished about 95 per cent of the immigration movement from Europe to the United States between 1819 and 1883.

During the entire period for which statistics are available—July 1, 1819, to June 30, 1910—a total of 25,528,410 European immigrants, including 106,481 from Turkey in Asia, were admitted to the United States. Of these, 16,052,900, or 62.9 per cent, came from the northern and western countries enumerated, and 9,475,-510, or 37.1 per cent, from southern and eastern Europe and Turkey in Asia. For convenience the former movement will be referred to in the Commission's reports as the "old immigration" and the latter as the "new immigration." The old and the new immigration differ in many essentials. The former was, from the beginning, largely a movement of settlers who came from the most progressive sections of Europe for the purpose of making for themselves homes in the New World. They entered practically every line of activity in nearly every part of the country. Coming during a period of agricultural development, many of them entered agricultural pursuits, sometimes as independent farmers, but more often as farm laborers, who, nevertheless, as a rule soon became landowners. They formed an important part of the great movement toward the West during the last century, and as pioneers were most potent factors in the development of the territory between the Allegheny Mountains and the Pacific coast. They mingled freely with the native Americans and were quickly assimilated, although a large proportion of them, particularly in later years, belonged to non-English-speaking races. This natural bar to assimilation, however, was soon overcome by them, while the racial identity of their children was almost entirely lost and forgotten.

On the other hand, the new immigration has been largely a movement of unskilled laboring men who have come, in large part temporarily, from the less progressive and advanced countries of Europe in response to the call for industrial workers in the eastern and middle western States. They have almost entirely avoided agricultural pursuits, and in cities and industrial communities have congregated together in sections apart from native Americans and the older immigrants to such an extent that assimilation has been slow as compared to that of the earlier non-English-speaking races.

The new immigration as a class is far less intelligent than the old, approximately one-third of all those over 14 years of age when admitted being illiterate. Racially they are for the most part essentially unlike the British, German, and other peoples who came during the period prior to 1880, and generally speaking they are actuated in coming by different ideals, for the old immigration came to be a part of the country, while the new, in a large measure, comes with the intention of profiting, in a pecuniary way, by the superior advantages of the new world and then returning to the old country.

The old immigration movement, which in earlier days was the subject of much discussion and the cause of no little apprehension among the people of the country, long ago became thoroughly merged into the population, and the old sources have contributed a comparatively small part of the recent immigrant tide. Consequently the Commission paid but little attention to the foreign-born element of the old immigrant class and directed its efforts almost entirely to an inquiry relative to the general status of the newer immigrants as residents of the United States.

In pursuance of this policy the Commission began its study of the subject in the countries of Europe which are the chief sources of the new immigration, and followed the emigration movement to ports of embarkation, across the ocean in the steerage, and finally to every part of the United States and into practially every line of activity in which the new immigrants were to be found. . . .

The old immigration movement was essentially one of permanent settlers. The new immigration is very largely one of individuals a considerable proportion of whom apparently have no intention of permanently changing their residence, their only purpose in coming to America being to temporarily take advantage of the greater wages paid for industrial labor in this country. This, of course, is not true of all the new immigrants, but the practice is sufficiently common to warrant referring to it as a characteristic of them as a class. From all data that are available it appears that nearly 40 per cent of the new immigration movement returns to Europe and that about two-thirds of those who go remain there. This does not mean that all of these immigrants have acquired a competence and returned to live on it. Among the immigrants who return permanently are those who have failed, as well as those who have succeeded. Thousands of those returning have, under unusual conditions of climate, work, and food, contracted tuberculosis and other diseases; others are injured in our industries; still others are the widows and children of aliens dying here. These, with the aged and temperamentally unfit, make up a large part of the aliens who return to their former homes to remain.

The old immigration came to the United States during a period of general development and was an important factor in that development, while the new immigration has come during a period of great industrial expansion and has furnished a practically unlimited supply of labor to that expansion.

As a class the new immigrants are largely unskilled laborers coming from countries where their highest wage is small compared with the lowest wage in the United States. Nearly 75 per cent of them are males. About 83 per cent are between the ages of 14 and 45 years, and consequently are producers rather than dependents. They bring little money into the country and send or take a considerable part of their earnings out. More than 35 per cent are illiterate, as compared with less than 3 per cent of the old immigrant class. Immigration prior to 1882 was practically unregulated, and consequently many were not self-supporting, so that the care of alien paupers in several States was a serious problem. The new immigration has for the most part been carefully regulated so far as health and likelihood of pauperism are concerned, and, although drawn from classes low in the economic scale, the new immigrants as a rule are the strongest, the most enterprising, and the best of their class.

CAUSES OF THE MOVEMENT

While social conditions affect the situation in some countries, the present immigration from Europe to the United States is in the largest measure due to economic causes. It should be stated, however, that emigration from Europe is not now an absolute economic necessity, and as a rule those who emigrate to the United States are impelled by a desire for betterment rather than by the necessity of escaping intolerable conditions. This fact should largely modify the natural incentive to treat the immigration movement from the standpoint of sentiment and permit its consideration primarily as an economic problem. In other words, the economic and social welfare of the United States should now ordinarily be the determining factor in the immigration policy of the Government.

Unlike Canada, Argentina, Brazil, Australia, and other immigrant-receiving countries, the United States makes no effort to induce immigration. A law for the encouragement of immigration by guaranteeing in this country labor contracts made abroad was enacted in 1864 but repealed in 1868. Later legislation has tended to prevent the introduction of contract laborers and assisted or induced immigration, the purpose of the Government being that the movement should be a natural one. The law respecting assisted immigration, however, does not deny the right of a person already in this country to send for an otherwise admissible relative or friend, and a large part of the present movement, especially from southern and eastern Europe, is made possible through such assistance. The immediate incentive of the great bulk of present-day immigration is the letters of persons in this country to relatives or friends at home. Comparatively few immigrants come without some reasonably definite assurance that employment awaits them, and it is probable that as a rule they know the nature of that employment and the rate of wages. A large number of immigrants are induced to come by quasi labor agents in this country, who combine the business of supplying laborers to large employers and contractors with the so-called immigrant banking business and the selling of steamship tickets.

Another important agency in promoting emigration from Europe to the United States is the many thousands of steamship-ticket agents and subagents operating in the emigrant-furnishing districts of southern and eastern Europe. Under the terms of the United States immigration law, as well as the laws of most European countries, the promotion of emigration is forbidden, but nevertheless the steamship-agent propaganda flourishes everywhere. It does not appear that the steamship lines as a rule openly direct the operations of these agents, but the existence of the propaganda is a matter of common knowledge in the emigrant-furnishing countries and, it is fair to assume, is acquiesced in, if not stimulated, by the steamship lines as well. With the steamship lines the transportation of steerage passengers is purely a commercial matter; moreover, the steerage business which originates in southern and eastern Europe is peculiarly attractive to the companies, as many of the immigrants travel back and forth, thus insuring east-bound as well as west-bound traffic. . . .

IMMIGRATION OF CRIMINALS

While control of the immigration movement so far as physical and mental defectives are concerned has reached a high degree of efficiency, no adequate means have been adopted for preventing the immigration of criminals, prostitutes, and other morally undesirable aliens. The control of the latter classes is a much more difficult matter. In spite of the stringent law, criminals or moral defectives of any class, provided they pass the medical inspection, can usually embark at European ports and enter the United States without much danger of detection. A considerable number of criminals or aliens with criminal records are debarred annually at United States ports, but this results from the vigilance of immigrant inspectors or from chance information rather than from our system of regulation.

While it does not appear from available statistics that criminality among the foreign-born increases the volume of crime in proportion to the total population, nevertheless the coming of criminals and persons of criminal tendencies constitutes one of the serious social effects of the immigration movement. The present immigration law is not adequate to prevent the immigration of criminals, nor is it sufficiently effective as regards the deportation of alien criminals who are in this country. . . .

THE PADRONE SYSTEM

In the case of the earlier immigration of several southern and eastern European races to the United States the control of some individuals in this country by padrones has occurred. Under this system persons have taken advantage of their better knowledge of our language and conditions to control the labor of the new immigrants of the same race. The system was somewhat prevalent in the case of the earlier Italian immigrants and in such case the padrones controlled the labor of their fellow-countrymen in construction and other work. Later a good many Syrian peddlers were controlled by padrones who furnished them with stocks in trade and profited unduly by their labor. With the development of immigration of any such race, however, and the establishment of such races as factors in the population of the country, the padrone system has substantially disappeared. At the present time practically the only aliens under the control of padrones in any considerable numbers are the Greek boys employed in shoe-shining establishments or in peddling flowers, fruit, or vegetables in the larger cities. This evil became so prevalent that when the immigration law of 1907 was enacted the following were included in the debarred classes:

> All children under 16 years of age unaccompanied by one or both of their parents at the discretion of the Secretary of Commerce and Labor, or under such regulations as he may from time to time prescribe.

Under this provision the importation of boys by padrones has been curtailed and the Bureau of Immigration makes persistent and continual efforts to stamp out the evil. While this condition in the case of the Greeks may continue for some time, it seems altogether probable that as persons of that race progress in the United States the influence of the padrones will largely disappear, as has been the case with other European races. . . .

IMMIGRATION AND CRIME

It is impossible from existing data to determine whether the immigrant population in this country is relatively more or less criminal than the native-born population. Statistics show that the proportion of convictions for crimes according to the population is greater among the foreign-born than among the native-born. It must be remembered, however, that the proportion of persons of what may be termed the criminal age is greater among the foreign-born than among natives, and when due allowance is made for this fact it appears that criminality, judged by convictions, is about equally prevalent in each class. It is obviously impossible to determine whether the proportion of unpunished criminals is relatively greater among the foreign- or among the native- born. It is sometimes stated that the detection and conviction of criminals, especially for higher crimes, is more difficult in the case of the foreign-born. Probably this is true of certain localities and perhaps generally true in the case of certain nationalities, but there is no proof that this condition applies to the foreign-born elements as a whole in the country at large. It is possible that in some localities prejudice against or sympathy for foreigners influences convictions or acquittals. In large cities a part of the apparent criminality of the foreign-born consists merely of violations of ordinances, which are offenses only because the persons who commit them are not naturalized. Prominent in this class of offenses is street peddling without a license in cities where such licenses are granted only to citizens.

The proportion of the more serious crimes of homicide, blackmail, and robbery, as well as the least serious offenses, is greater among the foreign-born. The disproportion in this regard is due principally to the prevalence of homicides and other crimes of personal violence among Italians and to the violation of city ordinances previously mentioned. . . .

Views of the Minority

I recognize the great value of the work of the Immigration Commission and unite in the conclusions, so far as they are based on the reports, whether they coincide with my personal and previously formed opinions or not.

A slowing down of the present rate of the immigration of unskilled labor is justified by the report, and, according to the report, restriction should be limited to unmarried male aliens or married aliens unaccompanied by their wives and families. The reports show that in the main the present immigrants are not criminal, pauper, insane, or seekers of charity in so great a degree as their predecessors. The educational test proposed is a selective test for which no logical argument can be based on the report. As the report of the Commission is finally adopted within a half hour of the time when, under the law, it must be filed, there is no time for the preparation of an elaborate dissent. I sincerely regret that I can not fully agree with the remainder of the Commission, and if time permitted I would point out the many excellent provisions contained in the report, some of my own suggestion. My main ground of dissent is the specific recommendation by the majority of the educational test, though there are other instances in which it has not my full approval.

WILLIAM S. BENNET

27.   Finley Peter Dunne,
"Immigration" and "The Rising of the Subject Races"

WHAT collection of documents for the early twentieth century could omit selections from Finley Peter Dunne's "Mr. Dooley"! Dunne was one of the leading journalists of his day, possessed of an ability as a punster that has usually invited comparison with Mark Twain and Will Rogers. Born in Chicago in 1867, he reached the height of his powers and popularity during the period 1895 to 1915, mostly while serving on the editorial staff of the Chicago Journal. His chief outlet was a regular column featuring one Martin Dooley, a shrewd, honest, and simple Irish-American barkeeper who shared his social and political views with his friend and customer, Mr. Hennessy.

In the first of two pieces included here, Mr. Dooley sounds off on the Immigration Problem, taking as his cue the Immigration Act of 1903 (which one historian has referred to as "a real loss of nerve and of faith in the virtue of freedom"). Inspired by the assassination of President McKinley in 1901, Section 2 of the Act made "anarchists, or persons who believe in or advocate the overthrow by force and violence of the Government of the United States, or of all government, or of all forms of law, or the assassination of public officials" ineligible for entry into the country. Any alien arrested as an anarchist within three years of his entry was deportable. Since the law did not define "anarchists," it was often used to deport aliens whose political views were deemed "radical" by local judges. The "Snolgosh" referred to on page 257, was of course Leon F. Czolgosz, McKinley's assassin; he was indeed, as Mr. Dooley notes with due irony, born in Michigan ("Mitchigan").

In the second article, inspired by Japan's defeat of Russia in 1905, the very Celtic Mr. Dooley mocks the pretensions of "Anglo-Saxon" missionary expansion.

SOURCE: Finley Peter Dunne, "Immigration" in *Observations by Mr. Dooley* (New York: Harper & Brothers, Publishers, 1906), pp. 49–54; "The Rising of the Subject Races" in *Mr. Dooley Says* (New York: Charles Scribner's Sons, 1910), pp. 50–58. Copyright 1910 Charles Scribner's Sons; renewed 1938 by Margaret Dunne. Reprinted by permission of Charles Scribner's Sons.

Immigration

"Well, I see Congress has got to wurruk again," said Mr. Dooley. "The Lord save us fr'm harm," said Mr. Hennessy.

"Yes, sir," said Mr. Dooley, "Congress has got to wurruk again, an' manny things that seems important to a Congressman 'll be brought up befure thim. 'Tis sthrange that what's a big thing to a man in Wash'nton, Hinnissy, don't seem much account to me. Divvle a bit do I care whether they dig th' Nicaragoon Canal or cross th' Isthmus in a balloon; or whether th' Monroe docthrine is enfoorced or whether it ain't; or whether th' thrusts is abolished as Teddy Rosenfelt wud like to have thim or encouraged to go on with their neefaryous but magnificent entherprises as th' Prisidint wud like; or whether th' water is poured into th' ditches to reclaim th' arid lands iv th' West or th' money f'r thim to fertilize th' arid pocket-books iv th' conthractors; or whether th' Injun is threated like a depindant an' miserable thribesman or like a free an' indepindant dog; or whether we restore th' merchant marine to th' ocean or whether we lave it to restore itsilf. None iv these here questions inthrests me, an' be me I mane you an' be you I mane ivrybody. What we want to know is, ar-re we goin' to have coal enough in th' hod whin th' cold snap comes; will th' plumbin' hold out, an' will th' job last.

"But they'se wan question that Congress is goin' to take up that you an' me are inthrested in. As a pilgrim father that missed th' first boats, I must raise me claryon voice again' th' invasion iv this fair land be th' paupers an' arnychists iv effete Europe. Ye bet I must—because I'm here first. 'Twas diff'rent whin I was dashed high on th' stern an' rockbound coast. In thim days America was th' refuge iv th' oppressed iv all th' wurruld. They cud come over here an' do a good job iv oppressin' thimsilves. As I told ye I come a little late. Th' Rosenfelts an' th' Lodges bate me be at laste a boat lenth, an' be th' time I got here they was stern an' rockbound thimsilves. So I got a gloryous rayciption as soon as I was towed off th' rocks. Th' stars an' sthripes whispered a welcome in th' breeze an' a shovel was thrust into me hand an' I was pushed into a sthreet excyvatin' as though I'd been born here. . . .

"Annyhow, I was rayceived with open arms that sometimes ended in a clinch. I was afraid I wasn't goin' to assimilate with th' airlyer pilgrim fathers an' th' instichoochions iv th' counthry, but I soon found that a long swing iv th' pick made me as good as another man an' it didn't require a gr-reat intellect, or sometimes anny at all, to vote th' dimmycrat ticket, an' befure I was here a month, I felt enough like a native born American to burn a witch. Wanst in a while a mob iv intilligint collajeens, whose grandfathers had bate me to th' dock, wud take a shy at me Pathrick's Day procission or burn down wan iv me churches, but they got tired iv that befure long; 'twas too much like wurruk.

"But as I tell ye, Hinnissy, 'tis diff'rent now. I don't know why 'tis diff'rent but 'tis diff'rent. 'Tis time we put our back again' th' open dure an' keep out th' savage horde. If that cousin iv ye'ers expects to cross, he'd betther tear f'r th' ship. In a few minyits th' gates 'll be down an' whin th' oppressed wurruld comes hikin' acrost to th' haven iv refuge, they'll do well to put a couplin' pin undher their hats, f'r th' Goddess iv Liberty 'll meet thim at th' dock with an axe in her hand. Congress is goin' to fix it. Me frind Shaughnessy says so. He was in yisterdah an' says he: ' 'Tis time we done something to make th' immigration laws sthronger,' says he. 'Thrue f'r ye, Miles Standish,' says I; 'but what wud ye do?' 'I'd keep out th' offscourin's iv Europe,' says he. 'Wud ye go back?' says I. 'Have ye'er joke,' says he. ' 'Tis not so seeryus as it was befure ye come,' says I. "But what ar-re th' immygrants doin' that's roonous to us?' I says. 'Well,' says he, 'they're arnychists,' he says; 'they don't assymilate with th' counthry,' he says. 'Maybe th' counthry's digestion has gone wrong fr'm too much rich food,' says I; 'perhaps now if we'd lave off thryin' to digest Rockyfellar an' thry a simple diet like Schwartzmeister, we wudden't feel th' effects iv our vittels,' I says. 'Maybe if we'd season th' immygrants a little or cook thim thurly, they'd go down betther,' I says.

" 'They're arnychists, like Parsons,' he says. 'He wud've been an immygrant if Texas hadn't been admitted to th' Union,' I says. 'Or Snolgosh,' he says. 'Has Mitchigan seceded?' I says. 'Or Gittoo,' he says. 'Who come fr'm th' effete monarchies iv Chicago, west iv Ashland Av'noo,' I says. 'Or what's-his-name, Wilkes Booth,' he says. 'I don't know what he was—maybe a Boolgharyen,' says I. 'Well, annyhow,' says he, 'they're th' scum iv th' earth.' 'They may be that,' says I; 'but we used to think they was th' cream iv civiliza-tion,' I says. 'They're off th' top annyhow. I wanst believed 'twas th' best men iv Europe come here, th' la-ads that was too sthrong and indepindant to be kicked around be a boorgomasther at home an' wanted to dig out f'r a place where they cud get a chanst to make their way to th' money. I see their sons fightin' into politics an' their daughters tachin' young American idee how to shoot too high in th' public school, an' I thought they was all right. But I see I was wrong. Thim boys out there towin' wan heavy foot afther th' other to th' rowlin' mills is all arnychists. There's warrants out f'r all names endin' in 'inski, an' I think I'll board up me windows, f'r,' I says, 'if immygrants is as dangerous to this counthry as ye an' I an' other pilgrim fathers believe they are, they'se enough iv thim sneaked in already to make us aborigines about as infloointial as the prohibition vote in th' Twinty-ninth Ward. They'll dash again' our stern an' rock-bound coast till they bust it,' says I.

" 'But I ain't so much afraid as ye ar-re. I'm not afraid iv me father an' I'm not afraid iv mesilf. An' I'm not afraid iv Schwartz-meister's father or Hinnery Cabin Lodge's grandfather. We all come over th' same way, an' if me ancestors were not what Hogan calls rigicides, 'twas not because they were not ready an' willin', on'y a king niver come their way. I don't believe in killin' kings, mesilf. I niver wud've sawed th' block off that curly-headed po-tintate that I see in th' pitchers down town, but, be hivins, Presarved Codfish Shaughnessy, if we'd begun a few years ago shuttin' out folks that wudden't mind handin' a bomb to a king, they wudden't be enough people in Mattsachoosetts to make a quorum f'r th' Anti-Impeeryal S'ciety,' says I. 'But what wud ye do with th' offscourin' iv Europe?' says he. 'I'd scour thim some more,' says I.

"An' so th' meetin' iv th' Plymouth Rock Assocyation come to an end. But if ye wud like to get it together, Deacon Hinnissy, to discuss th' immygration question, I'll sind out a hurry call f'r Schwartzmeister an' Mulcahey an' Ignacio Sbarbaro an' Nels Lar-sen an' Petrus Gooldvink, an' we 'll gather to-night at Fanneilnovi-ski Hall at th' corner iv Sheridan an' Sigel sthreets. All th' pilgrim fathers is rayquested f'r to bring interpreters."

"Well," said Mr. Hennessy, "divvle th' bit I care, on'y I'm here first, an' I ought to have th' right to keep th' bus fr'm bein' over-crowded."

"Well," said Mr. Dooley, "as a pilgrim father on me gran' nephew's side, I don't know but ye're right. An' they'se wan sure way to keep thim out."

"What's that?" asked Mr. Hennessy.

"Teach thim all about our instichoochions befure they come," said Mr. Dooley.

The Rising of the Subject Races

"Ye'er frind Simpson was in here awhile ago," said Mr. Dooley, "an' he was that mad."

"What ailed him?" asked Mr. Hennessy.

"Well," said Mr. Dooley, "it seems he wint into me frind Hip Lung's laundhry to get his shirt an' it wasn't ready. Followin' what Hogan calls immemoryal usage, he called Hip Lung such names as he cud remimber and thried to dhrag him around th' place be his shinin' braid. But instead iv askin' f'r mercy, as he ought to, Hip Lung swung a flatiron on him an' thin ironed out his spine as he galloped up th' stairs. He come to me f'r advice an' I advised him to see th' American consul. Who's th' American consul in Chicago now? I don't know. But Hogan, who was here at th' time, grabs him be th' hand an' says he: 'I congratulate ye, me boy,' he says. 'Ye have a chance to be wan iv th' first martyrs iv th' white race in th' gr-reat sthruggle that's comin' between thim an' th' smoked or tinted races iv th' wurruld,' he says. 'Ye'll be another Jawn Brown's body or Mrs. O'Leary's cow. Go back an' let th' Chink kill ye an' cinchries hence people will come with wreathes and ate hard-biled eggs on ye'er grave,' he says.

"But Simpson said he did not care to be a martyr. He said he was a retail grocer be pro-fissyon an' Hip Lung was a customer iv his, though he got most iv his vittles fr'm th' taxydermist up th' sthreet an' he thought he'd go around to-morrah an' concilyate him. So he wint away.

"Hogan, d'ye mind, has a theery that it's all been up with us blondes since th' Jap'nese war. Hogan is a prophet. He's wan iv th' gr-reatest prophets I know. A prophet, Hinnissy, is a man that foresees throuble. No wan wud listen a minyit to anny prophet that prophesized pleasant days. . . .

"He's a rale prophet. I wudden't pick him out as a well-finder. He cudden't find a goold mine f'r ye but he cud see th' bottom iv wan through three thousand feet iv bullyon. . . . He's predicted ivry war that has happened in our time and eight thousand that haven't happened to happen. If he had his way th' United States navy wud be so big that there wudden't be room f'r a young fellow to row his girl in Union Park. He can see a war cloud where I can't see annything but somebody cookin' his dinner or lightin' his pipe. . . .

"Hogan says th' time has come f'r th' subjick races iv th' wurruld to rejooce us fair wans to their own complexion be batin' us black and blue. Up to now 'twas: 'Sam, ye black rascal, tow in thim eggs or I'll throw ye in th' fire. 'Yassir,' says Sam. 'Comin',' he says. 'Twas: 'Wow Chow, while ye'er idly stewin' me cuffs I'll set fire to me unpaid bills.' 'I wud feel repaid be a kick,' says Wow Chow. 'Twas: 'Maharajah Sewar, swing th' fan swifter or I'll have to roll over f'r me dog whip.' 'Higgins Sahib,' says Maharajah Sewar, 'Higgins Sahib, beloved iv Gawd an' Kipling, ye'er punishments ar-re th' nourishment iv th' faithful. My blood hath served thine f'r manny ginerations. At laste two. 'Twas thine old man that blacked my father's eye an' sint my uncle up f'r eighty days. How will ye'er honor have th' accursed swine's flesh cooked f'r breakfast in th' mornin' when I'm through fannin' ye?'

"But now, says Hogan, it's all changed. Iver since th' Rooshyans were starved out at Port Arthur and Portsmouth, th' wurrud has passed around an' ivry naygur fr'm lemon color to coal is bracin' up. He says they have aven a system of tilly-graftin' that bates ours be miles. They have no wires or poles or wathered stock but th' population is so thick that whin they want to sind wurrud along th' line all they have to do is f'r wan man to nudge another an' something happens in Northern Chiny is known in Southern Indya befure sunset. And so it passed through th' undherwurruld that th' color line was not to be dhrawn anny more, an' Hogan says that almost anny time he ixpicts to see a black face peerin' through a window an' in a few years I'll be takin' in laundhry in a basement instead iv occypyin' me present impeeryal position, an' ye'll be settin' in front in ye'er cabin home playin' on a banjo an' watchin' ye'er little pickahinnissies rollickin' on th' ground an' wondhrn' whin th' lynchin' party'll arrive.

"That's what Hogan says. I niver knew th' subjick races had so much in thim before. . . .

"I don't see what th' subjick races got to kick about, Hinnissy. We've been awfully good to thim. We sint thim missionaries to teach thim th' error iv their relligyon an' nawthin' cud be kinder thin that f'r there's nawthin' people like betther thin to be told that their parents are not be anny means where they thought they were but in a far more crowded an' excitin' locality. An' with th' missionaries we sint sharpshooters that cud pick off a Chinyman beatin' th' conthribution box at five hundherd yards. We put up palashal goluf-coorses in the cimitries an' what was wanst th' tomb iv Hung Chang, th' gr-reat Tartar Impror, rose to th' dignity iv bein' th' bunker guardin' th' fifth green. No Chinyman cud fail to be pleased at seein' a tall Englishman hittin' th' Chinyman's grandfather's coffin with a niblick. We sint explorers up th' Nile who raypoorted that th' Ganzain flows into th' Oboo just above Lake Mazap, a fact that th' naygurs had known f'r a long time. Th' explorer announces that he has changed th' names iv these wather-coorses to Smith, Blifkins an' Winkinson. He wishes to deny th' infamyous story that he iver ate a native alive. But wan soon succumbs to th' customs iv a counthry an' Sir Alfred is no viggytaryan.

"An' now, be Hivin, all these here wretched millyons that we've done so much f'r ar-re turnin' on us. Th' Japs threaten us with war. Th' Chinese won't buy shoes fr'm us an' ar-re chasin' th' missionaries out iv their cozy villas an' not even givin' thim a chance to carry away their piannies or their silverware. There's th' divvle to pay all along th' levee fr'm Manchurya to Madagascar, accordin' to Hogan. I begin to feel onaisy. Th' first thing we know all th' other subjick races will be up. Th' horses will kick an' bite, th' dogs will fly at our throats whin we lick thim, th' fishes will refuse to be caught, th' cattle an' pigs will set fire to th' stock yards an' there'll be a gineral rebellyon against th' white man.

"It's no laughin' matther, I tell ye. A subjick race is on'y funny whin it's raaly subjick. About three years ago I stopped laughin' at Jap'nese jokes. Ye have to feel supeeryor to laugh an' I'm gettin' over that feelin'. An' nawthin' makes a man so mad an' so scared as whin something he looked down on as infeeryor tur-rns on him. If a fellow man hits him he hits him back. But if a dog bites him he yells 'mad dog' an' him an' th' neighbors pound th' dog to pieces with clubs. If th' naygurs down South iver got together an' flew at their masters ye'd hear no more coon songs f'r awhile. It's our conceit makes us supeeryor. Take it out iv us an' we ar-re about th' same as th' rest.

"I wondher what we'd do if all thim infeeryor races shud come at us together?" said Mr. Hennessy. "They're enough iv thim to swamp us."

"Well," said Mr. Dooley, "I'd have to go on bein' white or, to speak more acc'rately, pink. An' annyhow I guess they've been infeeryor too long to change. It's got to be a habit with thim."

VII

America Enters Foreign Affairs

28. President William McKinley, The War Message, April 11, 1898

WHY did the United States go to war against Spain in 1898? There are no easy answers besides the dodge that it was a mixture of commercial ambition, patriotic enthusiasm, and democratic ideals. Commercially, Cuba was no very juicy plum, and there were a few contemporary businessmen who would have exerted themselves to have opened Cuba to American investors without the costs of a war. Yet it could be said with accuracy that many Americans viewed Cuba as symbolically the thin end of the wedge that would open up Asia as well as Latin America to United States interests. At the same time, patriotic fervor had been rising, possibly in response to the sense of social disintegration growing in America during the Populist Era. "While it might be putting it too strong to say that war is needed in this country now," wrote the editors of one Kansas newspaper in October 1895, "yet who is there who does not . . . in fact know that such a thing would clear the atmosphere and stamp out the growth of socialism and anarchy, discontent and sectional prejudice that is gaining a foothold in this nation?" For some, especially among the old "aristocracy," like Theodore Roosevelt and Henry Cabot Lodge, patriotism offered an alternative criterion to wealth by which a man might be compared favorably with the "vulgar nouveaux" such as the Rockefellers and Goulds. War rather than wealth, according to such sentiments, tested a man's worth. "We hearken not to rhymers on universal peace," rhapsodized Indiana's Albert Beveridge as early as 1892, "for we know that with the sword the world has ever out of error carved its good estate. . . . I subscribe to the doctrine of war. It is the divine instrument of progress. Every lasting victory of freedom was won upon the field."

It was ultimately, of course, the cry "Free Cuba!" that rallied thousands of young men, radicals and stalwarts alike, to the colors against Spain. "We will have this war for the freedom of Cuba," Roosevelt wrote to his sister early in 1898, "in spite of the timidity of the commercial interests." William Jennings Bryan no less than the Roosevelts and Leonard Woods rushed headlong to the training camps and fretted miserably that the war might end too quickly for them to see action. In the final analysis, the idealistic notion—however misbegotten—that the United States served the cause of liberty must figure most eminently among the forces impelling McKinley to his war message, printed below.

SOURCE: James D. Richardson (ed.), *A Compilation of the Messages and Papers of the Presidents*, Vol. X (Washington, D.C.: Government Printing Office, 1899), pp. 139–150.

Executive Mansion, April 11, 1898

TO THE CONGRESS OF THE UNITED STATES:

Obedient to that precept of the Constitution which commands the President to give from time to time to the Congress information of the state of the Union and to recommend to their consideration such measures as he shall judge necessary and expedient, it becomes my duty to now address your body with regard to the grave crisis that has arisen in the relations of the United States to Spain by reason of the warfare that for more than three years has raged in the neighboring island of Cuba.

I do so because of the intimate connection of the Cuban question with the state of our own Union and the grave relation the course which it is now incumbent upon the nation to adopt must needs bear to the traditional policy of our Government if it is to accord with the precepts laid down by the founders of the Republic and religiously observed by succeeding Administrations to the present day.

The present revolution is but the successor of other similar insurrections which have occurred in Cuba against the dominion of Spain, extending over a period of nearly half a century, each of which during its progress has subjected the United States to great effort and expense in enforcing its neutrality laws, caused enormous losses to American trade and commerce, caused irritation, annoyance, and disturbance among our citizens, and, by the exercise of cruel, barbarous, and uncivilized practices of warfare, shocked the sensibilities and offended the humane sympathies of our people.

Since the present revolution began, in February, 1895, this country has seen the fertile domain at our threshold ravaged by fire and sword in the course of a struggle unequaled in the history of the island and rarely paralleled as to the numbers of the combatants and the bitterness of the contest by any revolution of modern times where a dependent people striving to be free have been opposed by the power of the sovereign state.

Our people have beheld a once prosperous community reduced to comparative want, its lucrative commerce virtually paralyzed, its exceptional productiveness diminished, its fields laid waste, its mills in ruins, and its people perishing by tens of thousands from hunger and destitution. We have found ourselves constrained, in the observance of that strict neutrality which our laws enjoin and which the law of nations commands, to police our own waters and watch our own seaports in prevention of any unlawful act in aid of the Cubans.

Our trade has suffered, the capital invested by our citizens in Cuba has been largely lost, and the temper and forbearance of our people have been so sorely tried as to beget a perilous unrest among our own citizens . . . so that issues wholly external to our own body politic engross attention and stand in the way of that close devotion to domestic advancement that becomes a self-contained commonwealth whose primal maxim has been the avoidance of all foreign entanglements. . . .

The war in Cuba is of such a nature that, short of subjugation or extermination, a final military victory for either side seems impracticable. The alternative lies in the physical exhaustion of the one or the other party, or perhaps of both. . . . The prospect of such a protraction and conclusion of the present strife is a contingency hardly to be contemplated with equanimity by the civilized world, and least of all by the United States, affected and injured as we are, deeply and intimately, by its very existence.

Realizing this, it appeared to be my duty, in a spirit of true friendliness, no less to Spain than to the Cubans, who have so much to lose by the prolongation of the struggle, to seek to bring about an immediate termination of the war. To this end I submitted on the 27th ultimo, as a result of much representation and correspondence, through the United States minister at Madrid, propositions to the Spanish Government looking to an armistice until October 1 for the negotiation of peace with the good offices of the President.

In addition I asked the immediate revocation of the order of reconcentration, so as to permit the people to return to their farms and the needy to be relieved with provisions and supplies from the United States, cooperating with the Spanish authorities, so as to afford full relief.

The reply of the Spanish cabinet was received on the night of the 31st ultimo. It offered, as the means to bring about peace in Cuba, to confide the preparation thereof to the insular parliament, inasmuch as the concurrence of that body would be necessary to reach a final result, it being, however, understood that the powers reserved by the constitution to the central Government are not lessened or diminished. As the Cuban parliament does not meet until the 4th of May next, the Spanish Government would not object for its part to accept at once a suspension of hostilities if asked for by the insurgents from the general in chief, to whom it would pertain in such case to determine the duration and conditions of the armistice. . . .

With this last overture in the direction of immediate peace, and its disappointing reception by Spain, the Executive is brought to the end of his effort.

In my annual message of December last I said:

> Of the untried measures there remain only: Recognition of the insurgents as belligerents; recognition of the independence of Cuba; neutral intervention to end the war by imposing a rational compromise between the contestants, and intervention in favor of one or the other party. I speak not of forcible annexation, for that can not be thought of. That, by our code of morality, would be criminal aggression.

Thereupon I reviewed these alternatives. . . . I commented especially upon . . . the inconveniences and positive dangers of a recognition of belligerence, which, while adding to the already onerous burdens of neutrality within our own jurisdiction, could not in any way extend our influence or effective offices in the territory of hostilities.

Nothing has since occurred to change my view in this regard . . .

Nor from the standpoint of expediency do I think it would be wise or prudent for this Government to recognize at the present time the independence of the so-called Cuban Republic. . . . To commit this country now to the recognition of any particular government in Cuba might subject us to embarrassing conditions of international obligation toward the organization so recognized. . . .

The only hope of relief and repose from a condition which can no longer be endured is the enforced pacification of Cuba. In the name of humanity, in the name of civilization, in behalf of endangered American interests which give us the right and the duty to speak and to act, the war in Cuba must stop.

In view of these facts and of these considerations I ask the Congress to authorize and empower the President to take measures to secure a full and final termination of hostilities between the Government of Spain and the people of Cuba, and to secure in the island the establishment of a stable government, capable of maintaining order and observing its international obligations, insuring peace and tranquillity and the security of its citizens as well as our own, and to use the military and naval forces of the United States as may be necessary for these purposes.

. . . Prepared to execute every obligation imposed upon me by the Constitution and the law, I await your action.

Yesterday, and since the preparation of the foregoing message, official information was recieved by me that the latest decree of the Queen Regent of Spain directs General Blanco, in order to prepare and facilitate peace, to proclaim a suspension of hostilities, the duration and details of which have not yet been communicated to me.

This fact, with every other pertinent consideration, will, I am sure, have your just and careful attention in the solemn deliberations upon which you are about to enter. If this measure attains a successful result, then our aspirations as a Christian, peace-loving people will be realized. If it fails, it will be only another justification for our contemplated action.

WILLIAM McKINLEY

29. Mark Twain, "Glances at History"

THE SPANISH WAR led the United States inexorably to the problems of empire. "We don't want more territory," wrote Lyman Abbott, editor and lay preacher, "but God doesn't permit us a choice." "There was nothing left for us to do," said McKinley in explaining his decision to annex the Philippines, "but to take them all, and educate the Filipinos, and uplift and civilize and Christianize them, and by God's grace do the very best we could by them, as our fellow-men for whom Christ also died." Some Filipinos, however, had been led to believe the Americans had come as liberators, and when they learned otherwise, they engaged the United States in a full-scale war under the leadership of Emilio Aguinaldo. The "organized" stage of the war had ended by January

1900, but guerilla warfare continued relentlessly until 1902. Meanwhile, many Americans suffered the spectacle of their country conducting the ruthless suppression of a proud and valiant people. Henry Adams wrote of how he "turned green at midnight" contemplating the barbarism perpetrated in the name of America's mission, while William James observed that if "the Anglo-Saxon race would drop its sniveling cant it would have a good deal less of a 'burden' to carry."

But probably few expressed their chagrin over America's imperialist venture better than Mark Twain. The passages presented below represent the major part of some fragments found in the Twain papers, probably intended for a book-length work that never materialized.

SOURCE: Mark Twain, "Papers of the Adam Family," *Letters from the Earth*, ed., Bernard De Voto (New York: Harper & Row, Publishers, Inc., 1962), pp. 107–109. Copyright © 1962 by The Mark Twain Company. Reprinted by permission of Harper & Row, Publishers.

We, free citizens of the Great Republic, feel an honest pride in her greatness, her strength, her just and gentle government, her wide liberties, her honored name, her stainless history, her unsmirched flag, her hands clean from oppression of the weak and from malicious conquest, her hospitable door that stands open to the hunted and the persecuted of all nations; we are proud of the judicious respect in which she is held by the monarchies which hem her in on every side, and proudest of all of that lofty patriotism which we inherited from our fathers, which we have kept pure, and which won our liberties in the beginning and has preserved them unto this day. While that patriotism endures the Republic is safe, her greatness is secure, and against them the powers of the earth cannot prevail.

I pray you to pause and consider. Against our traditions we are now entering upon an unjust and trivial war, a war against a helpless people, and for a base object—robbery. At first our citizens spoke out against this thing, by an impulse natural to their training. Today they have turned, and their voice is the other way. What caused the change? Merely a politician's trick—a highsounding phrase, a blood-stirring phrase which turned their uncritical heads: Our Country, right or wrong! An empty phrase, a silly phrase. It was shouted by every newspaper, it was thundered from the pulpit, the Superintendent of Public Instruction placarded it in every schoolhouse in the land, the War Department inscribed it upon the flag. And every man who failed to shout it or who was silent, was proclaimed a traitor—none but those others were patriots. To be a patriot, one had to say, and keep on saying, "Our Country, right or wrong," and urge on the little war. Have you not perceived that that phrase is an insult to the nation?

For in a republic, who *is* "the Country"? Is it the Government which is for the moment in the saddle? Why, the Government is merely a *servant*—merely a temporary servant; it cannot be its prerogative to determine what is right and what is wrong, and decide who is a patriot and who isn't. Its function is to obey orders, not originate them. Who, then, is "the Country"? . . .

In a monarchy, the king and his family are the country; in a republic it is the common voice of the people. Each of you, for himself, by himself and on his own responsibility, must speak. And it is a solemn and weighty responsibility, and not lightly to be flung aside at the bullying of pulpit, press, government, or the empty catch-phrases of politicians. Each must for himself alone decide what is right and what is wrong, and which course is patriotic and which isn't. You cannot shirk this and be a man. To decide it against your convictions is to be an unqualified and inexcusable traitor, both to yourself and to your country, let men label you as they may. If you alone of all the nation shall decide one way, and that way be the right way according to your convictions of the right, you have done your duty by yourself and by your country— hold up your head! You have nothing to be ashamed of.

Only when a republic's *life* is in danger should a man uphold his government when it is in the wrong. There is no other time.

This Republic's life is not in peril. The nation has sold its honor for a phrase. It has swung itself loose from its safe anchorage and is drifting, its helm is in pirate hands. The stupid phrase needed help, and it got another one: "Even if the war be wrong we are in it and must fight it out; *we cannot retire from it without dishonor.*" Why, not even a burglar could have said it better. We cannot withdraw from this sordid raid because to grant peace to these little people upon their terms—independence—would dishonor us. You have flung away Adam's phrase—you should take it up and examine it again. He said, "*An inglorious peace is better than a dishonorable war.*"

30. Woodrow Wilson, "Democracy and Efficiency"

THIS remarkable little article from the Atlantic Monthly, written just as the new century opened, reveals much about the premises of leading American opinion on both domestic and foreign policy. Woodrow Wilson was professor of history at Princeton and a Democrat in political affinities. Yet it is striking how much Wilson had in common with the aggressive Roosevelt-Beveridge-Lodge group that epitomized "the enemy" for him after he entered partisan politics. Wilson first of all presents the theme of "the closing of the frontier" with a discussion of the problems to democracy which that development seemed to portend (compare the Turner and Croly articles, Documents 1 and 4 above). Second comes Wilson's contention that the true raison d'être of American economic and political institutions is their role in individual character building; American institutions, he argues, have been valuable most particularly because of the way they depend on character in order to function effectively, and thereby they help to develop character. Third, he feels that the United States must solve its problems not simply for its own sake but because America stands before the world as the herald of progressive democracy. Finally, Wilson argues that America must accept its new-found international responsibilities, "The East is to be opened and transformed whether we will or no. . . . It is our peculiar duty, as it is also England's, to moderate the process in the interests of liberty."

This last was an unbeatable argument, especially in an era when Americans took for granted their superior enlightenment in matters economic and political. McKinley of course had used it to justify the taking of the Philippines ("we could not turn them over to France or Germany —our commercial rivals in the Orient—that would be bad business and discreditable"). Roosevelt used it to justify his "Corollary" to the Monroe Doctrine, and Taft to justify "Dollar Diplomacy (see Document 32). And it was probably Wilson's commitment to the idea that constituted the final argument in his decision to intervene in World War I; specifically, that if the United States were not a belligerent, and therefore not on hand at the peace table, the peace would be made by nations less committed to democracy and progress.

SOURCE: Woodrow Wilson, "Democracy and Efficiency," The Atlantic Monthly, LXXXVII (March 1901), pp. 289–299.

It is no longer possible to mistake the reaction against democracy. The nineteenth century was above all others a century of democracy; and yet the world is no more convinced of the benefits of democracy as a form of government at its end than it was at its beginning. The history of closeted Switzerland has not been accepted as proving the stability of democratic institutions; the history of the United States has not been accepted as establishing their tendency to make governments just and liberal and pure. Their eccentric influence in France, their disastrous and revolutionary operation in South America, their power to intoxicate and their powerlessness to reform,—except where the states which use them have had in their training and environment what Switzerland or the colonies and commonwealths sprung from England have had, to strengthen and steady them,—have generally been deemed to offset every triumph or success they can boast. When we praise democracy, we are still put to our proofs; when we excuse its errors, we are understood to have admitted its failure.

There need be in this, however, no serious discouragement for us, whose democratic institutions have in all large things succeeded. It means nothing more than that the world is at last ready to accept the moral long ago drawn for it by de Tocqueville. He predicted the stability of the government of the United States, not because of its intrinsic excellence, but because of its suitability to the particular social, economic, and political conditions of the people and the country for whose use and administration it had been framed; because of the deliberation and sober sagacity with which it had been devised and set up; because it could reckon upon a sufficient "variety of information and excellence of discretion" on the part of the people who were to live under it to insure its intelligent operation; because he observed a certain uniformity of civilization to obtain throughout the country, and saw its affairs steadied by their fortunate separation from European politics; because he found a sober, religious habit of thought among our people, and a clear sense of right. Democracy was with us, he perceived, already a thing of principle and custom and nature, and our institutions admirably expressed our training and experience. No other people could expect to succeed by the same means, unless those means equally suited their character and stage of development. Democracy, like every other form of government, depended for its success upon qualities and conditions which it did not itself create, but only obeyed.

Many excellent suggestions, valid and applicable everywhere, we have given the world, with regard to the spirit in which government should be conducted. No doubt class privilege has been forever discredited because of our example. We have taught the world the principle of the general welfare as the object and end of government, rather than the prosperity of any class or section of the nation, or the preferment of any private or petty interest. We have made the law appear to all men an instrument wherewith to secure equality of rights and a protection which shall be without respect of persons. There can be no misgivings about the currency or the permanency of the *principles* of right which we have exalted. But we have not equally commended the forms or the organizations of the government under which we live.

A federal union of diverse commonwealths we have indeed made to seem both practicable and efficient as a means of organizing government on a great scale, while preserving at the same time the utmost possible latitude and independence in local self-government. Germany, Canada, Australia, Switzerland herself, have built and strengthened their constitutions in large part upon our model. It would be hard to exaggerate the shock which has been given to old theories, or the impetus which has been given to hopeful experiment, in the field of political action, by our conspicuous successes as constitution-makers and reformers. But those successes have not been unlimited. We have not escaped the laws of error that government is heir to. It is said that riots and disorders are more frequent amongst us than in any other country of the same degree of civilization; justice is not always done in our courts; our institutions do not prevent, they do not seem even to moderate, contests between capital and labor; our laws of property are no more equitable, our laws of marriage no more moralizing, than those of undemocratic nations, our contemporaries; our cities are perhaps worse governed than any in Europe outside the Turkish Empire and Spain; crime defies or evades the law amongst us as amongst other peoples, less favored in matters of freedom and privilege; we have no monopoly either of happiness or of enlightened social order. As we grow older, we grow also perplexed and awkward in the doing of justice and in the perfecting and safeguarding of liberty. It is character and good principle, after all, which are to save us, if we are to escape disaster.

That moral is the justification of what we have attempted. It is for this that we love democracy: for the emphasis it puts on character; for its tendency to exalt the purposes of the average man to some high level of endeavor; for its just principle of common assent in matters in which all are concerned; for its ideals of duty and its sense of brotherhood. Its forms and institutions are meant to be subservient to these things. . . .

Representative government has had its long life and excellent development, not in order that common opinion, the opinion of the street, might prevail, but in order that the best opinion, the opinion generated by the best possible methods of general counsel, might rule in affairs; in order that some sober and best opinion might be created, by thoughtful and responsible discussion conducted by men intimately informed concerning the public weal, and officially commissioned to look to its safeguarding and advancement,—by discussion in parliaments, discussion face to face between authoritative critics and responsible ministers of state.

This is the central object to which we have devoted our acknowledged genius for practical politics. During the first half century of our national life we seemed to have succeeded in an extraordinary degree in approaching our ideal, in organizing a nation for counsel and coöperation, and in moving forward with cordial unison and with confident and buoyant step toward the accomplishment of tasks and duties upon which all were agreed. Our later life has disclosed serious flaws, has even seemed ominous of pitiful failure, in some of the things we most prided ourselves upon having managed well: notably, in pure and efficient local government, in the successful organization of great cities, and in well-considered schemes of administration. The boss—a man elected by no votes, preferred by no open process of choice, occupying no office of responsibility—makes himself a veritable tyrant amongst us, and seems to cheat us of self-government; parties appear to hamper the movements of opinion rather than to give them form and means of expression; multitudinous voices of agitation, an infinite play of forces at cross-purpose, confuse us; and there seems to be no common counsel or definite union for action, after all.

We keep heart the while because still sure of our principles and of our ideals: the common weal, a common and cordial understanding in matters of government, secure private rights and yet concerted public action, a strong government and yet liberty also. We know what we have to do; what we have missed and mean to find; what we have lost and mean to recover; what we still strive after and mean to achieve. Democracy is a principle with us, not a mere form of government. What we have blundered at is its new applications and details, its successful combination with efficiency and purity in governmental action. . . .

"If only we had our old leisure for domestic affairs, we should devise a way of our own to be efficient, consonant with our principles, characteristic of our genius for organization," we have heard men say. "How fatal it may prove to us that our attention has been called off from a task but half done to the tasks of the world, for which we have neither inclination nor proper training nor suitable organization,—from which, until now, we were so happily free! We shall now be forever barred from perfection, our own perfection, at home!" But may it not be that the future will put another face upon the matter, and show us our advantage where least we thought it to lie? May it not be that the way to perfection lies along these new paths of struggle, of discipline, and of achievement? What will the reaction of new duty be? What self-revelations will it afford; what lessons of unified will, of simplified method, of clarified purpose; what disclosures of the fundamental principles of right action, the efficient means of just achievement, if we but keep our ideals and our character?

At any rate, it is clear that we could not have held off. The affairs of the world stand in such a case, the principles for which we have battled the long decades through are now put in such jeopardy amidst the contests of nations, the future of mankind faces so great a peril of reactionary revolution, that our own private business must take its chances along with the greater business of the world at large. We dare not stand neutral. All mankind deem us the representatives of the moderate and sensible discipline which makes free men good citizens, of enlightened systems of law and a temperate justice, of the best experience in the reasonable methods and principles of self-government, of public force made consistent with individual liberty; and we shall not realize these ideals at home, if we suffer them to be hopelessly discredited amongst the peoples who have yet to see liberty and the peaceable days of order and comfortable progress. We should lose heart ourselves, did we suffer the world to lose faith in us as the champions of these things. . . .

Our almost accidental possession of the Philippines has put us in the very presence of the forces which must make the politics of the twentieth century radically unlike the politics of the nineteenth; but we must have taken cognizance of them and dealt with them in any event. They concern us as nearly as they concern any other nation in the world. They concern all nations, for they shall determine the future of the race. Fortunately, they have not disclosed themselves before we were ready. I do not mean that our thought was prepared for them; I do not mean that our domestic affairs were in such shape as to seem fairly well ordered, so that we might in good conscience turn from them as from things finished and complete, and divert our energies to tasks beyond our borders. I mean that this change in the order of the world came, so far as we are concerned, at the natural point in our national development. The matter is worth looking into.

There has been a certain singular unity in our national task, hitherto; and these new duties now thrust upon us will not break that unity. They will perpetuate it, rather, and make it complete, if we keep but our integrity and our old-time purpose true. Until 1890 the United States had always a frontier; looked always to a region beyond, unoccupied, unappropriated, an outlet for its energy, a new place of settlement and of achievement for its people. For nearly three hundred years their growth had followed a single law,—the law of expansion into new territory. . . . There was always space and adventure enough and to spare, to satisfy the feet of our young men.

The great process put us to the making of states; kept the wholesome blood of sober and strenuous and systematic work warm within us; perpetuated in us the spirit of initiative and of practical expediency which had made of the colonies vigorous and heady states; created in us that national feeling which finally put sectionalism from the field and altered the very character of the government; gave us the question of the extension of slavery, brought on the civil war, and decided it by the weight of the West. From coast to coast across the great continent our institutions have spread, until the western sea has witnessed the application upon a great scale of what was begun upon a small scale on the shores of the Atlantic, and the drama has been played almost to its last act,—the drama of institutional construction on the vast scale of a continent. The whole European world, which gave us our materials, has been moralized and liberalized by the striking and stupendous spectacle.

No other modern nation has been schooled as we have been in

big undertakings and the mastery of novel difficulties. We have become confirmed in energy, in resourcefulness, in practical proficiency, in self-confidence. We have become confirmed, also, so far as our character is concerned, in the habit of acting under an odd mixture of selfish and altruistic motives. Having ourselves a population fit to be free, making good its freedom in every sort of unhampered enterprise, determining its own destiny unguided and unbidden, moving as it pleased within wide boundaries, using institutions, not dominated by them, we have sympathized with freedom everywhere; have deemed it niggardly to deny an equal degree of freedom to any race or community that desired it; have pressed handsome principles of equity in international dealings; have rejoiced to believe that our principles might some day make every government a servant, not a master, of its people. Ease and prosperity have made us wish the whole world to be as happy and well to do as ourselves; and we have supposed that institutions and principles like our own were the simple prescription for making them so. And yet, when issues of our own interest arose, we have not been unselfish. We have shown ourselves kin to all the world, when it came to pushing an advantage. Our action against Spain in the Floridas, and against Mexico on the coasts of the Pacific; our attitude toward first the Spaniards, and then the French, with regard to the control of the Mississippi; the unpitying force with which we thrust the Indians to the wall wherever they stood in our way, have suited our professions of peacefulness and justice and liberality no better than the aggressions of other nations that were strong and not to be gainsaid. . . . Our interests must march forward, altruists though we are: other nations must see to it that they stand off, and do not seek to stay us.

It is only just now, however, that we have awakened to our real relationship to the rest of mankind. Absorbed in our own development, we had fallen into a singular ignorance of the rest of the world. The isolation in which we lived was quite without parallel in modern history. . . .

Misled by our own splendid initial advantage in the matter of self-government, we have suffered ourselves to misunderstand self-government itself, when the question was whether it could be put into practice amidst conditions totally unlike those with which, and with which alone, we have been familiar. The people of the United States have never known anything but self-government since the colonies were founded. They have forgotten the discipline which preceded the founding of the colonies, the long drill in order and in obedience to law, the long subjection to kings and to parliaments which were not in fact of the people's choosing. They have forgotten how many generations were once in tutelage in order that the generations which discovered and settled the coasts of America might be mature and free. . . .

It is of the utmost importance that we should see the unmistakable truth of this matter and act upon it with all candor. It is not a question of the excellence of self-government: it is a question of the method of self-government. . . . It is a matter of separating the essentials from the non-essentials, the principle of self-government from its accidental forms. Democracy is unquestionably the most wholesome and livable kind of government the world has yet tried. It supplies as no other system could the frank and universal criticism, the free play of individual thought, the open conduct of public affairs, the spirit and pride of community and of coöperation, which make governments just and public-spirited. But the question of efficiency is the same for it as for any other kind of polity. . . .

It is our present and immediate task to extend self-government to Porto Rico and the Philippines, if they be fit to receive it,—so soon as they can be made fit. If there is to be preparation, we must know of what kind it should be, and how it ought to be conducted. Although we have forgotten our own preparatory discipline in that kind, these new tasks will undoubtedly teach us that some discipline—it may be prolonged and tedious—must precede self-government and prepare the way for it . . . that character and the moralizing effect of law are conditions precedent, obscure, and difficult, but absolutely indispensable. An examination of our own affairs will teach us these things; an examination of the affairs of the peoples we have undertaken to govern will confirm us in the understanding of them.

We shall see now more clearly than ever before that we lack in our domestic arrangements, above all things else, concentration, both in political leadership and in administrative organization; for the lack will be painfully emphasized, and will embarrass us sadly in the career we have now set out upon. Authority has been as much dispersed and distributed in the making of law and the choice of policy, under the forms we have used hitherto, as it has been in administrative action. We have been governed in all things by mass meetings. Committees of Congress, as various in their make-up as the body itself, sometimes guided by the real leaders of party, oftener guided by men whom the country at large neither knew nor looked to for leadership, have determined our national policy, piece by piece, and the pieces have seldom been woven together into any single or consistent pattern of statesmanship. There has been no leadership except the private leadership of party managers, no integration of the public business except such as was effected by the compromises and votes of party caucuses. Such methods will serve very awkwardly, if at all, for action in international affairs or in the government of distant dependencies. . . .

We did not of deliberate choice undertake these new tasks which shall transform us. All the world knows the surprising circumstances which thrust them upon us. Sooner or later, nevertheless, they would have become inevitable. If they had not come upon us in this way, they would have come in another. They came upon us, as it was, though unexpected, with a strange opportuneness, as if part of a great preconceived plan for changing the world. Every man now knows that the world is to be changed,—changed according to an ordering of Providence hardly so much as foreshadowed until it came; except, it may be, to a few Europeans who were burrowing and plotting and dreaming in the mysterious East. The whole world had already become a single vicinage; each part had become neighbor to all the rest. No nation could live any longer to itself, the tasks and the duties of neighborhood being what they were. Whether we had had a material foothold there or not, it would have been the duty of the United States to play a part, and a leading part at that, in the opening and transformation of the East. We might not have seen our duty, had the Philippines not fallen to us by the willful fortune of war; but it would have been our duty, nevertheless, to play the part we now see ourselves obliged to play. The East is to be opened and transformed, whether we will or no; the standards of the West are to be imposed upon it; nations and peoples which have stood still the centuries through are to be quickened, and make part of the universal world of commerce and of ideas which has so steadily been a-making by the advance of European power from age to age. It is our peculiar duty, as it is also England's, to moderate the process in the interests of liberty: to impart to the peoples thus driven out upon the road of change, so far as we have opportunity or can make it, our own principles of self-help; teach them order and self-control in the midst of change; impart to them, if it be possible by contact and sympathy and example, the drill and habit of law and obedience which we long ago got out of the strenuous processes of English history; secure for them, when we may, the free intercourse and the natural development which shall make them at least equal members of the family of nations. In China, of course, our part will be indirect, but in the Philippines it will be direct; and there in particular must the moral of our polity be set up and vindicated.

This we shall do, not by giving them out of hand our codes of political morality or our methods of political action, the generous gifts of complete individual liberty or the full-fangled institutions of American self-government,—a purple garment for their nakedness,—for these things are not blessings, but a curse, to undeveloped peoples, still in the childhood of their political growth; but by giving them, in the spirit of service, a government and rule which shall moralize them by being itself moral, elevate and steady them by being itself pure and steadfast, inducting them into the rudiments of justice and freedom. In other words, it is the aid of our character they need, and not the premature aid of our institutions. Our institutions must come after the ground of character and habit has been made ready for them; as effect, not cause, in the order of political growth. It is thus that we shall ourselves recognize the fact, at last patent to all the world, that the service of democracy has been the development of ideals rather than the origination of practical methods of administration of universal validity, or any absolute qualification of the ultimate conceptions of sovereignty and the indispensable disciplinary operation of law. We must aid their character and elevate their ideals, and then see what these will bring forth, generating after their kind. . . .

The best guarantee of good government we can give the Filipinos is, that we shall be sensitive to the opinion of the world; that we shall be sensitive in what we do to our own standards, so often boasted of and proclaimed, and shall wish above all things else to live up to the character we have established, the standards we have professed. When they accept the compulsions of that character and accept those standards, they will be entitled to partnership with us, and shall have it. They shall, meanwhile, teach us, as we shall teach them. . . . We must learn what we can, and yet scrupulously square everything that we do with the high principles we brought into the world: that justice may be done to the lowly no less than to the great; that government may serve its people, not make itself their master. . . .

31. Theodore Roosevelt, The "Roosevelt Corollary"

BEFORE THE END of his first administration, Theodore Roosevelt laid out the principal guidelines for United States foreign policy in the twentieth century. Characteristically, he did not shy away from asserting that our foreign policy should serve our own interests but, also characteristically, he averred that such policies as the United States chose to pursue could not but serve "the interests of humanity at large." There was sufficient substance to that argument—at least as most Americans viewed their role in history, and especially if one emphasized that if the United States did not intervene, the "less noble" nations, such as Germany, Russia, Japan, or France, inevitably would—to silence most serious dissent on the subject.

Nevertheless The Nation, under Oswald Garrison Villard's editorship, took the measure of the Roosevelt posture: the President, it remarked, could not understand "the obstinate preference of people that have tasted liberty and seen that it is good, for doing things in their own way. . . . [Roosevelt] is almost painfully conscious of his own benevolence, but he does not see that benevolence at the tip of a bayonet may be hateful."

SOURCE: The Fourth Annual Message of President Theodore Roosevelt, December 6, 1904, reprinted in Fred Israel (ed.), The State of the Union Messages of the Presidents, 1790–1966, Vol. II (1967); and The Fifth Annual Message of President Theodore Roosevelt, December 5, 1905, in ibid., Vol. III (1967).

It is not true that the United States feels any land hunger or entertains any projects as regards the other nations of the Western Hemisphere save such as are for their welfare. All that this country desires is to see the neighboring countries stable, orderly, and prosperous. Any country whose people conduct themselves well can count upon our hearty friendship. If a nation shows that it knows how to act with reasonable efficiency and decency in social and political matters, if it keeps order and pays its obligations, it need fear no interference from the United States. Chronic wrongdoing, or an impotence which results in a general loosening of the ties of civilized society, may in America, as elsewhere, ultimately require intervention by some civilized nation, and in the Western Hemisphere the adherence of the United States to the Monroe Doctrine may force the United States, however reluctantly, in flagrant cases of such wrongdoing or impotence, to the exercise of an international police power. If every country washed by the Caribbean Sea would show the progress in stable and just civilization which with the aid of the Platt amendment Cuba has shown since our troops left the island, and which so many of the republics in both Americas are constantly and brilliantly showing, all question of interference by this Nation with their affairs would be at an end. Our interests and those of our southern neighbors are in reality identical. They have great natural riches, and if within their borders the reign of law and justice obtains, prosperity is sure to come to them. While they thus obey the primary law of civilized society they may rest assured that they will be treated by us in a spirit of cordial and helpful sympathy. We would interfere with them only in the last resort, and then only if it became evident that their inability or unwillingness to do justice at home and abroad had violated the rights of the United States or had invited foreign aggression to the detriment of the entire body of American nations. It is a mere truism to say that every nation, whether in America or anywhere else, which desires to maintain its freedom, its independence, must ultimately realize that the right of such independence can not be separated from the responsibility of making good use of it.

In asserting the Monroe Doctrine, in taking such steps as we have taken in regard to Cuba, Venezuela, and Panama, and in endeavoring to circumscribe the theater of war in the Far East, and to secure the open door in China, we have acted in our own interest as well as in the interest of humanity at large. There are however, cases in which, while our own interests are not greatly involved, strong appeal is made to our sympathies. Ordinarily it is very much wiser and more useful for us to concern ourselves with striving for our own moral and material betterment here at home than to concern ourselves with trying to better the conditions of things in other countries. We have plenty of sins of our own to war against. . . .

Moreover, we must make it evident that we do not intend to permit the Monroe Doctrine to be used by any nation on this Continent as a shield to protect it from the consequences of its own misdeeds against foreign nations. If a republic to the south of us commits a tort against a foreign nation, such as an outrage against a citizen of that nation, then the Monroe Doctrine does not force us to interfere to prevent punishment of the tort, save to see that the punishment does not assume the form of territorial occupation in any shape. The case is more difficult when it refers to a contractual obligation. Our own Government has always refused to enforce such contractual obligations on behalf of its citizens by an appeal to arms. It is much to be wished that all foreign governments would take the same view. But they do not; and in consequence we are liable at any time to be brought face to face with disagreeable alternatives. On the other hand, this country would certainly decline to go to war to prevent a foreign government from collecting a just debt; on the other hand, it is very inadvisable to permit any foreign power to take possession, even temporarily, of the customshouse of an American Republic in order to enforce the payment of its obligations; for such temporary occupation might turn into a permanent occupation. The only escape from these alternatives may at any time be that we must ourselves undertake to bring about some arrangement by which so much as possible of a just obligation shall be paid. It is far better that this country should put through such an arrangement, rather than allow any foreign country to undertake it. To do so insures the defaulting republic from having to pay debts of an improper character under duress, while it also insures honest creditors of the republic from being passed by in the interest of dishonest or grasping creditors. Moreover, for the United States to take such a position offers the only possible way of insuring us against a clash with some foreign power. The position is, therefore, in the interest of peace as well as in the interest of justice. It is of benefit to our people; it is of benefit to foreign peoples; and most of all it is really of benefit to the people of the country concerned.

32.   William Howard Taft,
"Dollar Diplomacy"

IN MODERN Marxian parlance, "Dollar Diplomacy" is merely another phrase for imperialism. The United States generally rejected territorial colonialism (especially after the Philippine War) but, in keeping with modern corporate innovations, American capitalists found they might earn the full fruits of colonialism by means of overseas investments. There is enough truth to that viewpoint to make it appear sufficient, especially to a generation of students that has come of age in the cynical atmosphere generated by the Vietnam war. It nonetheless neglects several essential points, not least the genuine idealism that underlay the "Dollar Diplomacy" concept. Marx himself had emphasized the service to mankind which commerce and capitalism had performed in subduing the feudal system of social organization—a system founded on violence. In international affairs, the world is still governed by that system. It was the hope of many in the early twentieth century that international commercial rivalry might replace violence—warfare—as the main ordering principle of competition among nations. Peace might then become, as Woodrow Wilson put it in an article written in 1907, "a matter of conference and international combinations." What remained unavoidable were the tensions that developed between the United States and the less advanced and relatively unstable nations whose economies American investors penetrated—tensions that in general any patron-dependent or creditor-debtor relationship produces. The American people's unwillingness to recognize that its "benevolence" sometimes precludes national "self-determination" among the people of the smaller client states has served to aggravate already sore sensitivities.

SOURCE: The Fourth Annual Message of President William Howard Taft, December 3, 1912, in Israel (ed.), *The State of the Union Messages of the Presidents, 1790–1966*, Vol. III.

The diplomacy of the present administration has sought to respond to modern ideas of commercial intercourse. This policy has been characterized as substituting dollars for bullets. It is one that appeals alike to idealistic humanitarian sentiments, to the dictates of sound policy and strategy, and to legitimate commercial aims. It is an effort frankly directed to the increase of American trade upon the axiomatic principle that the Government of the United States shall extend all proper support to every legitimate and beneficial American enterprise abroad. . . . Because modern diplomacy is commercial, there has been a disposition in some quarters to attribute to it none but materialistic aims. How strikingly erroneous is such an impression may be seen from a study of the results by which the diplomacy of the United States can be judged. . . .

It is not possible to make to the Congress a communication upon the present foreign relations of the United States so detailed as to convey an adequate impression of the enormous increase in the importance and activities of those relations. If this Government is really to preserve to the American people that free opportunity in foreign markets which will soon be indispensable to our prosperity, even greater efforts must be made. Otherwise the American merchant, manufacturer, and exporter will find many a field in which American trade should logically predominate preempted through the more energetic efforts of other governments and other commercial nations. . . .

America can not take its proper place in the most important fields for its commercial activity and enterprise unless we have a merchant marine. American commerce and enterprise can not be effectively fostered in those fields unless we have good American banks in the countries referred to. We need American newspapers in those countries and proper means for public information about them. We need to assure the permanency of a trained foreign service. We need legislation enabling the members of the foreign service to be systematically brought into direct contact with the industrial, manufacturing, and exporting interests of this country in order that American business men may enter the foreign field with a clear perception of the exact conditions to be dealt with and the officers themselves may prosecute their work with a clear idea of what American industrial and manufacturing interests require.

Abrams, Richard M *comp.*
The issues of the Populist and Progressive eras, 1892–1912, edited by Richard M. Abrams. ₍1st ed.₎ New York, Harper & Row ₍1969₎

viii, 283 p. 21 cm. (Documentary history of the United States)
3.25

Library has: Columbia, South Carolina, University of South Carolina Press ₍1969₎

1. U. S. — Social conditions — 1865–1918. 2. U. S. — Politics and government—1865–1933. I. Title.

E661.A5 1969   309.1′73   71–8957
                                        MARC